IMPROVE the WORLD
GO FISHING!

IMPROVE the WORLD
GO FISHING!

By world-renowned outdoor writer and fisherman
HARTT WIXOM

Copyright © 1998 by CFI

All Rights Reserved.

No part of this book may be reproduced in any form whatsoever, whether by graphic, visual, electronic, filming, microfilming, tape recording, or any other means, without prior written permission of the author, except in the case of brief passages embodied in critical reviews and articles.

This book is not an official publication of The Church of Jesus Christ of Latter-day Saints.

ISBN: 1-55517-360-8

10 9 8 7 6 5 4 3 2 1

Published and Distributed by:
925 North Main, Springville, UT 84663 • 801/489-4084

Cover Design and Page Layout by Corinne A. Bischoff
Printed in the United States of America

Table of Contents

Preface vii
Chapter 1 1
Chapter 2 11
Chapter 3 19
Chapter 4 27
Chapter 5 37
Chapter 6 47
Chapter 7 55
Chapter 8 63
Chapter 9 75
Chapter 10 83
Chapter 11 93
Chapter 12 103
Chapter 13 109
Chapter 14 119
Chapter 15 129
Chapter 16 135
Chapter 17 143
Chapter 18 151
Chapter 19 159
Chapter 20 165
Chapter 21 171
Chapter 22 181
Chapter 23 195
Appendix 198

Preface

What follows must be labeled fiction. Yet, the incidents are based on historical fact which can be researched and proven even today. For example, the state prison mentioned was located in "Sugarhouse" as depicted and the trustees were encountered by the main character in the story as described. The author was held at gunpoint by a "shaky" old man and the murder of a young girl did take place along the creek bank. In some places, the time element has been changed to include events together which occurred at more distant times. Some points are exaggerated in the telling, such as the author trying to cheer on professional tournament golfers just as they were about to strike the ball. This is true enough as stated but it could have been the author's imagination that said golfers even noticed the young boy at their elbow.

In some cases, but not all, names are changed to protect the innocent.

The author vouches for the validity of angling principles presented, allowing for a few biases common among dedicated (fanatical) anglers. They are given as they happened and most remain as valuable afield in the author's life today as the precious moment first learned.

Of course, anyone who reads the book merely to (acutely) refine angling skills will be shot at sunrise, if not well before.

Chapter One

When I was 12, my parents broke my heart. They moved from the country with its emerald meadows and casual trout streams to the city. Not just to suburbia. Inside the incorporated limits of a major western metropolis. Salt Lake City, Utah.

Rows of houses. Pavement. As far as the eye could see. No greenery or natural waterways in sight.

To be sure, my parents explained that the move was necessary economically; my father wanted to open his own business where the people were located. I asked why we couldn't get the people to move to Idaho. I didn't understand and I was totally devastated.

My only earthly salvation would be to find nature on the edge of megalopia. Having nothing better to do one July afternoon, the second after arriving in Terra Incognita, I wandered down a street labeled "20th East." Beneath a bridge, I made a startling discovery. A creek. Not a large one, but one with running water. I could hear it gurgling, and I could see orange-hued pebbles. The gully not only held water, but clear, flowing water.

Peering closer, I saw something which at first appeared as an apparition. If so, it had a tail which waved like a fan in the breeze. And gills. A fish! It was, in fact, as I studied it…a trout.

I had seen trout before, but they were mostly an enigma. Being born and raised in the hamlet of Logan in northern Utah, my cousin took me as an 8-year old to the Logan River. I loved the smell of moss, even decaying moss, and I followed my mentor, three years older than I, along miles of wondrous moss smells. The river twisted and bent in between homes and yards, and occasionally, my cousin would say quietly, as if in awe himself, "There…there is a trout! See how it rises alongside the far moss bank to take that insect…how delicately…and then retreats below the surface so it won't be seen by all its enemies?"

"Who are its enemies?" I asked Dennis.

"Minks and herons and kingfishers and us, mostly."

"When we try to catch them?"

"Yes, that too. But mostly people who dam the stream and pollute it and dry it up for irrigation."

"Do you see any pollution in the water now?"

"No but we will soon. Wait until about noon and you'll see when old Mr. Johnson washes the gravel from his pit and the river turns chocolate brown." We watched more trout slurp insects from the water, what my cousin called German brown trout, and also caddis flies. We were about to get an imitation caddis fly in front of a rising fish when sure enough, mud began to ooze around us like one of the Egyptian plagues. First, the water around our feet turned brown, and then precisely where the fish rose from beneath a half-submerged cottonwood branch. With the mud, the fish did not rise again and soon the entire stream was silted opaque.

"That's it for the day," Dennis announced. "We can try the outlet irrigation canal."

We walked half a mile to the outlet canal that lapped around the hill holding the town of Logan from slipping into the valley and for a while we saw trout as if in rows sipping at something on the surface. We began casting our flies to the spot where they lie in wait but soon the plague of silt inundated the canal. "Canal comes from the river," said Dennis. "We may as well go home."

"But can't someone make Mr. Johnson stop polluting the river?" I asked. "Isn't it selfish of him to…"

"No," my mentor stopped me. "He pays corporate taxes and when you do that, the zoning board lets you do whatever you want." I told my cousin I didn't understand corporate taxes and after a while, my cousin allowed he didn't either. "He just does what he wants," Dennis said finally. "It's called progress. And when you call it that, no one can do anything about it."

"Oh," I said. I mulled it all over best I could. But I didn't really understand that either.

Now, in examining "20th East Creek" carefully, I saw no mud. Good so far. But what about later today. I must come back later and see if the creek was still clear.

When we lived in Idaho, my father had on occasion driven me a few miles from home to fish the Bear River. It was murky much of the time but the carp and suckers didn't seem to mind like the trout. I concluded that trout are more elite; they like cleaner, more beautiful surroundings, and live in the kind of places I want to be.

Here on "20th East Creek" (its correct appellation later proved to be Parleys Creek, named after a local pioneer) I could not only see trout but witness them within easy casting distance. In fact, I could crawl along on my belly and dabble a fly directly over a trout's head. The stream remained clear all day, and I suspected then that I had discovered a treasure more valuable than any coveted by ancient pirates, for one could easily observe whatever happened in the creek. It was even better than an aquarium; it was not hand-controlled by man tinkering about and mostly messing things up but rather by a mostly unseen force called nature. I could learn about the mysteries of this strange force called nature by simply lying down by side the of the creek and watching the water flow by. I did so for hours at a time those first few days in July.

I tried often to catch some of the trout I saw. I could see them clearly enough all day long on Parleys Creek. The only problem, at least to begin with, was this: the fish were far too wary for me. They swam away at the slightest bankside vibration. If my toe itched, they'd be certain to feel me kick at it. If I waved my rod tip overhead trying to cast toward them, they saw it. Or the shadow. Then they remained in hiding and ignored me.

I vowed then and there that I would learn all I could in one lifetime about this creature, the wild trout. I experimented. I shouted at them. No reaction. They did not hear sounds above the water. I tossed a pebble 10 feet away at the tail of the pool. They scattered upstream. I waved a limb upstream, creating a shadow. They scattered downstream. At first I didn't know what to make of it all, but I wrote all my scientific findings down dutifully in my diary. Some day I would need all this data to become a world-renowned icthyiologist (one who studies fish). Or at least to catch my first trout.

But they eluded me over and over, and I began to suspect I would die an old man before I would learn how to outwit the species *Salmo*.

Meantime, I studied most carefully what the fish ate. Here and there I would watch the fish dimple or bulge the surface to partake of some unknown menu and return to feeding position, heads always up-current, even if the flow eddied. On the Logan, my cousin had told me to watch for the little caddis flies hatching out, but I could find none here. Most of the flies here had three tails which I found from a book were *Ephemeroptera* or

May flies. I suspected these Parleys trout were feeding on the May flies; yet, they ignored the May fly imitations I dabbled before them. Just as I suspected them of having lockjaw, they dined arrogantly on something unknown to my left or right. Or they would snap at something near the bottom, displaying cotton-white mouths as they opened and closed their jaws. They remained frustrating and cryptic to me for some time. I didn't think I would ever solve it. But one thing I did determine: no one could call me a quitter. This day, for example, I vowed I would not quit until one of them surrendered. In fishing or in life, my Dad had long ago taught me, one doesn't stop short of success. But then I got very, very hungry, too weak to even properly cast the fly. When I went home for vittles, I discovered my mistake in quitting. My parents were planting a new lawn and I was trapped. I did not see the creek for the remainder of that day and thus, my ichthyological education was further delayed.

Mostly, I got to the creek every day thereafter for the rest of the summer. Except Sundays. I was forbidden to fish on Sunday, or swim, or go to movies or anything but go to church and read "good" books. So, I began to acquire good books at the library and spent my Sundays reading good books. A few of the titles were *Trout, Sport Fishing* and *A Fisherman's Bible*.

My first three weeks on Parleys Creek, I used only artificial flies because I'd read in books and outdoor magazines that fly fishing was the only real, honest, sporting way to catch fish. I owned no flies myself; but my father had fly-fished occasionally, and I appropriated both his 8 1/2-foot split bamboo fly road and his packet of hooks covered with fur and feathers. Most were named "grey hackle yellow" and grey hackle whatever other colors. I focused on the "yellow" and cast it hundreds of times to trout I could see without enticing a single strike. One reason was probably that my leader and fly landed in a heap on the water like a bird's nest and frightened every fish away. I soon concluded through clever deduction that there was only one type of fish in Parleys Creek: alert fish. I searched diligently for dumb or even slightly backward cutthroat trout. I never found any in Parleys Creek.

My first breakthrough came in early August. I watched an older angler cast a fly into a small opening in the brush over deeply shadowed water. His rod bent and he pulled out a near quarter-pound of thrashing silver. It seemed only silver at first anyway. As he held the prize in his palm, I marveled at the beauty of a most sublime creation. Barely 10 inches long, the fish reflected a kaleidoscope of golden-caramel hues decorated with black splotches, scarlet gills and head, with bright orange slashes beneath the throat. It was as streamlined for speed as a torpedo with fins.

For openers I asked, "What kind of trout is that?"

"You from some other planet, kid? This here fish is a wild native cutthroat trout. See the orange slashes under the neck? That is, of course, why they call it a cutthroat trout."

"I've never seen one," I admitted. And I gave the most sophisticated answer I could think of at the moment. "Just brown and rainbow trout like we have where I used to live in Idaho. And in Logan. On the Logan River."

If I ever needed to save face, I mentioned that the Logan had in 1937 (I was 4 years old then, but did not stress that point) produced a whopper 36 3/4-lb. brown trout. It was world-famous and made the McClane *Angling Encyclopedia* but no official record books. It had been illegally snagged.

"Oh," said the older boy, now convinced I was not completely ignorant to piscatorial pursuits.

"And the fly…" I announced. "That looks like a…a grey hackle yellow."

"Very good," the boy said respectfully, creeling the fish and motioning wildly for me to get the heck back and give him more back-casting room.

I sat on a rock to ponder this new revelation. Cutthroat trout. Grey hackle yellow. He had cast the fly beneath dark shadows alongside the brush. I followed his example meticulously all that day and the next. Nothing but silent water. I decided at last to focus on one fish, finding a trout deep in the brush and lagging to him repeatedly. On about the 50th toss, he moved a little farther from his hideaway beneath the overhanging oak. On about the 75th, he eyed the surface more intensely. On about the 100th, he opened and closed his jaws, appearing restless. Five casts later, miracle of miracles, he rose and struck. I was so mesmerized by this phenomenon that I watched him swim with the fly protruding from his jaw to the bottom where, being an alert trout like all Parleys Creek trout, he decided it was a phony. He dispelled the fly.

I sat there wondering what I should have done. Strike back. Ah! Yes, I was supposed to strike back! Only in that way could I hope to hook the fish.

But at what precise moment should I do so? How quickly? How hard? I perused once again my treasure of outdoor magazines. Alas, none spelled it out precisely except to say it should "not be too soon nor too late." It should be "just right." Well, that wasn't much help.

But at least I had discovered something valuable. I had created an artificial hatch. I had cast the fly at the fish so many times that he thought insects were hatching upstream in large quantities and drifting down to him in numbers worth his time. The latter was, of course, as good a theory as any

I could come up with at the time. I could not be sure, since I was not a fish, nor had I ever managed to talk with one, nor have I since talked with a fish, and I don't know anyone who has—other than with dolphins which are not really fish at all but mammals.

In the book called *Trout,* by one Ray Bergman, he decided that nothing was for sure when it came to trout fishing. The field of endeavor was comprised almost entirely of myriad theories, and one man's theory could be as good as the next. So long as it caught fish. Clearly, I would have to put my own postulates to work.

If most came by trial and error, Parleys Creek was my laboratory. I went to it for answers as a mad scientist trying to create Frankenstein. Only I couldn't create anything; I could only observe and try to learn.

Many were the times I pondered it all over most carefully. My daily observations indicated quite clearly that trout would not begin feeding until convinced enough insects were available to be worth their while. I soon stumbled onto something big: fish follow a "caloric formula," i.e. if you are a fish, you cannot grow bigger unless you expend fewer calories than you take in. I expressed it mathematically as S (size) = A (availability of food) + E (energy expended in the capture thereof). Thus, a big stream fish would be found where currents brought food but not swim directly in the current because to do so would burn more calories than the fish took in. Put another way, in order to attain size, a fish would take up a position near current bringing in food but where little body energy was needed to hold position to actually gather that food. At the same time, seeking security (not expressed in my formula) the over-sized fish would try to hide under cutbanks, logs, moss, boulders or other structure where he could watch the flow safely without having to fight it.

But discovering the rudiments of how fish feed, I had to learn how to hook a fish after he fed on what I fed him. Following my initial experience in failing to set the hook as a trout rose and hit, I resolved to respond more quickly. Alas, next time, I raised my rod tip on nothing but air. I experimented relentlessly to find the perfect timing, neither too late nor too soon. Then came the day when I raised my rod tip just right and lo, the trout's head tilted toward me. It was a memorable experience, indelibly imprinted in my memory, the catching of that first trout, although I tried not to make too much of it. I recorded the event in Diary No. Two under the letter C ("Catching") as occurring at 9:33 a.m. Aug. 5, a Friday, under an overhang of Gambel oak with dark clouds approaching from the south-southwest, 11 paces from nearest path to the railroad track.

It was, of course, a monster cutthroat of some, well, at least eight inches and it was honorably taken on a fly as the magazines meticulously prescribed. My grey hackle yellow had no wings and thus, it was not technically a dry fly, which was considered the most sporting and exciting way. (I still feel that way today.) But I had read somewhere that my fly pattern would qualify as a nymph and that nymping required more skill than any other way of catching trout. (I still believe that today, too.)

I could not, however, lay claim to displaying any particular skill in the process of actually landing my first trout. Having watched in horror as finny adversaries of other anglers tangled in submerged brush and got away, I determined that would not happen to me. Thus, when I watched my first trout engulf a fly, I jerked. Actually, I jerked rather hard. The fish sailed over my head. I found it flailing about in a pile of scrub oak leaves well away from the stream. Bathed as the fish was in thick leaves, I couldn't find the creature for several minutes. Anyone watching the scenario would not describe it as pretty. And I couldn't have been prouder.

After that, there was no holding me back.

I caught four trout in all that first summer. One of my favorite fishing holes was a waterfall pool beneath a concrete spillway about a block below 20th East. The falling white water carved a pool some three- four feet deep which slacked in velocity until ebbing gently against a lacework of willows on the west bank. I could toss out my grey hackle yellow and drift it downstream to the willows and fetch a strike, or I could skip the fly upstream against the current. The latter almost always enticed response but sometimes the trout miscalculated the direction of my zig-zagging artificial and snapped at nothing. A hungry fish would strike several times at the same fly provided I didn't actually feel the hit. If I did, so did the fish, and it learned quickly that the "insect" didn't act like an insect at all. Indeed, it carried a strange, hard, un-insect-like zap very much to be avoided.

For years I harbored the theory that these were "smart" fish which knew what was going on, i.e. a *Homo sapiens* land-lubber sought to separate them from a life-sustaining habitat. In time, I decided that a theory holding more water was one in which the fish was "alert" sure enough, but not really "smart." That is, the fish was not capable of abstractly reasoning that I was an enemy bent on putting it in a frying pan but it could sure as hell see when something was not natural and avoid it. I hold to that same hypothesis to this very day, 51 years later.

It didn't take long before I noticed that boards placed in the concrete spillway (creating a higher waterfall) could be removed. When I did, dozens of trout scurried in a frenzy from middle of the pool into shadows beneath the willowed banks. It was a revelation to see how many trout could live in a pool only eight feet in diameter and a few feet deep. From that moment, I focused much of my angling attention below the concrete spillway. Of course, when fishing I also left the board dam in place to avoid spooking the pool's many inhabitants. If I did not bring my rod (which was almost never) I amused myself and perhaps a few friends by pulling the boards and watching dozens of fish scramble to safety.

The waterfall hole was, to be true, something of a social gathering place. Men in uniform sometimes converged at the small diversion just upstream from the spillway. One day I arrived to see such men gathered. They lifted an orange piece of canvas and instantly, flow fled to the ditch rather than the waterfall. Without a thousand blue-white air bubbles to mask their whereabouts, trout in the waterfall pool seemed to look up in surprise. Then they melted quickly into the shadows.

"That enough?" one of the men asked.

"No," said another apparently in charge. "The garden'll need more than that. We couldn't even grow enough to feed the warden. Shut the creek off completely."

I acted with visceral response more instinctive than intelligent. "You men have destroyed my fishing!" I blurted.

Two rough-looking fellows walked over and towered above me. "Clyde, see what we've done here. Scared all the fish for this poor young fisherman."

Clyde scowled. "Th' hell with 'im. The prison garden is nearly dry. We got more people coming. We need more water." He lit a cigarette and glared at me.

Being a relatively bright young lad, I deduced these men were prisoners. The one who spoke up was probably being incarcerated for murder. Maybe even of a young boy.

Finally, Clyde busied himself opening a burlap bag. The men stepped into the reduced flow below the waterfall and began netting fish with the bag. After fetching five trout in this manner, Clyde announced that it "was enough for supper." Before long, the men departed down the ditch from whence they'd come.

I followed them. Three-fourths of a mile away, on a bluff behind high stone walls, I discovered the Utah State Penitentiary. People called it the "Sugarhouse Pen." Not far away was a city suburb called "Sugarhouse." It had been named from an old sugar factory built by pioneers in the late 1800s and for many years it incarcerated Mormon men convicted of living "cohab," or in polygamy. Now, I was told, it held mostly robbers and murderers. Beneath the bluff, sure enough, there was indeed a garden; its rows were even now filling with water.

The trustees, as they were called, had told the truth; yet they had also broken the law. It was illegal in the state to catch game fish other than with rod and reel. They had claimed to be catching fish by hand "for the warden." I pondered the irony of it. Should I report them? But who would I report them to? Definitely, if they ever destroyed my fishing again I was at least going to write a letter to Gov. Maw.

But next time they showed up, they exhibited greater compassion. They let me fish for a while before shutting off the water. I was too afraid to say anything the second time they came, but on the third, I grew bolder and gently suggested they catch their fish upstream from the waterfall and not in the waterfall. I explained that it was my favorite fishing hole. This seemed to come as a revelation to the men. They pondered it over. One trustee said I reminded him of himself as a young boy. I didn't know at the time whether to take that as a compliment or not. Said one of his comrades, "I never even thought of going fishing as a boy. I was too busy getting into trouble."

Clyde mulled it over very thoughtfully, and decided it "would be harder" not damming off the waterfall but they could manage. He gave the order and the men turned their faces upstream. Whether they caught a trout meal for the warden, I never learned.

I told my mother in great detail and with very few garnishments what the prison people said about never going fishing as boys. It had the desired effect. If I ever again mentioned I was going fishing (and it was not Sunday and I kept my room clean and school was out), I was mostly allowed to go.

Chapter Two

When I went near the creek, it was usually to go fishing. Occasionally, it was to swim. One day, an adult male photographer approached the diversion dam and discovered several boys and myself diving and swimming. The man began taking pictures, even though none of us modeled a swimming suit. My parents were quite disturbed by this intelligence and discussed whether I should be allowed to swim in the creek at all. The water was numbing cold but I did not want to see one of my individual freedoms washed away. I pleaded my case and waited.

Two weeks later, the stranger returned with photographs taken at different angles, but displaying no private parts…other than the barest hint of buttocks. One showed me standing in the water with the concrete dam abutment masking my body from the waist down. I must have had a funny look on my face. The photographer labeled the picture "I Dare Ya!"

I had never considered myself to be an "I dare ya" type, but the photos were approved by my parents. Things returned to normal. I was allowed to swim in the creek, sans swim suit. In my childhood naivete I never really understood until years later what had concerned them so.

A few months after that, a girl complained she had been walking along 20th East when a man tried to force her into his car. I never told my parents about this. Instead, I turned detective, sneaking around the streamside brush looking for clues and suspicious people in old cars. I put sheets of paper down to record car tracks. I found plenty of tracks on the paper but I was at a loss to know what to do with them. I finally threw them away. And I saw weird strangers but no stranger who could be truthfully labeled dangerous. At least not at first.

Any true stream, of course, especially a trout stream (not a concrete-lined canal) is a mini-strip of wilderness with dense vegetation, even in an (otherwise) desert. Parleys Creek seemed blessed with much underbrush and natural cover which attracted various types of people seeking solitude. One sat in a stupor in his car drinking as I watched one day, throwing beer bottles across the D & RGW (Denver and Rio Grande Western) railroad tracks. But he soon left and I never saw him again. I brought a plastic bag from home and picked up the bottles and took them home to the family trash barrel. I felt sorry for the man. Anyone who would litter a trout stream would have to be a desperate and unhappy man. But he was salvageable, I decided, for he did not desecrate the creek by throwing any bottles in the water itself.

Another man who seemed homeless drained bottles of something and after tossing them in the creek, tried to break them with rocks. His aim was very bad and he never hit anything. I needn't worry about cutting my feet swimming or wading but I was angry. I prayed for this man that Heaven might forgive him.

Still another group of young men wandered about and look bored. A friend of mine happened through the area with a bicycle and they threw rocks at it, ruining the front wheel so bad he had to carry the bike home.

I could never understand aimless destruction of this sort. But one thing I noted among all who came to Parleys Creek: none of the sad-looking people ever carried fishing poles.

When stream flow naturally subsided in November and ice covered the waterfall pool, I broke the gleaming white mantle with a large rock and rested the area for an hour. When I returned, it was to catch the fifth trout of my life. Surprisingly, I enticed it on a commercially-dried grasshopper. What would a 'hopper be doing in such a place in the dead cold of winter?

I didn't know. Everything I'd read said you can't entice fish with a food that is out of season. But since I'd just done it, I never from that time forth trusted anyone's final pronouncements on trout. The only real experts on trout were trout. I decided a successful fisherman must be an iconoclast. He/she must break with cherished tradition, never quit experimenting, never accept anyone as the last word. That was my watchword later in life when I was told that striped bass must be caught at night from boat with bait. My first six striped bass were caught at noon with artificial jigs from the bank.

Thus, it was that I became distrustful about "fishing advice." There was much to be learned from reading or watching, of course, but the only real teacher was experience itself. I sought that experience as a drowning man seeks air.

Occasionally, I tried to simulate sophisticated trout fisherman I saw pictured in the pages of Ambercrombie and Fitch. But when I noted the prices in their catalogs, I concluded there was only way I could continue to go fishing: on a shoestring, as I'd been doing. I could not afford the fly fishing vest with the brook trout embroidered on the shoulder, let alone the much-in-vogue Harding reel and Fenwick rod, nor the chest waders with suspenders. I fished mostly in tennis shoes. If I waded, I rolled up my Levis and stuffed my socks in a back pocket. True, I did have a nice wicker basket creel inherited from my father. But when ready to go fishing, as I looked at myself in the mirror, I resembled none of the gentlemen portrayed in *Outdoor Life, Field and Stream,* or *Sports Afield*. I wore "freedom" clothes. Afterall, I could always dress up for school or church any time but only on special occasions like fishing could I wear comfortable clothes.

One of my heroes was Huckleberry Finn, even if he did only catch the lowly catfish. Mostly I admired Huck because he had the liberty to fish and seek adventure when and where he wanted up and down the Mississippi on a home-made raft. Unfortunately, Parleys Creek was not large enough to launch a home-made raft, nor for that matter, any other kind of raft. The creek was not even listed on any maps anywhere as a "navigable" stream. In fact, most maps did not show the creek at all. But Parleys Creek did have something Huck didn't: trout. I showed some pages of Huck to my father, but he frowned. "Mark Twain did not do parents any favors," he said. What did he mean by that? I asked myself. After becoming a parent I think I partly understood.

Meanwhile, I concluded that while I fished to catch fish, there was more to fishing than catching fish. I liked to be in the kind of places where trout lived. It was not just the creek itself, but the creek was the center of the world I liked to live in. The creek was a place to reflect, to think, to observe nature. A creek possessed discipline and order in its channeled flow, yet was deep and unfathomable in its infinity. A creek conveyed inspiration in the sight and sound and smell of its impenetrable magnitude.

In time I learned that the strip of wilderness brush and water that was Parleys Creek was born high in the Wasatch Mountains eastward, rushing down eagerly until reaching Salt Lake Valley and the Great Basin at a place called Suicide Rock. Legend was that an Indian brave had leaped to his death here when his only true love repudiated him for another. That was the legend. But I never did place much stock in Indian folklore. There were many local Piute and Shoshone Indian stories afoot at the time and it was hard to separate one from another. They seemed mostly far-fetched to me, like a fox turning into a bird and then being transformed into a beautiful maiden. I never saw a fox that looked like a maiden. I tried to reason how it could be but it was beyond me. I never knew if they were real legends or something made up by the local chamber of commerce.

One could see, however, upon visiting Suicide Rock that it would, indeed, be an excellent place to commit suicide. But as far as I knew, no one climbed it any more except to write love messages. Since I was only 12 at the time, I never found any reason to climb Suicide Rock.

The reason that I mention Suicide Rock at all is that below the pinnacle was a spillway chute which dumped gleaming white water into the Suicide Rock Hole. I spent many days there at the edge of this deeply- cut chasm casting to dozens of sun-tanned cutthroat trout finning in endless back eddies. One day, fishing for the first time with a worm, I lay the pole down on an elongated boulder and gazed at my scenic surroundings. Suddenly, my father's fly rod nearly jumped into the churning cauldron. I saved the rod, but alas, missed the fish. In my mind's eye it was at least a 10-pounder, although I never saw any fish in Parleys Creek more than a tenth that size. There were rumors of large trout being washed down from the reservoir above, but I placed them in the same category as the Indian legends.

Some 15-inch hatchery rainbow trout were placed at times in the canyon sector of the creek, always near the road. But being directly out of concrete raceways, they were pale, flaccid, chewed up from dorsal fin to tail, and dumb. Most lasted only a day or two before succumbing to the first crude offering. When these exotics were gone, serious fishermen found themselves alone once again trying to entice the creek's native residents, the born-free, wise (and always alert) cutthroats.

After entering the valley, the creek flowed down "Parleys Gully" into the largest metropolis between Denver and San Francisco. At Sugarhouse the little stream vanished into a storm drain. I was saddened peering into the black hole. How many people might enjoy the rivulet if allowed to remain aboveground a few more miles? People said the creek flowed imprisoned in an underground pipe until joining the Jordan River to the west and then it all flowed into Great Salt Lake. Examining the work of Don Bernardo Miera y Pacheco of Father Escalante's expedition in 1776, I was amazed to see that his map showed a river draining from this inland sea to the Pacific Ocean. Yet, I was able to float easily in the lake's nearly 30 per cent saltine solution because it had no outlets to anywhere. Salt came in but didn't go out. In the Fall the lake was seven times more salty than the ocean. Floating was not only easy but it was impossible to sink. One problem I found though, was that if a body had any sores, the salt would find it. And sting. One swim was enough.

During its approximately 15-mile sojourn of live flow, the creek provided a haven for much wildlife and a few unhurried people who came by to seek out its tranquil wake as did I. I determined to explore all 15 miles.

Walking upstream one day, I saw three doe deer. I also trapped a young valley quail against a bush. I examined this treasure for several minutes, noting the delicate wings and legs, the regal top notch. Quail always seemed so docile and trusting, sauntering about as if not having a care in the world. Yet, they somehow flourished. There were always a lot of quail. They had large broods; maybe that was nature's way of making up for their lack of wariness. Nature always seemed to have an answer for everything.

One day I observed a quail saunter into a rusted, squashed coffee can. Tiptoeing up, I placed my hand over the opening. Looking through my fingers, I saw eggs inside. Taking the prize home, my mother asked me what I intended to do with the young family. I thought about it, concluded I had rudely intruded upon nature, and returned can, mother quail and her 11 eggs to the same place I found them.

After that, I occasionally gathered bird eggs, pin-blowing them (cutting a hole in each end and then going puff!) and arranged them in neat boxes for display although I don't recall ever displaying them to anyone other than my friends who also collected bird eggs. But they were there if any college professor ornithologist wanted to see them. Mostly they were English sparrow eggs, although we found a few starlings. Why was it that the non-native birds were always plentiful? It was not nature who had goofed in bringing them to America but mankind. The same was true of carp and other aliens. I concluded that man should not mess with nature.

One day I found a robin's nest and marveled at the mud and straw construction. The Children of Israel couldn't have done any better making bricks for the Pharaoh, except that they had kilns to bake the stuff hard and the robins didn't. And the eggs were the most beautiful blue-green I had ever seen. Later I heard the term "robin's egg blue" and thought it was a most appropriate label, except were they really blue or were they green? Often, I would sit in the woods and listen to the robin's song, a kind of cheery-mournful chorus at sunset. I noted that robins lived everywhere. I saw them near the city and I saw them at top of the mountains where Parleys Creek began. Later, I gathered up two abandoned robin's nests and put them up for auction at a neighborhood garage sale. No one came, or at least no one who wanted to buy a robin's nest. Where were the world's robin lovers?

Flanking Parleys Creek for nearly a mile was a golf course. A private country club, it was patrolled by an off-duty policeman who summoned me from the oak brush one morning, casually eyed my fishing rod, told me I was trespassing on private property and trying to steal golf balls from land I had no business being on, then gave me a hard kick to the rear. Today with a witness, I could sue for enough money to go bonefishing in the Bahamas. Looking back on it, I was probably actually trespassing on the railroad right of way, not the golf course. But being a simple boy not certain of his personal rights, I took the pragmatic approach. I kept a sharper eye out for the golf course cop and his blue motorcycle. It could also be that he decided in observing me that I had far more interest in fish than golf balls. In any event, I had little trouble with him after the initial conflict. One reason might be that he switched from motorcycle to horseback and tore up the 9th green galloping in pursuit of would-be golf ball thieves. The damage was greater than tons of golf balls. He was summarily dismissed. If there was a replacement, I never saw him/her/it. I could then resume fishing without watching over my shoulder.

One day, I noticed that the course was full of golfers and gallery.

A tournament was in progress. An older man standing near me said: "Big names. Big. Arnie Palmer, Billy Casper, Gary Player." They were, indeed, a wonder to behold. Their approach shots hit the back of the green and spun back toward the hole as if on a string. Was it the ball they used? If so, I couldn't find any golf balls like those at any of the stores and no one seemed to know of any.

I practiced trying to hit the ball so that it landed at rear of the green and rolled back toward the cup and succeeded only in cutting deep grooves in the ball. And divots. Some divots went farther than the ball. But since I had decided to become a great golfer, I borrowed a friend's two-iron, went to the elevated 10th tee, and swung with all my might. The shot sliced across the railroad tracks and caromed beyond the prison irrigation ditch. I immediately returned the club to its owner. I would concentrate on fishing.

At the golf tournament, most of the celebrity names knew very little about fashion. They wore chartreuse pants with purple shirts and orange blazers with blue trousers. The only competitor with any sense of color coordination was Gary Player and he didn't wear any color at all. He dressed in total black from cap to shoes. Someone heard someone say that wearing black made Player feel "more powerful." I tried it and concluded there was nothing to it. Mr. Player's theory was like some fishing theories I knew and didn't pass muster at all.

One thing I noticed right off is that the golfers didn't like you cheering for them. I had heard much good about Mr. Casper and as he was about to hit an approach shot, I gave a cheer for him. "Go, Billy! Go!" The people next to me gave me a dirty look and Mr. Casper didn't look so happy himself. It was easy to see that golfers are prima donnas. Everyone had to remain dead quiet. (Later in life, I was to cover a golf tournament as a newspaper reporter in which Mr. Casper gave a clinic. I didn't dare mention that I was the boy who shouted at the country club and I was relieved that Mr. Casper did not seem to remember. I was, however, 13 years older then, nearly two feet taller and 75 lbs. heavier.)

It was hard to figure. Enthusiasm in tennis or basketball, or any other sports for that matter, could be expressed and in fact, is much encouraged. One does not exuberate in golf. A single incident taught me this. A quiet, almost taciturn golfer named Dow Finsterwald was about to hit a short putt on No. 11 at the aforementioned country club tournament. If Dow parred the hole it would tie him with Mr. Palmer. At that precise moment, my friend Jay Funk hooked a big trout just below the 11th green. I could tell it was big from Jay's shouting. Jay always shouts when he catches a big trout. Mr. Finsterwald did not seem to appreciate the fact that Jay had just caught a big trout. Mr. Finsterwald fell suddenly to his knees, then stood up, desperately tried to regain his composure, and badly missed his putt. I told Jay about it that same afternoon and he felt terrible. Then he held up the lunker cutthroat for me to see and I shouted myself when I saw it.

Chapter Three

One day I hiked to a place on the creek where I rarely went, beyond the second railroad bridge and even past the golf course. There I sat down alone, nearly buried in willows, looking at a crooked canopy of blue overhead and listening to the musical gurglings of the creek. The sweet smell of creosote wafted to my nostrils, a smell I had learned to love the year before while walking railroad ties to my best fishing.

With everything perfect, I let my mind reflect.

Why did I so like fishing? I didn't know. None of my close relatives fished, not my Dad unless I regaled him into it; none of my past peers except that I talked them into it. No one but my cousin in Logan and I was nowhere near him now. So why did I so enjoy fishing?

I was born on April 26, 1933, but no one put a fishing rod in my hands while in the cradle and said I was going to be a fisherman. I read no early books about fishing. Some uncles took me up Logan Canyon and we enjoyed a picnic and even killed a rattlesnake, but no one took my hand and walked me down to the river and said, "Fish live in there. You should pay attention."

Most of my early boyhood days, at least in physical leisure, were spent playing football, although I seldom got to be quarterback or captain because that honor went to the kid across the street who owned the football. On occasion, my family took me to Grandmother's farm in Idaho, where I rode horses bareback without knowing there was such a thing as a saddle and went swimming in the hot afternoons after working in the sugar beet fields, gathered chicken eggs in my pockets and had them break there, and learned to hate weeds, and wondered why vegetables couldn't grow with as little effort as weeds, concluded that weeds were of the devil, and went to church and read books on Sunday. But I decided I had much to learn about being a Christian. If faith was so important (and one must have it to be saved) but it was based on a declaration from within, why not just declare it done and be assured a place in Heaven? It seemed to me that adults delighted in making things far more complicated than necessary. And I had a question: if "good works" didn't save us, why do any?

I was stuck for an answer on that long into the afternoon. Then I thought about my original question that I came to ponder and was stuck on that as well. Some of my first efforts at trout fishing were with knowledgeable older guides, but they caught trout and I didn't. My father and cousin Dennis took me to the Narrows on Bear River where the water was cold and swift and the mountains high. Dennis succeeded in catching several rainbow trout on salmon eggs clusters which came in a bottle and I don't know why trout ate them because there were no salmon in the Bear River. I nearly landed one fish on the eggs but it fell on the steep bank and rolled back into the water. I stood there and watched that same spot for several minutes until my cousin asked if I thought the fish would commit suicide and jump back in my hands. I said I guessed not.

But fishing was a physical challenge and I deduced that I liked physical challenges. Yet, there was more to it than that. Hiking to the top of the ledge above me would be a physical challenge but I had little interest in it. The attraction must be that there was no guarantee of success in fishing and I liked the fact a person could fail or succeed depending on his own skill and personal preparation. Nature played no favorites. That was it, the challenge. At least partly. I looked at my arms and legs and body and decided I was somewhat muscular and had some physical endurance, playing tackle in kindergarten and loving it until the teacher saw the grass stains on our pants and made us stop...but it was not that only. There was something intellectual...even spiritual about fishing. The attraction to fishing came from both within and without.

Finally, it struck me that I felt differently about myself and the world when I went fishing. Everything fell into perspective. In the city it seemed that people fumed at one another. Here, everyone seemed to have more patience and were more in harmony with all about them.

But I must also admit that I had an aversion to the societal world of mankind as I perceived it. Clearly, I was no genius in social matters. Put me out in nature and I said, "Hi," as quickly and easily as the next guy. At school, church, on the street, and even at home, I was more likely thinking about something else when someone else was talking. I may have been thinking about what was happening at the creek. Years later I couldn't remember for sure. I'm not sure now.

But I had difficulty away from the creek fusing ego and humility. Which one was it that got things done? Fishermen seemed full of ego but every time I confronted a fish, I felt humble. And I had trouble with preciseness in things like math. One couldn't inject one's own feelings into math. It was just there. Other than the algebraic formula I had brilliantly devised for catching fish, S=A+E, I could not fathom anything at all in the sphere of mathematics. In the seventh grade, for example, every new math assignment was a crisis. I could never get my teacher, Mr. Archibald, to explain to me why the circumference of a circle equaled Pi r^2.

"What is Pi?" I asked Mr. Archibald.

"Don't worry about it, my boy. All you need to know is that the formula is Pi 3.14. Just do what it tells you."

I *did* worry about it. I wanted to know how the formula was devised and how come they called it "Pi" which seemed a stupid name and how come the formula *was the formula*. I concluded, rather correctly as it turned out, that I could never be a famous mathematician because I always wanted to know how they got the formula.

Along Parleys Creek, it made no difference. I needn't know math except to catch fish and to make sure I didn't catch over my limit which was 15 in those days and there was little danger of that. And I didn't need math to feel the presence of deity in my life. On the creek, I knew my place and it was beneath nature and God and the universe and most everything. And I felt happy being overwhelmed with humility as I tried to catch a fish. Humility was happiness. Or at least trying to overcome humility to feel important was happiness. It was the endless pursuit thereof which I finally construed to be true happiness.

I had long been hung up on rewards. Clearly, some rewards were bigger than others. To catch a fish, as with anything else, one must be willing to pay a price. Big fish were harder to catch than small fish. Thus, there was a greater reward in catching a large fish than a small fish.

But one could have expectations that were too high. What if you didn't succeed right away? What if the big fish was elusive or got away? Was joy negated in only trying?

It seemed that if you worked directly for rewards, or happiness, both fled. In religion, you are taught to "serve others because you will feel good about it and be rewarded." But will that happen if your main purpose is remuneration? No. The reward must be in providing a service without any thought of reward. Only then are you rewarded. The "reward" is in becoming strong enough within one's self to help others without any expectation of reward. Of course.

The foregoing did not come as an instant flash of inspiration at the age of 12. Only years later did I comprehend that happiness is a by-product.

Why did it take me so long to learn this truth? Was it delayed because I withdrew for a time, like the New England hermit Thoreau, to his pond? Or was the creek a catalyst in gaining this insight?

I believe the latter. I learned that I was more successful in catching fish if I focused on the energy and skills needed to meet the challenge, not only upon the reward. Put another way, I was more successful (and happier) if I temporarily forgot about the rewards and concentrated solely on what was needed to obtain the rewards. With that attitude, I enjoyed the pursuit of catching fish, not the catching only.

While time seemed to stop when near the creek, meaningful experience sped up exponentially. Clearly, I looked to the creek as a schoolmaster. There seemed no end of insights I could gain from it.

One insight was that all mankind is different. Most of my friends, it seemed to me, preferred to remain at home rather than going out of their comfort zone to the creek. So I did most of my fishing alone. Sometimes, a friend would announced he'd go fishing with me or meet me at the creek, but mostly they backed out for one reason or another. Except Jay Funk. But the day came when his mother decided he should take piano lessons and after that, I rarely saw Jay at the creek. My uncles owned a piano company and my mother revered her brothers and I lived in fear my parents would make me take music lessons. My greatest fear was that they would have me take up the violin.

Most people, it seemed, preferred to do indoor things. They opted for security and status quo rather than physical challenge and adventure. They wanted to be in total control of their lives next to a thermostat dial and refrigerator. Television was coming on in that era, and many stayed home for hours to watch (in black and white) professional wrestling. I couldn't see much future in it. One pin apiece was clearly orchestrated; the third, the winning fall, was up for grabs. The third one seemed to be honest but I could never feel intelligent or comfortable watching the first two. Every wrestler also had a gimmick, like "Gorgeous George" or the "Mad Bomber." I shunned such farcial programming, although later, when "Uncle Miltie Berle" came along I could see there might be more potential future to this new medium than I had first visualized.

It was true that a person could find more comforts at home than on the creek. With the latter, there was poison ivy (happily, I found I was immune to it) and there were thorns, briars and thistles, mud and cold and stifling heat, thirst, hunger, insects, snakes and spiders. Finding the poison ivy no deterrent, I sought out such places and crept in where others feared to go. One August behind a patch of ivy, I hooked and lost what was a trophy cutthroat trout for the little creek. Its crimson gills shone even in the brushy shadows. I took delight in the fact that this trophy fish lived less than a stone's throw from the 20th East Bridge where many people and cars trod daily. I lost this big fish the first year because a leader knot came untied on my grey hackle yellow. I vowed to never let such carelessness defeat me again.

But later stalking the fish I now called "Redgill," I made a different kind of mistake. I let my shadow cross the water's edge. A V-wake shot upstream. On the third try, I found still a different way to miscue. The casting motion of my rod tip overhead triggered a cloud of sand in the riffle below. I decided it was going to take much patience to catch "Redgill." I would have to learn much more about the habits and habitat of *Salmo clarki*.

I tried to envision how rewarding it would be catch this elusive fish. If not, I had done as Teddy Roosevelt, one of my heroes then and now, advised. "The credit belongs to the man who is actually in the arena, whose face is marred by dust and sweat and blood, a man who knows the great enthusiasm and the great devotions, who spends himself in a worthy cause, who in the end knows the triumph of high achievement so that his place shall never with those cold and timid souls, who know neither victory nor defeat."

If I did catch Redgill, it would be a bonus. At the same time, I must be careful not to rationalize. I must not be a quitter. I must do all I truly could to catch this special fish. I must not make excuses that it didn't matter. I knew it did.

It seemed that winter lasted forever. I helped speed it up by drawing outlines of trout on cardboard, painting them in natural colors, and placing them in the creek in "lairs" where they would look natural. All were monster 16 to 20 inchers. They looked fine for a while held in place by invisible leader. But by the second day, all the colors washed away and the fish themselves were torn away by the icy current. I never did learn whether anyone besides myself saw these substitute fish in their full, albeit ephemeral glory. At least they helped while away the days until spring.

The ice began to thaw in late April. But it was replaced with muddy snowmelt. I could find no fish in the watery onslaught which cascaded off the Wasatch. It was late June before I could cast into the creek without my line swishing past like a bull lassoed on twine. Finally, the time came when the stream returned to normal.

I caught a grasshopper along the railroad track and resumed my quest for Redgill. By now I had sense enough to tip-toe in lightly, maintaining a low profile, and moving very slowly into casting position from behind the final bush guarding Redgill's lair. I also kept my rod tip away from the water and kept my shadow in the ivy.

I twitched the 'hopper to make it appear as if struggling to avoid drowning. The critter suddenly disappeared. I lifted the rod tip gently but firmly, and saw a deep flash of scarlet glow from the dark water. It seemed forever until my opponent no longer thrashed around roots and brush and I could lift him from his sanctuary. A deep sense of satisfaction pervaded my being. I had persevered and won. Never before had I beheld such a resplendent entity as that cutthroat trout! The fish was not particularly large by most angling standards, just a plump 13 inches of gold, orange-brown and scarlet. Yet, it was the largest trout I had ever personally laid out strategy to catch. It had not been easy. But the fish had been reduced to the ecstasy of possession.

I had held larger trout in my hand. On forays with my cousin on the Logan River, I had watched him entice lunker brown trout by casting out "rock rollers", or as defined in a book of entomology, caddis larvae, which encased themselves in pebble homes and lived beneath stream rocks. But my cousin became disgusted one day when the fish were not biting and he had me hold a net on one side of a boulder while he poked a stick at the other. I felt a thud in the mesh and lifted. It was a beautiful brown trout of some 18 inches. We beheld our good fortune as if it was a rare dinosaur bone in a remote dig. But we had broken the law to catch the fish, as the prison trustees had done, and the result was remorse.

I enjoyed the beauty of our prize two hours later. But the reward was not as exultant as in catching Redgill.

True, I learned much about "stream strategy" with my cousin and I applied much of that now to Parleys Creek. For example, on the Logan, Dennis poked beneath cutbanks and boulders, predicting where the largest trout might lie. His stick revealed many hideouts of the big browns which the Logan River harbored in those days. I read in the *Herald-Journal* of trout to 17 lbs. taken by fly fishermen just below First Dam Reservoir. The lake held big fish, but I preferred running water to flat. You could predict the lies of big fish in running water. Besides, there was new personality around each bend of a stream, whereas a lake seemed in a single glance to be mostly a monotonous expanse of more water.

I tried to apply all I had learned on the Logan at Parleys, but I was on my own now. I decided that while I had learned much from my older cousin, much can also be learned by observing in solitude. With other people, there are distractions, mostly unnatural distractions, and one cannot be as absorbant of the natural world about them when talking to other people.

I was often caught in rain or windstorm on the creek. One morning, a mile from home, I had to nestle beneath a cottonwood tree to avoid a drenching downpour. There, I could watch the spectacular fury of lightning and thunder. It never occurred to me then that there was immediate and real danger associated with lightning. Looking back, I was too fascinated by this violent act of nature—all the more attractive because it was totally uncontrolled by man—to feel fear. For some perverted, or perhaps masochistic, reason, I enjoyed at that time gaining martyr status bucking the physical elements. If I was unprepared, nature taught me a vivid lesson I could not forget. There was unmitigated romance in being buffeted by nature-made adversity. It was a feeling which did not subside in the slightest until I was, well, at least going on 14.

After all was said and done, I concluded that the reason for my being awed by nature was this: one could compromise with mankind and manipulate one's way to truce or victory. There was no compromising with nature. It was resolutely absolute and gloriously unyielding. Thus, it was stronger than myself and a standard I could cling to. Man could not defeat nature. Man could triumph over nature only by obeying her.

Chapter Four

One night in late May a friend and I learned that a child was believed drowned in Parleys Creek. We joined crews searching the swollen stream until late hours into the night. I searched the muddy flow with flashlight, as did my friend Ulysses (yes, that was his real name). I pulled a mesh of brush from beneath a limb. Was there a body caught inside? No, it was just that, brush. My friend pulled a black something from a bridge abutment. It was an old tire. Downstream, I probed with my foot in a back eddy and felt a soft but solid object on the stream bottom. Was that the dead child? I reached down and retrieved the object from the water, and for a moment Uly (that was what I called him) and I were afraid we had found the girl. It was a dead cat in a burlap bag. We stopped and asked ourselves what we were doing here. Did we really want to find a dead *human* body?

Suddenly, my colleague and I looked at each other and walked away. We would leave the job for firemen and policemen. They were paid to do such work. Thank goodness there *were* people willing to do things like that, pay or no pay. I had learned my limitations. I was not as tough as I thought. I knew I could not bear to look into the face of a dead child. I could not even bear the thought of it in my mind.

The little girl's body was found downstream the next morning by a cop.

When my parents read about the child drowning, they worried about me "playing" near the creek. I assured them I would not go near the creek anymore when it was running high. This was true. Not to look for dead bodies, nor even to go fishing.

I'd learned the week before that there was no use trying to catch fish with the stream boiling out of its banks. For one thing, fish can't locate what the angler is throwing at them. Any trout sticking his snout into the main current that week might well have washed into Great Salt Lake.

One thing I did learn from observation that spring, however, was that larger trout become emboldened by slightly higher flows and emerged from places like overhung banks and brush to feed more openly. When Parleys flow subsided in July-August, the fish returned timidly to their old hiding places. One had to peer closely with eyes shaded to detect their tails beneath any obstacle they could find. I concluded that neither flood nor drought is a happy time for a trout; but of the two, the latter is probably the more frightening for them.

Yet, I concluded it is easier to catch fish in low water than high. In low water, it is easy to locate the fish, but one must also do many things to avoid spooking them. I could not wade upstream from my quarry, for mud or sand drifting down would make the fish suspicious. Shallow water meant keeping a low profile on the approach. Nor could I wave the rod overhead. I had to cast sidearm. I also had to use a long leader, for the line splatting on low, clear water (low water was always clear) was enough to send all alert fish (the only kind in Parleys Creek) into hiding for hours. In addition, I could only see the water's surface, so I had to use a dry fly. Wets and nymphs would sink to the bottom and in order to follow their path I would have to rise on my knees and inevitably frighten my opponent.

I learned to like fishing low water, however, for I enjoyed trying to catch fish I could see. Such a challenge was unmistakably lucid but one must be more painstakingly patient. Yet, I decided that painstaking patience was not a bad habit to cultivate for whatever might come along.

I also learned that all is not as it first seems in a creek. Light is refracted or bent when it strikes water. Fish which appear close are actually farther away. Fish are not as big when caught as they appear in the water. I filed that information away thinking it might be useful later.

Not long after the child drowning, headlines in the *Salt Lake Tribune* blared that a murderer had buried his young female victim in a shallow grave on the bank of Parleys Creek. It was where I had fished several times between the Gravel Pit and Suicide Rock holes. I do not pretend here to have been in any way witness to that event (although I might have as I tiptoed up and down the creek with fishing rod in hand). I envisioned the monster this man must be, grotesque head and twisted face. Later, I was introduced to the murderer who was being treated in the state mental hospital. I was given a tour by a friend who was the hospital chaplain. The murderer looked pleasant enough and seemed like a very nice man. He offered to shake my hand and I did so. My reasoning at the time was to be "nice" back, for the bars between us appeared fragile. But the man did not look at all as I had envisioned him. It was difficult to reconcile that this was the person I'd read about in the newspaper. I concluded that there was more to truth than one might see on the surface. On a creek. Or in life.

With others from my school I sometimes visited "Crazy Mary." Actually that term was an endearing one used for a warm but eccentric lady who lived for years at the gravel pit. It was rumored, especially around Halloween, that young people disappeared when visiting her alone. But I never read or heard about anyone actually disappearing. Some who were scared out of their wits vanished for a time, but they always showed up later. When my friends visited Mary, we always counted up afterward. Never did we have less than 100 per cent survival.

One time when fishing by myself, I saw "Crazy Mary." She waved and smiled and seemed friendly enough to me. I did not fear Crazy Mary. I feared her boy friend. His name was "Old Ed" and he lived near Mary. He was not Ed. He was "Old Ed." In any event, I climbed from the Gravel Pit Hole one day to see a pistol pointing at my head. Actually, the pistol did not just point at my head; it jiggled and wavered at my head.

Nervously holding the other end was the man said to be Mary's lover. I had apparently unknowingly trespassed too close to the crumbling railroad caboose he called home. Punctuating the end of each broken sentence with a scowl, he waved the muzzle which on occasion, I could look into directly. Considering his age, I suspect that the shaking might have been triggered from senility as much as fright or intent to kill. It made little difference if the thing went off.

My mind had been on other things. I'd just caught a brown trout in the pool below and was pondering how a *Salmo trutta* had gotten here in a cutthroat stream. I pondered how to catch more of the hole's browns on the next visit. But I now doubted that I would ever again fish the Gravel Pit Hole— even if I lived long enough to be tempted. I visualized the *Deseret News* reporting my death: "12-year old boy shot by Crazy Mary's Lover after Catching Brown Trout in Cutthroat Stream."

I had read that one should back away gently from a grizzly bear while talking all the while. Ed seemed to fit the image. I did so now. When out of pistol range, I quit talking and ran pell-mell down the railroad track as fast as I could go. Last time I looked, Ed was still there waving his firearm at all 12 points of the compass. Two more years passed before I dared fish the Gravel Pit Hole again. By then, Ed was no longer there. Alas, neither were the brown trout.

Another time I talked my father into taking a hike with me up the gully. We wondered at the sight of a three-point mule deer buck which seemed surprised to see us. We also saw a mink, hen pheasant, and many colorful flowers, including honeysuckle bushes yellow-bright with early summer's glory. My Dad rarely took walks with anyone, because as a young boy he had taken on rheumatic fever. It so weakened his heart that he had little energy save to work in his wood refinishing shop, eat supper and go to bed. On the one memorable time he strolled with me up Parleys Creek, I felt closer to him than ever before. I showed him where I had caught trout with his fly rod and he smiled. Never again did he gain the energy to take a long walk with me up Parleys Gulch. He did, however, seem to better understand its attraction for me. Before we left the creek that day he made an announcement: the split-bamboo fly rod which he had owned since a boy was officially mine. Forever. I used it from then on with greater pride and devotion while most other boys only had metal telescope rods. Those rods could be altered to any length desired up to seven feet or so but they were heavy and did not carry the distinction of being genuine split bamboo. I could cast my lightweight bamboo rod all day and never grow tired. Maybe I didn't dress like those gentlemen in the outdoor catalogs but no one could say I didn't carry equipment of distinction.

My second summer on Parleys Creek, I caught 61 trout, an indication of having learned much from the little stream. Two of them happened under particularly unusual circumstances; at least I thought so. It was early summer and the stream seemed too high for best angling. But at the last minute before taking a hike to look things over, I tossed a six-foot leader with a fly in my back pocket. The fly, of course, was a grey hackle yellow and I was careful to fold the whole thing in a piece of paper to avoid hooking the back pocket of my Levis. When well upstream, I noted one riffle I'd never fished before. It seemed fairly clear, though high, and it swept through a likely lair near heavy brush. I sat down and tied the leader with fly onto the end of a stick about four feet long. Then, I tossed it out and…was that a fish? I lifted the stick and voila! The other end fought back. In amazement, I pulled the creature out and had very little trouble finding it in the leaves behind me. I'd try it again. But this time I noticed the stick had cracked when pulling in my prize. It was too limber to use as a fishing rod, so I tossed out the leader by hand. A second trout struck and I pulled it in by hand.

Afterward, I tried to analyze what had happened. The previous summer I couldn't have caught a fish with the original angling pole owned by Izaac Walton on England's River Trask. Here I was catching two fish on the most primitive of equipment. I decided I had learned a few things but mostly it was luck.

Could I repeat what I had done if ever stuck in the mountains after a plane crash or something and had to feed a starving crew of pilots and passengers? I didn't know.

But two weeks later, I was very lucky again. The stream had dropped and cleared with much better fishing conditions. A friend named Richard told me he had been trying for more than a year to catch a certain large trout, a cutthroat, not a hatchery rainbow, for he had seen the orange gill slashes as the fish struck his fly. Once he had hooked the big cutt but it got away. Since then, he had not succeeded in coaxing the fish out from its home behind a large brush pile. He was not even certain the fish was still alive. Perhaps someone else had caught it, or it had died of old age. He cast several times without success as I watched, then bid me try it.

I looked through my fly book. I had lost my last grey hackle yellow and had not replaced it. But there sat an old bedraggled wingless nymph which if in a sporting goods store, no one would buy. The concoction did, however, look quite real, as if it might try to crawl off my hand. I held it to my ear and told Richard I expected to hear it buzz. He laughed out loud. Then I threw it out and there was an immediate blur of orange. I pulled and the fish sailed past my head almost into Richard's face. He looked stunned. I was somewhat stunned myself, and the fish never touched me. It was a 13-inch cutthroat, fat and sassy and as glorious a trout as I've ever seen.

"You did it," he said, half in lament, half shock. "You caught my fish!"

"Well," I apologized, "you can have it." But he shrugged it off and said it was my fish; he had invited me to cast and I caught it fair and square. "But he added, "I don't think it was right. All the time I've spent trying to catch that fish and you do it on the first cast."

"Sheer luck," I said, and I knew that was mostly right. But I sneaked a look at the fly he had thrown and it was a grey hackle yellow. Fishing caused a person to be full of conclusions and I came to one now: there was more to this business of fishing than merely casting out grey hackle yellows.

I learned most about the trout of Parleys Creek in sitting still and observing. I finally concluded that two things comprise the life of a trout: (1) feed (2) security. (Once a year, of course, in late spring, these cutthroats had their minds on sex and spent about two weeks spawning.) But food and security were their main concerns. Most anglers do not, I decided, realize the importance of the second part while seeking the first. Most of the fish I caught that second summer were because I got my fly or offering to them when they were not apprehensive about danger. One had to be patient in that respect, although a habit of impatience must also be cultivated. One must not wait around for fish who are not hungry, but move on to find those who are. Give them their chance and get out.

I conducted many more experiments to determine what spooks fish and learned that fish in shallow water are much more wary than those in deep. Yet, it was also worthwhile to search out trout in water less than a foot deep because there is only one reason they are there: to feed. They know they are exposed and conspicuous in shallow water and much more alert (that word again) to moving shadows or bank tremors. I learned to never attempt a short cast to fish in shallow water, but remain some distance away, preferably 15-20 feet or more. If closer, keep a low profile. A fish's eyes can see movement much more readily say, five feet above the bank, than two. It's the way nature has fashioned a fish's eyes on the side of its head. Any movement as with a fly rod tip should therefore be from well upstream. If in doubt, let your offering drift down.

The argument has raged over the years about casting up or down stream; but if the water is low and clear as it was on Parleys Creek in late summer, there is little argument: drift it down. If you cast upstream, not only will you have to get closer to the fish, but you will put the leader and possibly the line right over their heads. I've heard many arguments for casting upstream only, with the idea that behind the tail is the fish's blind side. True, but that is all negated if you must cast over their heads. Actually, a side position to the fish is ideal, but in a small stream that may be impossible.

I spent many hours observing drift and drag. Trout are like Pavlov's dog; they become conditioned in their search for food and if it appears to look familiarly real like the last food they partook of, a buzzer goes off in their heads. If not, they pass. Why bother if it doesn't look like food? It is as simple as that.

I decided therefore, that any serious fly fisherman must take time to study real insects and the way they drift. There are such things as wet flies and nymphs, of course, but they represent something other than *dry* flies. The latter is pretty much an insect which has recently hatched and died. Fish take note of what is happening and focus on it to the exclusion of all else—just as they did my artificial hatch, showing no interest until perhaps the 100th cast. When they do home in on that particular tidbit, their focus will not likely change until some other phenomenon sets in which is worth their time. The reason they do so is maximum feeding efficiency, calories in vs. calories out.

Insects hatch, of course, by emerging from the bottom where they have spent a year or more living under rocks; they then swim to the surface. Their wings are developed, but they are wet and useless for a time. The insect must drift to some safe place such as boulder or bank to dry out before flying away. Many trout which appear to be slurping insects off the top are actually intercepting insects moving up from the bottom. A second or two may be required for a fish to notice and calculate the insect's speed of ascent. Thus, the "take" often occurs just below the surface. The trout's dorsal fin and tail might well break water, but the angler using a dry fly does so in vain. The fish is focusing just below the surface for its food, and only there during this phase of the hatch. The fish probably doesn't even see an artificial on top.

One might think the fish would be an opportunist and take whatever food is available, especially larger fare, but this is seldom the case. A fisheries biologist explained to me that the fish can only do one thing at a time, like a human gathering berries; we might spot a pear or peach off to one side but we focus only on the berries in order to gather them in more quickly and efficiently.

Therefore, during a hatch, an observant fly fisherman must drift his offering at just the right level or he could well go fishless. It's a science I did not master for a few more years past my 13th birthday. Nor have I completely since. Nor I suspect, does any nympher in any one lifetime.

After the hatch has been on for an hour or two, the insects may die, become somewhat waterlogged and sink. Then, wet flies will be in vogue. I caught four trout one day from a Parleys riffle when noting they were feeding in open water, but jaws opened and closed on something well under the surface. Casting the grey hackle yellow as a dry fly on top brought no response. At the right (wet fly) level, however, those trout couldn't leave the artificial alone.

It is a fact that many fly fishermen don't understand "drag." No wonder these anglers are ignored. And frustrated. A fish gets in the habit of sipping a fly from current which conveys it down naturally without "side pull." An artificial with string attached is apt to pull toward the angler or at least toward the angler's rod tip. A real fly may ride very high in the current, at least if a may fly or other lightweight insect.

Once I tossed out small grasshoppers and noted that they also rode with few hackles denting the surface. The best imitation, I decided, was not a pattern labeled "Joe's Hopper" or some such designation, at least not to imitate small 'hoppers. An angler must learn to view the offering as a trout does, and a small grasshopper (or even a moth) is so light that it scarcely touches the water. The best imitation I found for both small hoppers and moths was a size 10-12 elk hair caddis. From an angler's view above, it looks absolutely nothing like an honest grasshopper. From underneath, it couldn't look more real.

As for the metal hook, it's true that it simulates nothing in nature. In fact, sophisticated fish (those hooked often) definitely learn to shun the barb, especially when obvious on the surface. But if a fish sees the positives it is looking for at first glance, I became convinced the rest often does not matter.

On Parleys Creek I noticed that many fish struck at what must have seemed a hatching insect trying to become airborne off the surface, or a female of the species attempting to deposit eggs on the water. In addition, drag could be rather easily avoided on a small stream. When I tried to fish larger waters, it seemed that a "dead drift" was preferred, with many currents between my rod tip and the fly placing drag on the latter. It was much simpler if the fish would accept an insect skipping around, but it seemed to happen less on the larger streams, probably because more food was available and they could be more picky. There were also far more currents to create drag on a carelessly drifted artificial.

I vowed to keep an open mind and keep learning, a thing which probably keeps so many astute and intelligent anglers hooked on fly fishing. The smartest thing I ever did in those early days was keep an open mind. I had not mastered fly fishing and I knew it. But I would keep trying.

In searching out what spooks trout, I found from my daily research lying at one side of the stream that overcast days were more productive than bright ones. When others said it "looked like it was going to rain," that was when I should be on the creek. Sunlight illuminating the water made everything in it, even the little fish, more edgy. A chickadee or Stellar's jay could flit by on a cloudy day and almost be ignored, if seen at all. On bright days, the trout would flee at the first overhead appearance of even a butterfly.

Of course, a fish in a small stream has many enemies: minks, herons, kingfishers, larger fish, man etc. That is why a large trout will often take up residency in the permanent shadows of a bridge or brush pile. There it is less seen. On Parleys Creek, there were many railroad ties that fish stationed themselves beneath. (Many smelled of creosote which to this day is a pleasant odor reminding me of good fishing on Parleys Creek.)

I observed that with sunshine comes more moving shadows beneath breeze-blown willows. Anything waving over the water, like my fly rod, would scatter far more fish in sunlight than on overcast days. On a bright day, one must wait dawn and dusk. I learned to avoid fishing altogether under bright mid-day sun on open meadow streams, especially if they were shallow. Sunless days were especially savored because one didn't have to be so wary. A super-lengthy leader, hard to cast, was not necessary.

This intelligence has had such a far-reaching effect on me even half a century later that what appears to be a "nasty day" for some is "bluebird" weather for me. It's like duck hunting. To say that foul weather is good for ducks is a oxymoron, for it is not good for ducks at all. It is only good for duck hunters who find birds more restless on such days and more likely to continue searching for calm water, hence remaining on the move.

I also learned from Parleys Creek that light clothing against a dark background is seen more easily. Wear clothing that matches your background whenever possible. Whatever you're wearing, move slowly; lift and place feet as if walking on egg shells when nearing potential trout lairs. I can always tell an inexperienced trout fisherman, for he trods the bank instead of tip-toeing it. He stands tall over the water. He makes false casts over the very water he will fish. When he does cast, he thrusts line down hard instead of soft and easy, failing to note that a real insect alights upon the water as gently as thistle down.

An alert angler (fishermen can be that too) must know the difference between the various insect phases in progress in the stream at any given time. We force our will upon the fish and demand they take what we want to give them instead of being observant enough to notice what it is they want. Perhaps that is why 10 per cent of the fishermen (the sensitive ones) catch 90 per cent of the fish.

In other words, most anglers just won't take the time to study what the fish have focused their dining ritual on at the moment. Humans do the same. Would we eat mashed potatoes when looking for ice cream?

Chapter Five

As I approached my second autumn on Parleys Creek, I came to realize that, socially, I was a nerd. I preferred to be alone in nature than among other human beings, i.e. I hated to ride the school bus. Others seemed to enjoy the experience, at least the ride home. It was dead quiet enroute to school, but everyone chattered like tree squirrels scolding a fox on the way home. One obnoxious kid sang a song, "Cement mixer, putsy, putsy, which end does the cement come out?"

I thought once about fighting him, but I had decided after getting in dozens of fights as a nine-year old that fighting was somewhat over- glorified. Even when you won. I will give an example to illustrate. A boy named Albert who had befriended me the first day of fourth grade in a new school suddenly began telling everyone that he could beat me "easy" and I was a Pastsy." I grew tired of it and knew the time had come to prove otherwise.

Five minutes later, I saw the terror on his face as he lay on the ground, blood spurting from his nostrils onto what had been a clean white shirt. As my fist clenched to hit him again, girls smiled at me as victor. The truth is, Albert and I were both losers. True, he never again taunted me again or claimed he was "tougher." I had accomplished that much. But Albert was humiliated and hung his head when near me and all I wanted was to be his friend and everyone else for that matter and he would never talk to me again.

And of course, reasons for not fighting when losing are obvious.

As for the kid in the school bus, there was another reason I didn't want to fight him. For one thing, he was bigger and he had an entourage who held him as a hero; I could never figure that out. He was a bully to the bus driver and wouldn't sit down or shut up. Boys patted him on the back and told him what a brave guy he was. Girls looked at him with admiration. I decided if I had to be one or the other, I would rather be a nerd.

Fortunately, this bully had his mind on more important matters than me, like singing his putsy song. He never bothered me in my silence, nor knew I existed. Another advantage of being a nerd.

I could, of course, walk down the creek past the prison to school and avoid the bus altogether. But I would arrive somewhat disheveled after busting through briars and willows. I was too young to care much about talking with girls, but old enough to care what they thought of me, and it seemed girls noticed one thing mostly, whether your clothes looked nice. So I tried to have my clothes look nice whenever I was around them.

My sister, Shari (she was named after "Shari" Parisian face powder, a rare name in those days but common now) three years younger, rode a bus to a different school and my little brother, Douglas, was not even a factor in my life except to cry at night. Mom, finding it bothered Dad less than her, would get up to take care of the matter. I slept downstairs alone where I couldn't hear him and it didn't bother me at all. Shari grew up to be a beauty queen but said she didn't try to. "It just happened." My brother would become a fishing technician and one of my closest angling partners, but that would not take place for another decade or more.

At school I hated math and wood shop but loved geography, science, and English. I liked art if I could draw what I wanted. I also took to P.E. if the right sport was in vogue; in football I was chosen captain of a team (no big deal since there were four squads and four captains). But we were not allowed to play tackle as I'd taken to in kindergarten. That might have been a good thing because the seventh grade school yard was concrete and gravel, all conducive to scraping arms and legs.

But most of the time I wished I could break away from school and resume my education on Parleys Creek. For example, I witnessed real redds there (not just pictures), nests that fish scooped out of the gravel to lay their eggs. The fish would not lay them in mud or even sand and that was probably best, for the eggs would not hatch unless in gravel. The male and female thing happened there as with all life (except amoeba-type single- celled animals) where eggs deposited by the female would not hatch unless the male dumped something called sperm on them. I guess it was so the fish could have families like humans do. But in some species like bass, the male fish guarded the eggs until they hatched and messed up the families anyway by gobbling up the young.

Trout eggs were about size of a small safety pin head and bright orange. The eggs lay in the creek water for some 30-50 days, depending on exact temperature, until hatching. Fish live on their egg sac until reaching an inch or two long, then feed on whatever is available in the stream, things like minute algae and young insects. Some three years later, the fish grow to "fingerling" stage, advancing food-wise to more delectable items such as caterpillars and spiders. It might require five years to reach seven inches long. In high altitudes, the fish might have such cold water and little feed it would take nine years to reach as many inches.

These insights made me respect every fish I saw, or at least the trout I knew something about. Some of the Parleys trout, even the medium-sized ones, were probably older than me. I could not look at them without wondering how they had survived so many enemies. Fish in lakes and large rivers were never in as much danger as those in small streams, where droughts, ospreys, kingfishers, herons and bitterns, minks and kids lurked nearby. Thus, my higher level of respect for the small stream trout.

Rarely in school classrooms did I learn things like that. Knowledge was always couched in some sort of "academic" language so it sounded official and important but it couldn't be more important than I already explained it.

Teachers sometimes also had different ideas of what was valuable to know. For instance, a home room teacher asked us one day what we had gained during the week that was a "valuable learning experience." I had been studying birds along with other natural life along Parleys Creek, and with a no-nonsense bird book in hand, learned there are no blue jays in my area, like you see painted on calendars all the time (Eastern-made calendars). The "blue jay" of the West was really a Stellar's jay. I learned to tell the difference between a yellow warbler and a goldfinch (the term "wild canary" meant only that a bird had escaped from someone's cage), and I learned about warblers, vireos, wrens and the like and hawks of various kinds. The creek harbored little-known species such as towhee, slate-colored junco, indigo bunting and other finches and thrushes.

I studied them in detail every chance I got. And for a time, I attempted to draw them. So when the teacher asked what I had learned of value that week, I wrote I had learned how to put a "fierce and angry look" in a bird's eye. It could be done, I explained, by drawing a curved line over the iris of a hawk or shrike eye.

With a tone of derision, the teacher read it to the class. They all laughed. I felt like running outside beneath the canal bridge and weeping. But on this occasion, her remark did not phase me in the least, for I realized my teacher did not know her birds and was ignorant of how important it was to those who did.

On Sundays when I couldn't fish I was a deacon who passed the sacrament in church and wore a white shirt and tie, except some days when I wore a plain red shirt with no tie and didn't look like any of the others and was told I couldn't do it any more. Well, was not this whole business of religion to test our free agency? I opted for a red shirt.

Except my parents would frown on that, and I didn't want to displease them. I would try to conform, if it wasn't too painful. My parents were, I had discovered by now, devout Christians and they expected me to be the same. But they put little direct pressure on me, letting me feel my own way through the "earthly testing process" as they put it. I was allowed to make mistakes, and correct them, although if I was near running water I could never see how it would be a mistake.

I would take my time. My parents were a happy couple and set good examples, people said, for honesty and industry, and I saw no reason not to be like them some day. Unlike some religions I'd read about, my parents had fun, went to dances and movies. But they believed in blooming where planted, not traveling around much, and I would be nearly 16 before seeing any other county than the three or four we had to pass through between where we lived and where we had lived. There wasn't much adventuring to it, considering the dozens of magazines I'd read extolling the virtues of far-away places like Paris and London and Rome. And the outdoor magazines! I lived for the day I could go fishing in New Zealand and Alaska. But I was only 13. I must wait.

Meantime, my father decided I would have to "learn how to work" and make some money for myself, as I was now too old for an allowance." I was required to go with him most Saturdays to his shop in downtown Sugarhouse where I "would learn a trade." My father was a refinisher, and like the Savior himself, also a carpenter, a "highly revered profession," my father reminded me. That was fine except that I had no proclivity whatsoever toward carpentry and only the barest minimum toward refinishing. One problem with carpentry was that it involved math. I had a decided inclination not to measure a piece of wood that needed to be fit into a vacant place on the piano but rather make an "accurate estimate" of it. The length would be one ruler long (12 inches) plus the length of a nearby nail and some two more inches. I thought at the time by sheer law of averages that I might come out right occasionally; but due to poor luck never once did the piece I cut fit the vacant space to be filled.

As for refinishing, I wasn't to be actually trusted with putting the varnish back on the furniture and pianos; my father did that. I was the "unfinisher." (Some called it "stripper" but I never liked the term.) What I did was take the finish off, a tedious and often painful process of applying paint and varnish remover to the wood and scraping it off. If any of the remover got on the hands or face it was invariably painful. One wore gloves, of course, but the remover had a fetish for human flesh and always found it sooner or later.

I thought many times that if my father had gone into the newspaper or printing business that I might have taken more interest in his work. He was a "born fix it" man, people said, and thereafter, I put no more stock at all in the term "heredity."

So, with winter coming on, I lost most Saturdays. The fishing season itself officially closed Oct. 31, leaving me maybe eight weeks before my learning opportunities on Parleys Creek ceased for another season. I must make the most of what I had left.

It was one day in mid-September when I went to the creek and found the dam on the waterfall permanently plugged. All flow diverted into the prison ditch. The stream flow had likely been halted for several days, for there were no trout at all to be seen in the pool below the runway. The fish had to be there, of course, somewhere, hiding in the low water. The next day I saw a trustee, one I'd never met before, near the diversion. He told me the prison warden had managed to obtain all water rights to Parleys Creek and what I was looking at was permanent. There would be no future flow to the waterfall pool or anything below it.

I knew that all trout below the diversion would die within weeks. There would be no more downstream fishing. I enlisted the help of my next door neighbor and we pitched in to salvage the fish. To be sure, we were illegal, catching fish with our hands; but we might as well do it before the fish died of natural causes—or the prison trustees got them.

We focused our initial efforts on the first brushy riffle below the waterfall pool, since it was shallow and the fish would die there first. I had seen several trout in the past, and managed to catch one. When I waded into the two-foot deep water, I got the shock of my life. Trout zoomed about my feet everywhere. But they were too fast to catch. I swept at them with a net in vain. Only one thing to do. We tore out all brush so the riffle was stripped clean, except for one small patch of willows. All the fish took refuge beneath the one willow patch and before we were finished, my friend and I had captured 13 exquisite cutthroat trout. One that I had never seen before was 12 inches long, trophy size for the little creek. Most bore dark and colorful markings rather than mere silver, a commodity I learned was reserved for trout living most of their lives in obscurity and darkness.

Improve the World...

In the weeks which followed, we hauled out many pounds of trout from the dwindling stream, by late September no longer even trickling slightly from pool to pool. I discovered trout trapped in tiny pockets of water, which I had no idea harbored anything but minnows. I found much biota in the water I'd never noticed before, including myriad rock roller caddis larvae, stone flies and scuds, or freshwater shrimp, and larger life such as crayfish. I also found sculpins, tiny and primitive-looking fish with large heads and brassy complexion. I knew it was a favorite food of oversized brown trout in the Logan River but had never witnessed them here. Well, I hadn't looked closely enough.

Mentally, I cussed at prison officials and those who let them do this to a once-living stream; but at the same time I learned much about streams and the key role they play in the environment to house life forms. In the process, I learned where trout hide and how they survive under adverse conditions and perhaps most of all this: no matter how observant you think you are, nature is a step ahead. There are always creatures living lives in complete secrecy, filling a vacant "niche" as it is called. But *Homo sapiens* do not notice with only casual looking.

When the waterfall pool dried up, it broke my heart. I stood looking for half an hour at the dead moss (decaying moss smelled aromatic but that is not the same as actually dead moss) and squirming little immature insects which lived beneath the now dry rocks. I caught with my hands a few trout beneath the one or two remaining wet rocks, and transplanted them via net above the diversion.

With the far downstream trout it was too far to "live water" and we took them home for a fish fry. My parents seemed to take the attitude that at last they were rewarded with some of my voluminous time spent on the creek. I observed that people who don't fish think fishermen catch fish to eat fish but that is rarely the case. Fish taste good but eating is not the real reason for catching fish. I could not tell any of my aunts about catching fish on Parleys Creek without them asking if the fish tasted good. They did, but that was of small matter.

A young teen-ager was often misunderstood, I decided. In the first year we moved to the city, World War 11 ended. I liked to draw pictures of aerial battles and showed one of my masterpieces to an aunt who said, "You show here fewer enemy plane being shot down than our own. You should have more faith in our side. Haven't you been listening to the president's [Franklin Delano Roosevelt] fireside chats?"

Indeed, I had sat around the radio with my parents listening to FDR saying, "We have only one thing to fear and that is fear itself." But I said to my aunt, "I like to portray life as it really is. I try to be objective and according to the newspapers, the Zeros and Messerschmitts have some flying aces as well as our own side."

When the war ended, I was at a boy scout camp in the High Uinta Mountains, and I remember it well because I fished most of the week without catching a single fish, or even feeling or seeing one on my line. I had much to learn about high altitude fishing. I remember thinking my aunt was right, our side won. Then when I drew pictures, I could show mostly enemy planes shot down, for that was the way it had to be at the end.

Yet, I was not caught up in the hoopla as some. Boys about me lamented they were "stuck" at boy scout camp, and hitch-hiked a ride to the nearest town, 35 miles away, celebrating well into the night. I remained at Scout Lake and fished until dark that evening, much like I had the other days of that week. To be sure, I returned to the campfire, attended mostly by the scoutmaster, empty-handed. But I had not really failed. I had learned many things which wouldn't work.

Shortly after my return from that fishless experience, my father announced that "no work had come in for several days" and he had some free time. My mother suggested he take me fishing and Dad asked if I was interested. By nightfall, we were in a tent near the shore of a place called Trial (not Trail) Lake, not far from Scout Lake. It was called Trial because it was an experiment of the water-users in the valley below and it was apparently working, for the lake was brimful of water. I was still convinced that fly fishing was the only sporting way to catch fish (something of a curse from reading too much I later decided) and my father walked more than a mile around Trial Lake with me, without so much as even seeing a fish.

The next day we cast flies around several more High Uinta roadside lakes, including one called Alexander which had just recently had a road access cut near it by a logging company. Floating out to the middle in a makeship log raft, the two of us cast for hours without catching anything.

Just at dusk, my father had two strikes as he was about to lift his fly pattern from the water. He missed them both. We had now gone two days without a single hit. Counting the week at scout camp, I had fished these same high lakes for eight days without a hit, or even a bump against my feathered artificial. We had by then deteriorated into making up silly ditties about "little fishy in the brook, please look upon my hook." These ditties did no good whatsoever, even sung loudly to the stares of other anglers.

Perhaps it was time for a change. We drove to Mirror Lake several miles away and at the lodge bought more than lunch. We bought some worms. We applied them to the end of our line, threw out and within a few minutes, my rod tip began to bounce. At the heighth of the bouncing, I pulled back. Too late. Well, the fish could taste the offerings we now tossed at them and that should make hooking much easier than with the phony, tasteless flies. I missed a second strike. On the third, I looked at the dancing rod tip in my hands, and shouted to my father. "Fish on!"

We caught two brook trout apiece that afternoon, one of the most colorful creatures God could have ever created. Amid bodies mottled with emerald, turquoise and even purple, the fish displayed fins of black and white, edged in scarlet. If I was in charge of the Universe, I told myself, I would construct such a fish myself, for it could be done no better. I marveled out loud about the imagination and power of deity in fashioning such a resplendent creation.

My father nodded. "Surely, mankind could not do this on his own," he said. My father was never one to overstate the obvious, even if an object lesson, and he left it at that.

It was a wonderful four days, although we caught no more fish. I looked at one huge trout, however, which cruised near the shore of Mirror Lake and ignored all we threw at him, flies, worms, plugs and spinners. Clearly, he was swimming about looking for food. After a while, he returned to the deep from whence he came and I could see there was much more to learn about fishing above 9,000 feet. Still, I had actually caught a fish, my first brook trout (scientifically, a char like lake trout, but a technicality which could be overlooked) and I determined to scour the earth to find brook trout where they were more plentiful and grew larger.

I had learned the value of using worms in these lakes, but one thing puzzled me: earthworms do not occur naturally in alpine lakes. If fish fed on the familiar, what did they think the worms were? The quandary was partially resolved when I found thin, black "blood" worms in Mirror Lake. They probably looked enough like earth worms for the trout to try the latter variety and liking the taste, ingested them enthusiastically.

I decided that the reason I missed some strikes on the worm-eating trout was because they felt line tension before I set the hook. The time to do so, I concluded, was at the first full enthusiastic jerk on the rod tip, or the second, if there two in brief succession.

I would use worms on alpine trout for many more years, although the time eventually came when I gained more faith in flies, although they were different types than found in the flatlands. I also had to gain more insight into mid-day breezes which waft insects about in high country. Fishing early in the morning, as was paramount in summer lowlands, was useless in the highlands because it was the rising sun's warming rays acting against cold ones in the canyons which caused breezes and blew insects about. Fish didn't bother until maximum calories made it worth the effort.

Specifically, the sun had to reach about 9 0' Clock before stirring enough winds to get the fish feeding.

Fishing after a rainstorm (frequent above 9,000 feet) was fruitful because the droplets knocked bugs down from the skies. Of all the fishing I ever did, then or since, I found that timing is the most important factor on upland waters.

I also found that water remained too cold the day ice went out, usually in mid or late June, but a few days later, the fish were ravenously hungry. The best fly patterns were small sizes 12-16 in yellow, brown, black or grey, the most frequent colors among natural insects, adult or immature, in alpine terrain. The least likely color in nature was purple. When a friend showed me the many fly patterns he had tied in purple ("It was the only color thread I had") I told him to throw them away.

I might have been a little harsh, but what I meant to say was, "Have you been out there observing what goes on?" I actually caught a fish on a purple fly once but it wasn't on Parleys Creek and I don't think it was very alert. The fish was a hatchery rainbow and I might have caught it faster if I had stomped on the bank like the feeding man does when he tosses out fish pellets at the hatchery.

Chapter Six

Although color of fly was important, my observations proved to me that size was most critical of all. Dry and wet flies worked well in sizes 10-14, but tinier midges and emergers constituted most of a trout's food. On occasion, a large grasshopper or moth imitation as large as 8 or 6 fetched strikes for me but basically, most of the food the Parleys trout ate averaged less than the size of a paper match head.

I hated small, but the proof was there after several months' experiments. Clearly, I had to simulate small, or miss out. I had shunned "small" because size 18-22 artificials made for difficult tying; the hook eye was about size of a pinhead. And of course, one needed extremely skinny leader to thread through the hook eye and get a proper knot tied. I hoped during those days that a technical breakthrough in leader would come along in the future.[1] Traditional "cat gut" leader sold by most stores had to be soaked for about 15 minutes in water prior to using. If not, it broke easily.

In addition, some leader strength was lost with even the best of knots. If the leader listed at 6-lb. test (it would hold that much dead weight), I soon learned that a simple overhand knot (the worst kind) would reduce it to 3-lb. test. No trout I ever cast to in Parleys Creek weighed that much, but the pound test listed was breaking strength without considering the pull factor. No striking fish I had ever hooked failed to pull, and if the angler panicked and pulled too hard on his end, he could pop a 6-lb. test leader on a fish as small as say, 10 inches. If the fish pulled left when you pulled right, one could even break 8-lb. test.

The response by the angler on a taking fish had to be firm but gentle

---

1. The "technical breakthrough" hoped for has happened. Leaders nowadays not only don't require pre-soaking, but come in much thinner diameters with greater test strengths. (See Appendix A.)

with any light leader; you couldn't use heavier ones or the leader would fail to fit through the eye of the hook. Of course, deciding on leader diameter-test strength was always a compromise between two things: (1) having leader thick and strong enough to hook and land a fish, (2) keeping the leader light enough that the fish wouldn't see it and shy away. I witnessed several anglers during my early boyhood days using 10-lb. test on streams where trout rarely exceeded 14 inches. Anglers who did this just didn't know their quarry. With the microscopic vision of a fish, 10-lb. test would resemble cable in clear water. Needless to say, anglers using such "whale bait" rarely bragged of enticing many fish to the hook.

As for tying leader to hook, I lost several fish using a figure 8 knot. One loop around just wouldn't do it. I learned to twist the leader around itself at least six times and insert the end through a loop near the hook no less than twice. There was so much to know and only one lifetime.

Whenever emergers were hatching, trout seemed prone to hone in on them to the exclusion of all else. One reason was likely that they were numerous and relatively easy to catch below the surface, compared to wets drifting through occasionally, or dries flitting about the surface. Emergers began moving late in spring and continued through early summer. I would find caddis, stone and may fly larvae beneath rocks in late April, rarely larger than my smallest fingernail; by August most were gone. During this period, I had to drift a fly no larger than 16 at best and if it was dawn or dusk or a dim day, and if the wind was blowing, getting such a small fly tied on was no easy task.

The hatching adult, of course, was rarely much larger in body size than the nymph, although wings and tail could make the overall insect a 14, say, instead of an 18. Still, I was dealing with small. I welcomed late July when a large and foppish 'hopper or cicada imitation would match streamside life around me. I could also use other "terrestrials" imitating ants, beetles and spiders. But there could be no doubt about it: these trout ate mostly minute fare and if the stream dropped way down in early fall, they became more fussy what they dined on. At times, I would drift a meal-sized morsel like a huge moth imitation near them, but if they were "berry picking" on gnats and midges, I doubt they even saw my alternative. If they did, they rarely let on, eyes glued on the "no see ums." Apparently, they preferred them because they were more abundant than all else.

I tried also to figure out the color dilemma. Purple was out, of course. Orange was in if imitating trout eggs during the spawn. Red was the color of blood and worked in lures but rarely in flies. I cast a scarlet ibis pattern around two different days for hours as an experiment and drew only a blank. Yellow was found in caddis flies (rock rollers when in immature form, as I had learn to call them on the Logan River); young "rollers" were often greenish in the first few months. Some streams, I learned through reading, also had a hatch of green drakes, a form of adult caddis which I never saw on the Logan or Parleys. Some insects hatched into blue hues, although they almost never carried that color in the immature stage. Many flies, adult and nymph, were brown and black or grey, including the stone and may flies. White was an easy "color" to follow in the water but rarely matched anything in the wild.

I kept a fly book of mostly brown, black, grey and yellow fly patterns. I tried at one time to tie them myself but found my fingers rather clumsy at tying tiny winged artificials and decided to just buy them. Later I began tying my own nymphs and streamers. Being mostly smaller than 13 inches, Parleys trout seemed little interested in spinners and/or minnow imitations, fly or otherwise; thus, they did not figure in my early angling education. (I would later rely heavily on muddler minnow streamers and other minnow simulations, and keep a large arsenal of "large flies" in my creel at all times. Smaller fare were, however, the bread and butter fare that trout generally preferred.)

I was also aware from reading outdoor magazines that a battle raged among fisheries biologists about whether fish could actually distinguish colors. There was no such quandary in my mind. They could. Many was the time I sat in one spot and dabbled flies of equal size and shape but of different hues to Parleys' trout. Some colors were ignored, while others seemed as Pavlov's dog, fetching instant attention. For example, during a caddis hatch, pale yellow or tan-cream hues were the decided preference. The blue-grey-black Adams fly generally worked well as did the renegade but the fish wouldn't touch either in the same size and shape as caddis imitations if caddis were hatching. There was no use my fighting it; if I tied on a ginger quill, elk hair caddis or other imitations in a tan-cream color, I scored.

Only years later did science conduct experiments much like Pavlov did on his dog to prove that fish can and do determine colors. Bumping certain color markers in aquariums meant food for the fast-learning fish, while other colors did not. Science finally realized what dedicated fishermen knew all along.

Shape is also important. I tossed out flies of same size and color to find out that winged artificials were like magnets during a "dry" fly hatch, and wingless just as popular when nymphs were what the fish wanted. With emergers, I wanted "slick" looking patterns; if they had wings, they must be tight against the body, for fish saw them that way as they made their way to the top to stretch and dry out. I was convinced the trout watched for certain "sight pictures" and when they got it, they responded. Such a picture might be upright wings, or drooping wings, or no wings at all, or skinny body, or fat, or jointed, etc.

Fish in current always made up their minds regarding sight picture faster than slow water counterparts, and thus were easier to fool. A trout watching current had perhaps half a second to make up its mind about striking; if hesitating, the tidbit was gone. I could tell that some fish guessed incorrectly, because in taking stomach samples of fish I caught, some sported spruce needles and twigs. What had the fish taken them for? Whatever, they would starve if letting all "possibles" pass by. If they guessed wrong, no matter. Stomach acids would dissolve what they couldn't convert to calories. I even found a relatively large rock in one stomach; I have no idea what it passed for, but it likely passed out via the vent without causing any particular problems to the fish.

Trout in slow water had more deliberation time and I seldom found non-edibles in their bellies. Therefore, if I couldn't coax fish in slow pools to strike, I tried riffles. One day I enticed no fish in pool water but caught eight out of riffles bubbling along briskly. Of course, I learned to avoid water that was so swift, for fish would have to burn up hundreds of calories per hour just to remain in place. Yet, at the same time, fish would take up feeding stations in broken flow where a rock or bank deflected current even slightly. This was true in large streams more than in small ones like Parleys. Security requirements dictated that trout have one of the following to remain in place for long periods: (1) deep water; (2) shadowed or covered water, (3) shallow water only if in a wide stream. In a small stream, fish were too easily seen by enemies on bank, including fishermen. Cover was also more important in small or narrow streams than wide streams like Montana's Madison River, Utah's Green, Idaho's Henrys Fork, et al.

I also found that fish preferred one type of stream bottom to another. I could usually assume trout were present, if in the stream at all, on dark-bottoms. Sand and light-colored rocks on a smooth bottom were less likely habitat. Broken flow and dark bottom were a winning combination; the reason for this, I think, is simply that nature's camouflage laws favor places where the black back of a trout makes it less conspicuous in dark water. With birds, of course, usually viewed by enemies from below, it is the opposite; light underparts blend in with sky and clouds.

I was often amazed at how difficult it is to see a fish even in shallow water. One mis-step often sent fish which "weren't there" scurrying. I learned to scan water carefully before stepping in. Shading one's eyes or wearing polariods helped, as did concentrating on searching for moving tails and fins against the unmoving bottom.

Most anglers I watched were not aware of hidden fish they spooked, especially when wading fast via large steps and sending out a tell-tale V-wake ahead of them. Blissfully, such anglers moved on and failed to understand why fish ignored them. It was when I walked in short, no-wake steps, lightly touching bottom, that I found unsuspecting fish. In streams with slippery rocks (one place I fished not far from home was known as "Soapstone"), an angler had to wear tennis shoes, or felt soles on boots, and be careful to walk with a stable step. Even a near-fall could alert fish for a dozen feet or more.

As time went on and I explored more of Parleys Creek, I discovered it could be divided into two sections. Most of what I've described was below Suicide Rock. Above that landmark, in the canyon, U.S. 40 paralleled the stream for some eight miles. People from California and New York and inbetween often stopped there to sleep, picnic, sometimes to wade or possibly fish. The water was colder here and brook trout comprised some 40 per cent of the catch. Rainbows were occasionally dumped in, especially near the big white Stillman's Bridge. On occasion, I would turn social and talk with tourists. "Boy, what a thing you got here, kid," they would say. "I wish we had a trout stream where I live in Los Angeles or Omaha or Philadelphia. Let's see if you can catch one!"

Such a challenge could not go unaccepted. Sometimes I did catch one as they watched, but it was less likely because if they watched, you grew more impatient and didn't take the pains to do things right like you always did when you were alone. Sometimes it happened and I enjoyed listening to them marvel at the magnificence and splendor of a wild trout. Some had never seen one before. They would go on and on about how important it was to have such "natural interludes" in life. Then they would go on their way and I would return to my solitude and wonder if they would ever take the time to catch a wild trout for themselves. I suspected not, for most of them seemed caught up in a "rat race" treadmill as they themselves termed it, with so many places to go and things they had to do, and the pressure was on to do more of it, and it had to be done now, and I was happy to just be a young boy with a fishing pole.

At times I did not even care if I caught fish, although it was always in the back of my mind. I enjoyed the creek gurgling by and the willows and the sky and told myself I was the luckiest creature in five counties.

I confess I had not as yet gained the skills to land a fish properly. I had learned much about how to entice and hook a fish but reducing to possession in classical style was something else. I got it done in the quickest and surest way.

One day I was surprised when a trout struck from a shallow riffle where I was just dragging my fly through to reach a better looking pool. It so startled me that I vastly over-reacted, flinging my rod tip into the air. The fish became disconnected at the apex of the swing and sailed at least 60 feet directly above me. I tried to catch the fish on the way down but I miscalculated.

The fish splatted on the large, flat rock beside me and I could see by looking at the pieces that it was a small brook trout. I vowed to become more sophisticated in the process of landing fish, although deftly stepping into the small stream to net or grab the prey was seldom possible. I could at least, I chastened myself, strike back barely enough to hook the fish without also making it airborne. But alas, a fish the very next day landed so far behind me that I couldn't find it. So much for sophisticated landing techniques for the time being.

When November ended fishing for the season, I went into a mild funk. The stream was iced over and the creek took on a different look. Icicles emprisoned the rose-colored bushes. Snow fell everywhere in equal doses but remained longest in the north slope shadows of every Gambel oak. Snow hung from swaying branches and if one wasn't careful, funneled down the neck. Chickadees showed up seemingly from nowhere to eat the dried fruit of serviceberry and chokecherry bushes. I often hiked the gully at this time of year, occasionally seeing cottontail rabbits and the ubiquitous quail.

It was a beautiful season but I yearned for the time when the water would become alive once again. I could always remain indoors and read about the places I wanted to visit but it was a restless business. On Saturdays it hurt less, of course, to accompany my father to his shop and concentrate on the work to be done.

In winter, I could, however, pay attention to something I had begun to take a new interest in: Boy Scouting. I wanted to advance from Tenderfoot to Second Class. But my papers had been lost in moving to the city and I lamented that I would have to start over again. A patrol leader named Jerry convinced me it would not be that difficult, especially if I'd done everything once, so I proceeded to run the scout pace and build a fire and cook something over it and take a 14-mile hike and do all the things I wanted to do anyway but Scouting would give me awards for it.

Rapidly that year I moved to First Class Scout and gloried in learning all the outdoor skills required, quickly launching into Fishing and Bird Study. Even the more academic ones, like the Citizenship merit badges, had a certain appeal in the setting given with boys competing against one another to see who could learn them all fastest.

Some Saturday nights I talked my parents into letting me go to a movie not far from the refinishing shop and come home on the bus. It required a three-block walk through dark cottonwood trees, a place where a boy could imagine the worst. Sometimes when I took a shortcut off the pavement across back roads I saw teenagers engaging in drinking and other behavior which seemed devious. Since the same had been deeply preached against by my parents, I perceived there were two worlds, the one of Walt Disney innocence I lived in, and the one my eyes now beheld in stark realism. I would place what I had learned on a shelf for future decision-making. The day would come when I would make up my mind which direction to take my own life. For now, there was much I didn't understand. For example, how could a large trout grow big by swimming around eating only tiny insects?

Chapter Seven

I was now nearly 14 years old. I had spent most of my time on the creek from June to November, except Saturdays when I had to work, and of course, Sundays, and often strolled along the banks during off-season. Truly, I loved the hazy days of autumn enjoying the rich scarlets of oak and maple, the golden sheen of quaking aspens. Most beautiful of all were the chokecherry bushes whose tangled web of branches hosted withered leaves with a thousand shades of purple ranging from magenta to indigo. The temperatures were also about right, at least into early October, and the sun seemed happier with less of a burden trying to heat up the high mountains.

But it was a harbinger of winter and I knew what lie ahead. I fought if not despair, minor depression. Ice would soon enprison and hold hostage until April all flat water and much that had hurried about, water or live creatures. There would be no more sound of evening crickets. The earth would become hard and unsympathetic to the touch of toe or finger. The fish would feel no hunger, being cold-blooded and their metabolism would wind down until they required little or no food. The books said they were in a state of semi-dormancy, almost like a hibernating bear. If they could be seen at all in the creek, they lay as if lifeless in a deep crevice where they could sleep; but having no eyelids, they appeared as if dead. In the middle of the day in spring-fed waters (rather than colder snow-melt), the fish might possibly feed now and then as temperatures warmed slightly. Ice fishermen on lakes could catch a few fish if they augured a hole directly over a mid-day feeding lane between moss. But mostly, the fish were not active. It was a time when life below the surface of water seemed as frozen as the world above it.

My parents observed that I was less interested in the creek during winter months and outlined a schedule which included two hours of work after school, and eight hours on Saturday. I could slip over occasionally to a hill nearby and do some skiing at dusk on Saturdays. But there was no biological challenge in it; one strapped on the skis and slid down the hill. (The day of tight-fitting bindings had not arrived, at least for me in my crude attempts, and most of my skiing was hoping the buckle would not give halfway down the hill.) The physical challenge was there but it didn't seem intellectually challenging. It would be years later in high school before I would take up skiing seriously. Then it was considered chic to be seen on Mt. Majestic. It appeared to me many students who didn't ski at all could be seen there and made certain they were seen there. But mostly, winter was just a time to pass quickly until April could finally penetrate the inscrutable hold of March.

That April I noticed a girl who sat behind me in my math class. She was brunette and smiled easily and I fancied that she looked a little like Elizabeth Taylor. I would wait until the teacher walked to the cabinet to fetch out an algebra chart and then turn around and try to make conversation with Elizabeth, only she said her name was Diane. No matter. I had limited time, about six to eight seconds as I calculated it, while Mr. World turned his back to the class. I had to select my words carefully to avoid the teacher seeing me, for I was already in trouble with Mr. World for handing in papers which were a variegation of vagueness. (He had forbade any erasures as if a student could figure out a complicated problem without ever making a mistake. I couldn't. My paper looked as if I had erased a dozen times; I had.) Most certainly, I did not want to draw the teacher's wrath now. But I did want to talk to the girl behind me.

The first time I turned to face her, I died a thousand deaths; maybe two thousand. My heart grew taut with the terrible trauma, but ah! she smiled that easy smile of hers and I was encouraged. To my utter shock and ecstasy, she watched Mr. World and coordinated her comments to mine so that we fooled the old teacher completely together and we began laughing about it. My first words were something like, "I'm not too good at math; how about you?" She allowed it was not her favorite subject either and that gave me an in. I told her I liked science, and asked her what she liked. She sort of liked science too! We had something in common! I allowed at the time that it was a wonderful coincidence.

Then Mr. World turned around and scowled at our side of the room generally, and I sat in agony for a full two minutes until he returned for more charts. I looked around then at the girl behind me and couldn't think of anything to say. But she saw it and couldn't think of anything to say either and we both smiled. Ah, what a glorious smile!

After class we stopped to talk in the halls and after school we strolled among trees turning to chartreuse with new buds and I had not realized before just how glorious the month of April really was. A week later I asked her to a formal church dance and she accepted and I realized what I had done. I would have to buy her a corsage! Ah, the wonderful and terrible world of social graces. Where would I buy a corsage? I couldn't just ask Diane. (By now I had decided she didn't really look like Liz Taylor but was a beautiful girl in her own right. That made it infinitely more scary.)

Then I noticed north of Sugarhouse a place called "My Flower Shop." I walked in to buy. But what kind of flowers would she want? I went home and pondered for half an hour. My 11-year old sister came to my rescue. "Find out what color formal she's wearing, dodo." Yes, yes! why hadn't I thought of that? I asked Diane at school the next day and she said she would have to talk to her mother and she would let me know the next day. She did. It was light green. There are no green flower blossoms, I lamented. I couldn't just present her with the stems. But she read the consternation on my face and quickly suggested white flowers. I bought her a corsage of white carnations.

There loomed the problem of transportation. I had no driver's license, nor did my two acquaintances who had asked girls to the dance. I had overstepped my bounds. Once before, I had asked a girl on a date and we had taken the bus to see a Roy Rogers movie. But there was no bus service to the dance and I couldn't expect a girl to walk half a mile in high heels. High heels...ah, the sheer wonder of womanhood. It seeped into my consciousness that I knew far more about fish than girls. It seemed girls I'd observed generally were not certain of what they wanted and one couldn't sit down and write scientific notes about them, at least which meant anything, and get anywhere with them as one could with fish.

With that realization, I sat down with my heads in my hands and cogitated my irrational boldness. But I did like her and I wanted to be with her and I would have to figure something out. It would not do to talk it over with Diane, for it was clear in talking to the other boys that a boy must take the lead; the girl expected him to, and he must figure out all these things as if it was only a casual concern and act as if it was no great matter, only it was, and make certain it was all done correctly.

Have my mother drive us to the dance? Her mother? And pick us up afterward? No, that wouldn't work. I worried more about it, but in time an older boy who had a driver's license agreed to take us to the dance, and I personally had a wonderful time, although there was much I needed to learn about dancing and vowed some day I would. She smiled the entire evening, although she always did, and I wasn't certain if she had a good time as well.

It was all platonic although I saw that she needed help walking across an icy street and held her hand and guided her tiny waist until we got inside. Conversation was easy but she was light years ahead of me in small talk. "Don't you like the decorations?" Yes, the decorations are fine." "That's Jim Alby there, the senior class vice president. Do you know him." "No." "Is the floor too slick?" "Yes." I sure do like your light green formal." "Thanks." And it went easy like that all evening.

The following Monday in school, she seemed pleased that I timed Mr. World's inevitable search for more charts and turned around to talk. That afternoon I walked her home from school. I did so the next afternoon as well. But the ecstasy I felt within my soul was to soon crash and burn ignobly. I arrived on the porch one day unannounced, rang the doorbell and glimpsing inside, saw an older boy talking to "my girl." It was a boy I recognized as captain of the football team. He was a very good player. I did the only intelligent thing possible under the circumstances. I panicked and jumped off the porch and fled from sight.

The next day, Diane smiled as usual, but I couldn't muster the courage as before to talk with her. My burst of bravado was gone. Older men had noticed the one I really cared for. I could not compete with the sophisticated swashbucklers of the world who could give a girl everything she ever wanted. He probably even owned a car, although I didn't see one parked in front. I would go back to drawing birds in math class.

A week later when I saw her openly flirting with the football captain, I knew I had no courage to intervene. I climbed beneath the canal bridge and wept. And I would not attempt to date again for several years.

This was not a subject I could talk with anyone about, especially my parents, for there was an unwritten rule in our church that a youth should wait until 16 or older before dating. The concept was not without some wisdom, I decided. But…

A friend up the street was the same age as I and dated girls, and drove a car without a driver's license and went to drinking parties, and talked of drugs and physical passion and called me a nerd. But he had no interest in fishing or the outdoors in general, and I concluded I had nothing in common with him. Years later, he died an alcoholic who would talk to no one, not even his three ex-wives and I concluded that maybe he should have spent more time being a nerd and going fishing.

During that year the call went out for everyone at school to audition for A'capella. They needed more voices. Everyone was supposed to try out. Finally I succumbed to peer pressure and sang for Mr. Willardson. I was rejected immediately. Yet, I was glad I went, since no one bothered me any more about it. Music, like wood shop, was something I had no natural talent for and I decided that a person is either born with talent or he isn't. Mozart was a genius at age 10 and there was no way he could screw up and be anything but a famous composer.

What I was destined to be I did not know but it seemed I had a natural affinity for science. Not physics, for it included math. Physics, I decided was math, only disguised as something useful. Chemistry...now that allowed for self-expression. I bought a chemistry set, and discovered many great things suggested in the experiment book and didn't blow up anything except what was supposed to blow up and decided that chemistry was my future. Through the winter months I spent many hours mixing things together and eventually delved into an adventurous quest to find a cure for cancer, or at least hives.

Taxidermy? When I got paid for two weeks' work in my father's shop, I immediately sent off to the Northwestern School of Taxidermy in Omaha, Nebraska correspondence school for all the tools and instructions needed to mount deer heads and other animals and fish. I went outside and shot a cedar waxwing stealing cherries from a neighbor's tree and proceeded to dissect it. I had a younger friend named Frank who wanted to help me, for his parents had prodded him to become a famous physician. To do so, he would have to learn how to cut living things apart. But upon the first sight of bird blood, I heard a thud. My friend had not fainted exactly but he had felt queasy enough that he quickly sought a seat on the floor. He went home and told his mother he would not become a famous physician after all but probably go into plumbing or something where, when you took things apart, there was no blood.

I didn't mind the blood so much but the rest of the insides were squishy and seemed forbiddingly clammy. I threw the bird away and was sorry I'd shot it and decided taxidermy was like looking for dead bodies. Only with taxidermy you had to already have one.

At times I would visit my cousin Ralph in Idaho where I used to live and we would go hunting. I had no qualms at all in shooting English sparrows, for they were quarrelsome and raised five to six broods a year and seemed destined to take over the Universe, or at least the graineries of southern Idaho. We used beebee guns and became rather accurate with them and killed as much as six "spugs" a day. I also took a .22 out in the country for rabbits and I heard of people being accidentally shot with the little rifle and got a safety lecture from my grandmother. But I never let the muzzle point at anything I didn't want to shoot, and neither Ralph nor I ever had any sort of mishaps in our hunting adventures. It seemed as safe as climbing out of a bathtub, only you had to keep track of what you were doing. Did I want to spend my life studying game animals and become a famous hunter? I wasn't sure. I would have to wait and see.

My grandmother encouraged me to shoot all "chicken hawks" (all hawks were "chicken hawks") which she insisted stole her young hens about to lay. But I read in books that hawks ate more mice and rodents than chickens. It was a fact, however, which my grandmother didn't agree with; she sermoned me that books didn't know everything there was to know. Whenever she was around, I scanned the skies for chicken hawks, although I never did see any near her chickens.

My grandmother was a pragmatic woman who had 26 hours of work to do every day, with a large family to care for, and much work to do. I spent several days pitching hay onto a wagon where a derrick would hoist it onto a huge pile where someone had the fun job of tramping it down. But this was saved for the older and heavier boys. I also weeded and "thinned" sugar beets and potatoes. At the end of the year, I approached my uncle to ask for some pay for the work and he said, "What about all the food and baked bread and apple pie you've eaten at your grandmother's table?"

I thought about it and felt humbled and repentant and never brought up the subject of pay again.

I learned early that I belonged to a large family on my mother's side, for she had more brothers and especially sisters than I could count. We had what were called "reunions" and they were often at my maternal grandmother's farm. It was a grand time. We had all we could eat and played Tarzan in the apple orchard, swaying from tree to tree and finding it difficult to choose between Roman and delicious apples.

I had an uncle who did feats of daring in the orchard like leaping from limb to limb, then graduating to a cottonwood tree high above the ground. I only went to one circus in my youth but he was better than any of the trapeze acts. He said that his brothers were blessed with intellect and musical skills and such but that the Lord had blessed him with only one thing, muscle. He entered a "Night of Pugilistic Skills" at the high school and was pitted against a renowned boxer from the Salt Lake Boxing Club and the man danced around my uncle until the former was "way ahead on points," people said. Toward end of the second round, my uncle threw his first punch and knocked his opponent flat to the canvas. They had to delay the next bout until they could get the renowned boxer out of the ring.

Another time my uncle got mad at a cow which wouldn't go where he wanted it. He lassoed the beast with a rope and tied it to a stake and "taught it a lesson" by killing it and the meat wasn't any good because the cow had gotten lathered up so and they had to throw the animal away. But my uncle had taught the cow a lesson, he said, which it would never forget.

I concluded that my uncle had, indeed, been blessed. But he was much like me, even moreso, in lacking social skills. He had set an underwater swimming record in the Navy but when mixed company all went swimming together in the Bear River and someone said, "There's a snake swimming toward you!" he let it come and bit its head off. I somewhat admired him for it, of course; but I knew it was something I could never do.

During the family reunion I encountered along the Bear River such rare phenomenons as black-crowned night herons, bitterns, and snowy egrets and rejoiced in it. There were many killdeer, a fascinating bird which said "killdeer! killdeer!" all day long and would pretend a wing was broken if you came near its eggs and then fly away after luring you away. I always wondered if they learned this or were just reacting to an instinct without knowing what they were doing. Did a time come along in a maturing killdeer's life when it said to itself, "There comes a mischievous boy near my nest, I better go into the broken wing routine I learned from my mother?" I yearned to know, but not being a killdeer, I could never find out.

And no one else seemed to know.

There was limited time for fishing, but with my cousins we cut poles and tied lines around them and tossed our bait out by hand into the muddy marshes of the Bear, catching perch, catfish, bluegill, and an occasional monster carp. I never considered these "trash" fish to compete with the loftier realm of fly fishing for trout. One mostly waited for something to swim along and find the worm and dance the pole tip. It was fun to fight the fish in, however, and I noted that if we had younger cousins with us, they cared little what the species might be so long as they could subdue the fish and hold it for others to see. The smile on their young faces was worth it just to help them catch a small carp, the lowest form of icthyological matter, but to a six-year old, a treasure.

Much fishing was relative, I perceived. I had read about people who revered channel catfish, perch or bluegill as a mighty catch, although the latter rarely grew over nine inches. The trouble was that these warm water species did not live in the same noble environment, the clean, pristine water of trout. The nearby vegetation was also more likely mired in lowland bulrushes than mountain bulwarks.

I didn't mind impaling worms on the hooks, although one had to be careful to wash the hands while eating lunch. One time I didn't remember after catching a fish and rebating my hook. I can here testify that a worm tastes bitter, much like the beer I sipped in my youth, although I never saw anyone shy away from beer for that reason. One forgetting was enough and I always remembered to wash my hands after that. Truly, fly fishing was less messy and like telling the truth or being honest; one didn't have to keep track of what he had just done.

Turning on 14, I was finding many more interests and diversions in life. Yet, I found myself time after time returning to my earlier quest: to learn more about the catching of the creature people called trout.

Chapter Eight

After two summers living near Parleys Creek, my parents made an announcement to me one day: we were moving to the inner city. My father decided he wanted to have his shop in a new location with more space next to living quarters. We drove as a family to look at the site. Never in my lifetime had I lived where one house touched another with neighbors pressing in all around. I could find no other word but for it but "slums." Yet, I knew it was not so in the sense of slums I'd seen depicted in movie plots set in New York, Chicago, Los Angeles. But it was a slums in that there was almost no yard, and you could hear people arguing in the adjacent duplex unit through what seemed paper-thin walls. The bus stopped at our corner and there was a drugstore across the street and nearly all was concrete as far as one could see save for a few trees.

Worst of all, the creek was no longer nearby. I could ride my bicycle to the creek but it would require an hour or more each way and I didn't have that much time after school. The only break in what was otherwise a bleak future was that a neighbor boy took several of us to the "Trestles." It was a canal which required a mile's walk each way across the industrial side of town across both U.S. 89 and a block long labyrinth of railroad tracks. There we caught a few mudcats and bluegills. One of the boys along, Deral, seemed a genius at catching bluegill. He baited with a tiny worm and lowered it into crevices and seeps along the broken channel where fewer people thought to fish. It was the same principle I'd witnessed on Parley's Creek; those who walked the main paths and easiest routes caught little. But Deral was willing to experiment even more than I on this new fishing hole. When it came to brackish, flat water fishing, I had a thing or two to learn.

True, catching this species was not the same as questing for trout. But the fish did possess a certain spunk all out of kilter with its size. One fishing expert named Henshall had said the bluegill "inch for inch and ounce for ounce, are the gamest fish that swims." Possibly. But I reasoned that he lived in the East and had probably never caught a trout.

I became close friends with Deral. It struck me that while I didn't like living in the "slums," there were some very fine people who did. Besides Deral there was a boy named Richard who shared my beliefs about Christian values (at least those of my parents, for I hadn't fully made up my mind yet); but he had no use for fishing and had to work after school every evening selling newspapers downtown. There was also Jimmy, our Boy Scout patrol leader, who loved scouting as did I, and Jerry, who would have nothing to do with religion, but loved fishing. How had all these good people emerged from a lifetime of living in the slums?

Deral and I gathered all the books we could find on fishing, using his library card and mine, and had a "seminar" to share unique ideas that appeared worth trying. On occasion, since he didn't have a bike, I "pumped" him on mine to Parleys, happy that he was somewhat smaller than myself. Trying out our various theories, we made some worthwhile discoveries. I abandoned flies for a time and tried various baits and lures, some I hadn't even read about.

I was convinced flies were still the best way to catch fish in Parleys Creek, but I was also interested in expanding my horizons. Most fishermen, of course, began with bait and lures, then moved to fly fishing. I was doing the opposite. We decided to focus on fishing with nightcrawlers and worms. I'd used them successfully in the Uinta high lakes, but never in current. We haunted the local city park with flashlight to capture nightcrawlers. One had to avoid direct light on the giant worms, or they would slide back into the holes from which they emerged on warm summer nights. One used a thin cloth across the lens to dim the light and looked wherever the grass or soil was damp. To catch them, we had to gauge which end was fastened into the soil and trap them from vanishing back in the ground. Then came the process of gently pull-coaxing them from their dens. It appeared at times that it was more difficult to capture the 'crawlers than the fish. But with trial and error, we got the knack of it.

I found I could not persuade any Parleys trout into taking a full crawler, although I did so when breaking it into halves or thirds. Trout liked the worm "bite-size." They also liked the lighter, tail end best. But in time, we made a startling discovery: city crawlers were not nearly as attractive to the fish as worms dug up alongside the stream bank. These small grey or red worms apparently worked better because they were what the fish had become accustomed to seeing and feeding on. Success skyrocketed when taking a shovel to the stream banks and digging out "native" worms. One of them was worth a dozen oversized 'crawlers from Liberty Park.

In addition, it was considered "proper" in the fishing books to impale a worm so that it covered the entire hook, including the barb. The idea was that the fish should not be allowed to see the metal. But when we tossed out worms and watched them drift with current flow, they never tumbled down in a round ball as they did in covering a hook but with ends wriggle- free. Thus, we baited the worm in a straight line down the shank of the hook, leaving both ends, or at least one free end, to look natural. Success quadrupled. The fish did not worry at all about the visible barb; likely they thought it was an attached stick or moss strand.

In this, I saw that human beings sometimes outsmart themselves. What appeared most logical was in fact, the least logical. One had to study closely what was happening from a trout's point of view, not man's.

It was also very important to let the bait sink as near bottom as possible. Trout did not look for worms near or on the surface as they did insects. Bait-feeding trout tended to remain near bottom because that was where the worms, being much heavier than insects, drifted. Thus, a small splitshot to weight the offering down, applied about a foot above the worm, was the best way to rig. If the fish had to chase it, they likely wouldn't. One had to make the drift directly into a trout's snout if seeking the larger, lazier fish. This precluded merely tossing in and sitting down and waiting (at least in a stream). It was the angler who followed his rod tip above the bait and kept it moving downstream with the current who caught far more fish.

The same principle, of course, is true with almost any offering. I watched flies being ignored if they drifted other than into a trout's feeding lane. Some trout wouldn't budge more than an inch or two to sip a fly, and I knew the same must be true near the bottom where fish sought the easiest meal possible. One had to study the currents and learn where trout lay; then become an expert enough caster to get the bait, fly, lure directly in front of the fish. Ideally, an offering should not land in front of a feeding fish, scaring it away, but three to four feet upstream.

Another thing we learned from fish we cleaned was that while they had moss in their stomachs—some is ingested via the gills through the process of breathing—that if any moss was attached to the bait, trout wouldn't touch it. The same was true with any hooked offering. One had to maintain a close vigil against even a small strand of moss. The same did not "tarnish" the hook. It apparently made the same look unnatural.

We also discovered that a little white serviceberry which grew along the stream was a favorite trout food. But just impaling it on the hook and tossing out with a splitshot as with worms wasn't good enough. The berry had to sink slowly, in "waves," carried with the vagaries of current. Sinkers could not be used. One had to be patient and let it sink naturally. One could help by casting slightly upstream and letting out line. It was the direct opposite of weighting a worm to the bottom with splitshot.

I was often amazed at how quickly a cutthroat would dart from submerged brush to "ambush" one of these free-falling berries just before it touched bottom. It didn't seem to make much difference how the berry was impaled on the hook; on the barb or shank worked equally well, probably because either looked like a stem accompanying the berry. Whenever breezes blew, the latter likely fell often with stem attached. Since the berries grew almost everywhere along Parleys Creek, one never was out of bait to fish with. Interestingly, in all the time I was growing up in mountain country, I rarely found a trout stream without a plethora of these berries lining the water's edge.

Another trout favorite was a tiny freshwater shrimp, attached to a size 16 hook or smaller. If trout were present, this bait was seldom ignored. It meant dealing with "small" again, for a "scud" was never large enough for a hook size of 14 or more. (Putting two scuds together didn't look natural.) Scuds were also difficult to catch, usually living in moss beds and were fast swimmers when disturbed. The shrimp were even more difficult to catch than nightcrawlers. Fortunately, we found a bait stand staffed by two boys selling both worms and scuds at reasonable prices. I learned later that they financed their way through college by selling these two bait items on a busy artery leading up Parleys Canyon.

In early summer, my father hired a man who loved to fish and was very experienced at it. We talked several times and when he saw my enthusiasm for "this lifestyle," as he put it, he invited me to go along on a 10-day trip to Jackson Hole and Yellowstone National Park. He would depart in mid-August. It was understood that I would have to pay my own share of expenses. It was, of course, a trip of a lifetime for me. I worked extra hours in the shop to both fulfill my obligation to my father, and to earn the necessary money. Jack planned to do some trolling, he said, and when I told him I had no trolling rod and reel, he showed me how to construct a "trolling board" with several hundred yards of heavy line which was hand-held.

He had one more thing to say. He was taking along his girl friend and they were going to be married in Jackson. He also took along a nephew which I was told had little interest in fishing but wanted to go along "for the scenery." I saw in this nephew the antithesis of myself, for it was true; he had little enthusiasm in talking about fishing and even less for the process itself. I could not fathom how this could be so, but soon found it to be true.

When we arrived in Jackson, the first thing Jack and his fiancee did was visit the local justice of the peace and get married. They stayed in a cabin somewhere, as my father had predicted. But the next day, we put up a big tent on the shore of Jackson Lake and all four of us slept under the same canvas roof for several nights.

I couldn't wait to get in the boat and let my line out. The nephew remained in the tent and slept. Jack took very good care of his bride until actually getting on the water and then he seemed transformed. He wouldn't take his eyes off the tip of his fishing rod. He didn't even look at his newly-wed wife. I could see right away that he was a dedicated fisherman.

As luck would have it, we hadn't been on the lake 10 minutes when I felt a sharp tug at my hand holding the line and hooked a good fish. It proved to be an 18-inch cutthroat trout. "Ninety per cent of the fish in Jackson are lake trout," Jack said, "but you said you had spent a lot of time learning how to catch cutthroat."

This was an anomaly, of course, because catching the species in creek and lake are two different things and I knew that Jack knew it. I remained at least relatively humble, for I felt that much of an angler's success in trolling depends on luck, whatever the species caught. Other than reaching the right depth for time and season, in matching "comfort zone" water temperature, much of trolling is simply a waiting game. I waited. But I experienced no other strikes during the afternoon's outing.

Yet, it was impossible to be bored what with the jagged Teton Mountains reflected in the lake's clear water. They rose almost straight up from the valley floor, losing their high summits in what seemed perpetual clouds. Wildlife abounded everywhere. We saw several deer and a cow moose. I had always felt that seeing a moose made any fishing trip special, although the time would come when I would be chased by the black beasts and wished I hadn't seen any at all.

Jack caught two respectable lake trout, or Mackinaw, as locals called them, before we quit. I had never seen a "Mack" up close, but noted the sharp teeth used to feed almost exclusively on minnows and small fish. They never bothered with insects, and in fact, were built by Mother Nature to live only in cold water of 45-55 degrees, which necessitated remaining in 100 or more feet deep during the warm summer months. Going so deep often required heavy weights, sometimes stifling a fish's fight. I decided that it was less sporting than casting a fly. Still, the possibility existed on these long-lived fish to catch specimens up to 30 lbs. or better. Jack said that the record was a 36-pounder caught by a woman who lay her pole with its pop-gear spinners down at mid-day to eat lunch. She barely grabbed the rig before it disappeared over the boat gunnel.

While camped on Jackson Lake, we fished the Snake River. Jack tied on a sandy mite fly resembling a caddis larvae, cast it upstream so it would sink quickly, and immediately began catching the pin-spotted strain of cutthroats which abound in the stream. Displaying a fisherman's wise judgment, Jack had driven an extra dozen miles to cross the bridge at Moose and take an old dirt road up the north, or seldom-visited side of the river. We parked on the canyon rim and walked a quarter mile almost straight down to the river. We saw not a single gum wrapper or beer-soda pop can. Jack understood fishing. Here was a man after my own heart.

Jack's bride did not weather the hike to the river well at all. Tired when reaching the stream bank, she sat down with her fishing rod and Jack did what I would have done: he gave her some worms to fish with so she could remain in one place and rest. She seemed content for 10 minutes but when her husband caught two trout on flies within her line of vision, she grew restless. She walked over and said she wanted to fish with what he was fishing with so she could catch some fish too. He told her firmly to stick with the worms.

She frowned and pointed her finger at him. "You don't love me, or you would let me fish with something that catches fish."

He looked down at the sandy mite pattern in his hand. "Oh, this? Well, flies are not easy to fish with. You're better off with the worms."

It did not appease her. She walked back where she had been and said in my direction, "Married only two days and already he doesn't love me."

I tried my best to explain it. "No," I said, "worms really are the best way to catch fish, normally. Flies are more difficult to fish with."

She gave me a hard look and cast her line in and looked at me once again. "You men are all alike, aren't you?"

I could think of nothing to say. Nothing at all.

Later, I assured her that I would have told her the same thing as her husband. She seemed partly satisfied with that and sat quietly for a while. But she caught no fish that afternoon and bedeviled her husband all the way back to camp about "making her fish with something that didn't work." I concluded thoughtfully that I would be careful who I married.

One thing I realized when looking out upon the vast expanse of the Snake River. It was 200 yards across and at least 5,000 Parleys Creeks. I didn't know where to cast. I was lost. I needed a class in hydrology. Did that current at the far end of my cast continue to swirl down, or back eddy slightly upstream? What about the current in front of it catching the belly of my line? How could I keep the artificial from "dragging" unnaturally against the flow? I had always felt that approximately 85 per cent of fishing was putting the offering where the fish were so that it appears natural to them. Here, they could be most anywhere in the Niagara of water before me.

Jack tried to be helpful. "Look, just think of it as 5,000 creeks with their own currents. Fish as if each one were a small stream of its own."

That helped a little. I tried not to be overwhelmed. I decided to focus on the current which swept along the near bank and then back-eddied in heavy current behind a log. I tossed one of Jack's sandy mites there and felt a small strike. A 10-inch cutt. So far so good. But in time, I decided there were larger fish in this black hole and rigged up with a spinner. I had used one but sparingly in the past and was not quite sure how fast to retrieve it. As the blades rotated past a submerged branch, a massive black form appeared suddenly from the depths and stopped just short of hitting the lure. I held my breath. The fish dropped back out of sight. I knew not what caused it to change its mind.

I sat down on the bank and removed my cap. Was I glad or sad the fish did not strike? In one way, I felt relief. Could I have held it, or would the levithian have just tangled me in the branches and broken me off in its mammoth fury? Never had I beheld such a gigantic fish. Was my heart strong enough to fight such a formidable foe?

Perhaps not. Maybe it would be better to stay with the flies and catch fish I could handle. I did so, but decided the day would come when I would catch such monsters as the one I had witnessed.

I asked rhetorical questions. Could a stream cutthroat grow so big? Were there other species in the river? A little later, I had my answer. Jack had switched to a spinner and caught a 22-inch lake trout. "Must have come down through the dam on Jackson Lake," he said. Should I tell him that I almost hooked a larger one? No, I would seem to be bragging and besides, I had nothing to show for it. I would wait until I could psychologically master such a challenge. It would take time but I would strive for the day I might be mentally prepared.

During the afternoon, I spotted a lone grasshopper on the bank, impaled it on a hook, and caught a 13-inch cutt. Jack saw me do it and praised my ingenuity in using the creature for bait, but asked if I always tossed fish so far back over my head when landing them. "I'm working on it," I told him. "I'm working on it."

"Another thing. When you become the fisherman I think you want to be, you'll find a fly to imitate a 'hopper or something you see on the bank or water and use that to fool the fish with." I pondered that. Jack was right. Someday I would have to learn how to catch any fish I saw with a fly. Even a monster lake trout living beneath a tree. Ah, there was so very much to learn.

Within a few days we moved on to the Yellowstone River. Upon first glance, I fell head over heels in love with this stream. What a mighty force! It rolled along in a crystalline majesty I had never before witnessed. I could not in my utmost imagination conjure up such a large river being as utterly and totally pristine as the smallest spring-fed brook. One could see a yellow pebble halfway across the river in eight feet of water. One could also make out the orange throat slash of cutthroat trout 40 feet away!

My heart leaped to my throat several times along the roadway stream when 17-18 inch cutthroats eagerly greeted my lures and plugs. They finned out quickly from brush and obstacles in most instances but had a slow quiet way of placing their mouth around the offering almost tenderly. It helped me learn to tighten the line to set the hook without sailing them over my head.

Later, I tied on a small grey fly and fished downstream to a gravel bar where people were lined up to fish. I saw that everyone quickly caught a limit of five trout on flies and then moved out to make room for the next angler in line. When it came my turn, I hooked several fish and lost them. I heard moaning behind me. In time, I caught my five trout, five of the largest I'd ever seen, and moved out. I wanted to do the same again the next day.

But Jack said the Yellowstone fish were "too easy to catch" and he hated fishing where it was crowded. We moved on to the Madison. There we had what he was looking for. I was completely baffled by the smooth glide of moss-strewn water. If there were no pools or broken riffles, where would the fish be? It seemed no problem for my host. He caught some on flies, others on a lure called a "flatfish," which fetched out 17-inchers almost anywhere. A favorite lair for the big browns was beneath cutbanks on bends. In one place, we observed seven huge trout feeding at the edge of current feeding from a marsh directly below us, a most resplendent sight that remained vividly in my mind half a century later. But we couldn't find a way to approach without spooking them. They turned tail and fled. I failed to catch a single decent trout in two days on the Madison.

Still, Jack said he admired my tenacity. "You never quit trying," he said.

I felt a surge of glory fill my head but allowed that working hard didn't do much good if you didn't know what you were doing. I was casting blindly, hoping, wondering. But Jack had mastered it. I reasoned that so could I.

Later, we fished the Gibbon River, a rose-hued tapestry of a stream that washed down in a table-smooth sheet through emerald meadows. It was even more difficult to fish than the Madison. Neither Jack nor I enticed a single strike from the Gibbon. But that evening, camped at Madison Junction, I felt rewarded. We viewed several dozen elk, including three massive bulls. And a clown of a black bear sampled all the nearby garbage cans, almost getting his head stuck in one. I had never seen a bear before. For most people I talked with, seeing the bears was the highlight of their trip.

The next day was Sunday and something of a crisis. It was my first Sunday away from my family—at least with a fishing rod nearby. What to do? It was not that I disbelieved my parents, but I sought verification. I wanted to know personally if their beliefs met life's earthly as well as celestial challenges. Clearly, I was developing into a serious pragmatist. In Scouting, I had taken an oath to "Do my duty to God and country...to be physically fit, mentally awake and morally clean." The entire admonition seemed like a good one and it had come not from a pulpit but from the comraderie of a campfire. I was a sucker for anything said around a campfire. Anything at all. It seemed that looking across leaping orange flames outdoors, I listened more intently and became more committed to act upon what I heard. I didn't know exactly why myself, and I have never to this day entirely figured it out. It just seemed that people became more earnest around campfires and a closer bonding took place between the various parties in whatever they agreed to do.

I also decided that while I'd received no personal witness that there was a God in Heaven—who would not forgive me for fishing on Sunday—that if was going to be in control of my life, I had to cultivate discipline. I had to be strong enough to make decisions I could stand behind. Only then could I be in control of my own life and not someone or something else. The same was true for every man, it seemed to me, whether he be white, black, yellow, red, or from any religious persuasion or ethnic background.

I had read of a Jewish man who was ridiculed for worrying about what he ate. "You're an adult now," he was told. "Can't you make up your own mind what you should eat?" His answer was that with billions upon billions of people on earth, he found it encouraging that a caring God would be interested in what he had for breakfast."

I was glad my faith allowed me to eat pork chops. But I admired the man who didn't in order to abide by his convictions.

As a budding pragmatist, it made no difference, it seemed to me, whether or not a watchful God required that we be honest in all our dealings with self or others. Even an atheist would be better off in this life being totally honest. The opposite would bring unwanted and unnecessary conflict. One would have to write down and remember every lie he uttered. If he made a promise and people learned he wouldn't keep it, he would never again be taken seriously. One had to make a commitment and stick with it or be blown about with every passing whim, whether from people or their programs.

Neighbors had at times regaled my parents with advice: "You can't let that boy just go fishing all the time. He needs to be told what to do. His life needs to be more structured by responsible adults." My parents told me about this but they did nothing to change my routine. They said they had confidence in me to make up my own mind what was best.

Jack went out fishing as usual the next morning. I focused on trying to photograph the elk, and explore the downstream meadows. There were signs of beavers. I saw two muskrats and several harlequin ducks, colored with bright spots as if paint had been dropped on a purplish iridescence. If one looked closely enough, he could also see the tracks of great blue herons. Overhead, an osprey wheeled. They were proof that fish could be found somewhere about. "Fish hawks" ate little else.

Jack's wife seemed to eager to talk with someone, anyone. Jack was gone, his nephew asleep. I talked of little but fishing. Mostly I listened. She seemed satisfied with that arrangement and we sat in camp chairs and enjoyed the setting sun over Madison Meadows until steam began to rise from the water now warmer than the air. Awhile after that Jack returned. He had hooked two monster rainbows on a large royal coachman, he said, but both "broke me off."

Our final two days we fished the Firehole River. I couldn't believe that a stream with so many steaming hot pots pouring in could sustain trout life. The stream bed was scorched with the reds and yellows of the boiling side flows. Somehow, the stream sustained trout life, although I was told by a park ranger that in the heat of summer, the Firehole's browns and rainbows sought refuge in hotpot-less tributaries. I cast to a wide range of waters, including the main stream itself but could not fetch any strikes. I was not convinced it held any trout at all in the steaming cauldrons of fire below Biscuit Basin.

Then, a fly angler cast out and hooked a trout in my presence. Now, I had to believe. Almost immediately upon doing so, I caught a small rainbow. It wasn't much, but I was proud of that fish. I could do it if I thought I could do it.

I yearned to return to the Yellowstone River but there was not enough time. We departed the park and drove straight home. It was a wonderful place, Yellowstone, if no for other reason than the plethora of clean water and wildlife. I would return.

Teddy Roosevelt was right. The park was worth setting aside. It was, indeed, a special place.

Chapter Nine

After returning from the Yellowstone trip I decided that I needed to learn more about fishing with a spinner. It seemed to entice larger fish. I experimented with various techniques in Parleys, but the fish were not very receptive to the blades. The fish were smaller and almost entirely atuned to insects. I needed a larger water to try various types of spinners and retrieves.

In time, my father and mother agreed we would take the entire family fishing for four days. We would camp near the Provo and Weber (Weebur) rivers. They were much larger than Parleys but only about a fifth the size of the Snake. They would be just right for a spinning rod and metal lure.

I cast conventionally at first, as I'd seen others do it, downstream reeling up. In a day and a half I never had a single strike. When I cast upstream and retrieved down, I found some takers. There was one problem with the downstream retrieve: if one didn't reel rapidly enough, the lure snagged on bottom. It was difficult to move the line at just the right speed to keep the spinner near the bottom but not in it. When I got the hang of near but not in, I was amazed at how many more fish I caught. I reasoned that a big, lazy fish would rather expend energy chasing a hapless or wounded minnow at mercy of the current (tumbling downstream) than a healthy one swimming upstream.

The very best technique was to cast up and across so the lure wouldn't move too fast and let it "flutter" past cut banks, logs and fish hiding stations. If it was impossible to lag up because of brush, I worked it from the upstream side but slowed the retrieve to make the lure go deep. Letting out line would accomplish the same purpose. I held the rod tip low so the spinner would dig deeper. Sometimes I suspended the blades in weak current and held them there. Always make things as easy for the fish as possible became my motto.

I found that a No. 3 lured out the most big fish. One needn't use sinkers with this spinner because it was heavy enough to cast easily and sink quickly.

Improve the World...

A weightless line was best because the spinner could rotate at slower speeds. On the theory that fish took the spinner to be a minnow, it made the latter look more vulnerable. With a weight, one could get a no. 2 spinner to sink quickly. But the weight stifled lure action.

Success didn't quickly overwhelm me. I also had to get the right size and color. Most attractive blade finishes were either silver or brass. I learned to use silver in waters with chubs, brass on waters with sculpin. Since the latter are favorite prey for brown trout, I caught most of my big browns on the sculpin imitations.

The worst case scenario I witnessed with novice anglers was to cast down and retrieve with rod tip held high. This forced line and lure to the surface where the trout were definitely not looking for minnows. If I saw an angler doing this, I usually also saw a fishless fisherman. I wanted to go over and face the angler upstream and push the rod top low to the water; I tried once but the fisherman wasn't convinced. I didn't try again.

It took me some time on the Provo before I saw the error of spinning downstream. When I began experimenting upstream, I lost three spinners on snags. When I learned to calculate water depth and speed correctly, I managed to reduce the number of snags, although not completely; if I didn't snag occasionally, I told myself, I wasn't fishing where the fish were.

Eagerly the second morning, I got on the stream and caught two small browns. I was on to something. I just needed more time to get the downstream retrieve perfected. But at lunch I got bad news: my father announced we were going home. The "four-day" dream trip was over. He explained that owing to the fact we had all slept out in an open trailer, my mother and sister had been badly bitten by bugs and mosquitoes.

I had no bites whatsoever. "I guess it's the hair spray and perfume," my father said. "Anyway, they are pretty badly bitten. It also looks like rain is coming tonight and we have no cover for the trailer." We headed home.

I had made many vows in my young life and one of them now was to get the right tent or trailer or whatever it took for everyone to enjoy camping. In addition, we had slept at the edge of a hayfield; a boy came out in the morning to say we were on his father's property and he thought we should pay something for it.

My father was not a big tipper. He handed the boy 50 cents and he went away. But why didn't we check the maps and learn where the approved campgrounds were located? There had to be some up the canyons on forest service property. (Thank goodness for federal land.) But at the time we had no sophistication in such matters. Thus, I made still another vow.

Later in the summer, I had occasion to talk with Jack about fishing while we worked in the refinishing shop. Jack invited me to go on an overnight fishing expedition with him to the eastern part of the state. He was divorced now. I never saw her again and I don't think he did either. In any event, there would just be the two of us on this trip. The nephew declined an invitation to go with us.

There were many streams in this country which flowed off the south slope of the Uinta Mountains, including the Duchesne (Doo shane) and Lake Fork, which ran out of huge Moon Lake. Jack trailered his boat in case we made it to the lake; but we tired of driving the rough dirt road and wound up stream fishing on Lake Fork. The drainage was a maze of beaver dams and ponds. They looked like pictures I'd seen of the Amazon jungle. Jack soon vanished downstream somewhere. I decided to sit down where I wouldn't cause a search and rescue later. When Jack returned it was with several large rainbows. Another angler showed me his catch. I wasn't certain why I had not been more adventurous. Never in my life was I so unsuccessful at catching fish. It seemed I was entering a more cautious period of my life. Or was I less foolhardy? I wasn't sure. Jack seemed mildly disappointed that I had remained in one place and fetched not a single strike. I felt disappointed in myself.

I remembered this singular defeat and decided to make up for it two years later when I got my driver's license. I brought a friend named Robert to this labyrinth of dams and ponds. Noting the landscape, nearby hilltops and appearance of stream channels and islands, I no longer feared getting lost. Venturing downstream with a fly rod, I caught 26 pansized rainbow and brook trout with a black barberpole fly pattern. I twitched the offering slightly and when seeing any surface activity near the fly, lifted my rod tip. Not a single fish was tossed over my head.

Robert caught nothing. I felt sorry for Robert. But I had avenged the earlier debacle. The only problem was that by then, Jack no longer worked for my father and had moved on. The main thing, however, was that I had shaken the fear of getting lost. I felt I was becoming more than a fisherman. I was becoming more skilled in woodsmanship. Soon I would take back pack trips 20 miles into the vastness of the High Uinta Primitive Area. Later, they would become 60-mile treks taking a week or more.

For some reason in my 15th year, my father moved his shop to a new location on the outskirts of the city. I was required to go with him every day toward the end of summer. I was told we couldn't afford to hire so much outside help and family members would have to pitch in and do more of the work. During noon hour the first day, I took my lunch down to a little line of trees. There was a creek there. It was called Mill Creek, someone said. Mill Creek didn't cut a large gully when it knifed from the Wasatch Mountains into the valley. It was apparently a younger stream geologically, and coursed only a few feet below the surrounding terrain. Many homes had been built along the creek. This pool by the bridge was, in fact, one of the few places not marked "No Trespassing."

While eating my lunch, an apparition appeared in the pool below me. I sat stunned. It was a cutthroat trout of some 12 inches and it began slurping insects off the surface of a back eddy right in front of me. I had never seen a cutt which looked like this. It was a slender, graceful fish. But what set it apart was that it exuded a drab-like brilliance. It was grey green across the back, a subdued gold-orange across the body. I wanted to behold it up close. I wanted to hold it in my hand for miniscule examination.

The next day I told my Dad I was going to catch the fish during my lunch hour. I took my fly rod and waited for what seemed days until the noon hour arrived. I left my lunch behind and rushed to the creek. No sign of the fish. I eased a size 14 Adams into the current where it would curl around to the trout's lie of the day before. Nothing but empty water. I was about to lift the fly from the surface when jaws appeared beneath the artificial. It was my cutthroat.

I watched the jaws close. I lifted. Nothing. I had missed! I sat down and mentally prepared myself for another try. Had I blown it? Did the fish feel the hook and know it was a phony floating through his territory? He would now have nothing to do with it?

I waited patiently while the fly floated once again to the point where he had struck before. Jaws rose again to intercept. Miss!

What was I doing wrong? I knew that luck alone sometimes dictated that the barb would not find home. Usually, it happened because a fish pulled one way, the line, by the way it lay, another. I decided I was striking too fast. But would the fish give me another chance?

The fish appeared a third time. I counted one, two. When I lifted, the trout was on! My rod tip plummeted. I held my breath as line whipped beneath submerged brush and overhead branches. I had made it a habit of asking myself before casting in any water, "Now if I hooked a good fish here, where would I land it?" High banks shadowed the pool from every side but downstream. I rushed there, wading in to grab the fish securely by the gills and race up the bank to examine it more closely. Exquisite!

I couldn't wait to rush in and show my father. He was talking to my uncle and I interrupted their conversation. "Wait your turn!" my father chastised me. He was right. I had barged in without invitation.

"No, wait!" my uncle said. "Let's see what you have there."

"The most beautiful trout I've caught this year," I almost shouted.

"Not terribly big," my uncle said, as if trying to find reason for my excitement.

"But look at it!" I said. "Just look at its markings! What a wonderful thing that such a wild and beautiful creature should live within half an hour of half a million people!"

With that, both my uncle and father looked at each other and then at me. My father seemed to view me through new eyes. "I see," said my father, now examining the fish. "I don't blame you for interrupting. This is, indeed, something special for you."

It struck me then and has since that people become too busy to notice nature, too busy to notice the Cornucopia that life has to offer. My father made a quick adjustment once called to his attention. But some people, it seems, never do.

Without much advance talking of the subject, my father announced to me one day he was going to make a delivery into Idaho and on the way back we could take half a day to fish a stream his brother-in-law had told him about. The brother-in law might even come with us. But when my father told him we would be camping out on the ground—what other kind of camping was there?—suddenly he decided he couldn't make it. He drew us a map to locate the Blackfoot River.

The stream was supposed to harbor some very large cutthroats. I wasn't fully prepared for how large. I saw them almost immediately after we followed the hand-scrawled map and walked to the river's edge. The fish were spawning from a downstream reservoir and it made my heart almost miss a beat to see in the clear water that some were longer than my arm. A few were the size of my leg.

I felt panic coming on. Did I want to cast my line in there with them? On Parleys Creek, a 12-incher was a monster. Some of these fish might eat a 12-incher. But I decided it had to be done. A battle raged within. Could I land such a fish after hooking it? To lose it would be to fail. But to not even try at all would be to lose in a larger sense.

After mustering my courage, I sat down on a log and checked all my knots very carefully. It would not take much here, a loose tie or a nicked leader, to separate fish and fisherman.

My father had bought some worms and handed me one. I would try that first. My initial cast hung up in moss. I removed the strands and cast again. This time the bait settled into the bottom of a slow riffle. After some five seconds, I lifted for another cast. The line wouldn't budge. It must be caught on the bottom. But then the bottom began to swim downstream. Fish on!

What should I do next? Oh yes, look for a place to land it. Why had I forgotten to do that now when I had always done it even for small fish?

Clearly, my meticulous and in-control demeanor was shifting if not shattered. Valiantly I stood my ground and fought the fish. Dad stopped his own fishing to watch me. Some five minutes went by and the fish seemed to be tiring. Then it took off on one more run, and…I accidentally stepped on the line accumulating at my feet. That was it. The leader popped and he was gone.

I'd heard that no one believed fishermen because the big one always got away. Well, it was true! The bigger fish were the ones to find weakness in your tackle or your technique. They were smarter because they were more experienced and they were certainly stronger because they were large. They were more of a challenge and I must meet it.

I re-rigged. On the third cast, I hooked another fish. I never learned how big it was, for it wrapped around a submerged log, and it, too, broke off. I tied on stouter leader, a new hook, fresh wriggle-free worm and cast again. Almost immediately, my line tightened. This time, I ran with the fish and kept the line tight so that it could dispel a loose hook and watched ahead for any snags. In time, the fish bellied up, and slowly, I eased it toward my father's outstretched net. Then, the mesh closed around the fish and he lifted my prize toward me.

It was not as large as the fish which had spurned me on the Snake River, but it was huge, perhaps four pounds, easily the largest trout I had ever caught. The cutt was in brilliant crimson spawning colors. What wasn't red was orange, except for the upper body and tail which were a caramel gold-brown. I lofted the trophy for a long, long time. I had prevailed!

I looped the fish on my belt. Every several minutes I would stop fishing to look at it. Yes, it was still there. It was…still there.

I lost one more fish which threw the hook and then the feed seemed to be over. Try as we might, we could not resurrect the frenzy of the past hour. Then it struck me; my father had not coaxed a single hit. Did he bait the worm in a ball? Did he fail to read the currents? No matter for him, he said.

It was worth the entire trip just to see me catch the big trout.

At the end of that summer, I returned to Parleys Creek on my bicycle and gloried in seeing the brushy riffles once again where I had caught my first fish. The cutthroats were still where they had been. Rock rollers and may fly larvae could still be found beneath the rocks. I sat down and rejoiced. The serviceberries were still there. Quail rummaged about in their naive invulnerability. Grasshoppers leaped from my steps. Some winged for the creek. I visualized them falling in the water and being greeted by crimson jaws. Golfers cursed their tee shots and sometimes even their approach shots and crashed through the streamside brush looking for lost golf balls. I smelled the creosote of the railroad track. All was normal. As I walked about and looked upon the Suicide Rock Hole once again, I felt nostalgia shaking me like an ocean tide. That it might be this way forever.

I was told by a railroad worker that the DRG and W train did not run anymore through Parleys Canyon to Sugarhouse. They were going to tear up the track. Change. Progress. It was inevitable. Would Parley Creek remain? What could they do to it? The waterfall hole had dried up, of course, with all flow coursing down the prison ditch. But from there upstream the creek of my boyhood seemed to be intact.

Several of my trips to Parleys in that year were with my uncle who had been wounded in World War 11. He had been in the Battle of the Bulge in Belgium, when the Allies thought Hitler had given up, or should have. Instead, Hitler threw everything he had into the vain hope he might turn his fortunes around. He was doomed to die, said my uncle, and Germany was doomed to lose. But first they had to kill more American soldiers. He and four brothers had made it safely through the war but only he had been wounded. A German artillery shell exploded in a pine tree overhead and exploded downward, with a piece of shrapnel shearing off his right hip.

He had spent five months in a veteran's hospital uncertain whether he would ever walk again. "I was bitter," he said. "And to a certain extent, I still am, I guess." But as I watched him now, I couldn't even detect a slight limp. Yet, the emotional scar remained.

He had time on his hands for now between college quarters on the G.I. Bill of Rights and decided to do some fishing. He had heard from family members I might be able to guide him. I selected the canyon sector of Parleys. It was not long before he lifted a fat brook trout from a shadowed riffle at my left. This was my first experience at guiding and I felt relieved to witness my first success. We also plunked .22s at targets in the foothills and had a memorable time together. Later, he committed suicide.

I could not reconcile it.

He had lamented the hatred and killing of the war. Eventually it must have eaten away at him. But there were so many who also loved him.

So very many.

He left a note saying he was too worried about finances to remain in this world. But his supervisor at work told me he had just received a year's end bonus of $30,000. I allowed that I did not understand much in life and probably never would. Was it the war? Only four years away was my own venture into war with Korea. Then I better understood. But always the question remained. Why had he not thought of all of us who loved him?

During the winter preceding my 16th birthday, I spent more time with my chemistry set. I envisioned a career as a famous chemist giving advice off the top of my head to anyone asking for it and helping build a bigger and better corporate America. I spent more and more time with my microscope received at Christmas and eventually, a James J. Audubon book on birds. My parents helped me in all this and I was grateful.

While they did not share my passion for the outdoors, nor even necessarily understand it, yet, they fully acknowledged the same. I was in no trouble with the law, nor did I join a neighborhood group of lads who were caught vandalizing a school. I had no sympathy for such activity and said so. Of all the actions of mankind, vandalism seemed the most senseless to me. No one benefitted. As far as my parents were concerned, I seemed to be on the right path.

But, I had gotten in trouble. Once I stated openly that I had tossed a match into a small pile of brush to watch it burn. Later, the forest service battled a fire on the same mountain. The two must be connected. Maybe they were. A ranger came to my house, said I owed money for the cost of fighting the fire and extracted $12 from my mother. It was all the money I had in the world. I had learned my lesson. Why did they have to take the $12? My mother sided with the forest service and I was not allowed any self-pity whatsoever. At least not around my parents.

Another time, I accompanied some boys to eat watermelon. The melons as it turned out were in a U.S. Government Agriculture Experiment Farm. We were taken to federal court where it was decided we were simply bored kids who needed something better to do. They proposed Boy Scouting. That was fine with me and the charges were dropped. But from it all, I concluded one thing: if I wanted to continue my life of relative freedom to go fishing, I'd better prove I could stay out of trouble.

Chapter Ten

After turning 15, I entered a crisis. I yearned more than ever to fish new horizons far from home, but it would be another year before I could get a driver's license. Yet, that was minor. I had begun to realize that not all I yearned for was possible to achieve. I had always taken the attitude I could accomplish anything I set my mind out to do or be. I had been encouraged in it. Now, there were rumblings of reality.

For example, my ninth grade chemistry teacher gave assignments that were mostly math. It was, of course, important to use the right ingredient, and I had nearly memorized the Table of Elements, at least usables ones like sodium and magnesium, if not the obscure and rare ones like radon and the inert gases. But it was not so much the element or compound used in a given equation to make anything such as an alloy of steel, strengthened by carbon; more important was the amount of each used.

"That's math," I told Mr. Garrish. "I thought this was a chemistry class."

"That's right, my boy. Chemistry is math."

"Why didn't someone tell me before this?" I wanted to know.

"Whatever, that's the way it is."

In addition, the several biology classes I took, in which I had previously been fetching A's, now began dissecting frogs and cats. I could stand the frogs. I drew the line at cutting into cats. "Well, that's what you'll have to do if you want to become a famous biologist," Mr. Smith said.

"Well, then I don't think I want to become a famous biologist."

As for dating, I still sought the necessary courage. If a girl could come along who was supremely confident in her own abilities, and liked me and I found I liked her and if she would take charge in a way that didn't bruise my embryo social ego and guarantee no heartbreak and…

But in all honesty, I knew I could not guarantee her the same security. How had so many millions of earthlings become married?

Making things worse, I had appealed to my father that I be allowed to fill the pores of pianos and furniture with something other than the "dirty hand method." A craftsman of the old school, my father would not allow any of his help to "fill" wood with any material by machine. It must be done by heat of the human hand. And the affection and love that came only with personal attention. Thus, one brushed the right filler, i.e. for oak, mahogany or walnut on the wood and rubbed it in by hand. I appealed to Dad that I might be allowed to use gloves. Thumbs down. I rubbed for what seemed like hours. And at end of the day, I could find no magic fluid which would remove the stain from my hands.

"It has to wear off," my Dad said.

"That's all fine for you to say," I lamented, fighting open anger. "You're married. What girl would talk to a boy with this stuff on his hands?" To complete the routine, I turned my hands toward him. He would give me a stern look and turn to his work.

My father was a patient man, not given to anger. Once I saw a circular saw blade fall off the tool rack above him and strike his hand, drawing blood. He said nothing but picked up the offending piece of metal and threw it out an open window. I assume he went out later and retrieved the blade, for I saw it in place two days later. But the bottom line for me was that I, too, was expected to harness negative emotion. There was no excuse for me to show anger in my Dad's presence and I knew it. But I hoped, often out loud, that as a woodworking artist, he might find some other effective way of doing the work besides the dirty hand method. He never did.

When autumn arrived, and I started senior high school, I tried out for the football team. I had been a reasonably successful neighborhood sandlot player. Now I found the coaches telling me I was too small. True, at 125 lbs. I was not likely to terrorize a 200-lb. lineman. How did high school kids grow so big? I did well in practice but couldn't even get the coach to look at me on the bench when game time arrived, even though rival teams were beating up on us.

One problem was that I hadn't been realistic in my planning. I should have tried out for defensive cornerback knocking down passes, or something where great size was not such an important factor. But the season was nearly over before I realized I would make a better impression with my peewee size playing in the defensive secondary than trying to ram through linemen twice my size. That was the problem: I hadn't made the right decisions before the fact; now it was too late.

It was time now to start making right decisions for the rest of my life. I was still, of course, a nerd. Some of my associates were looking cool in the parking lot adjusting their cigarettes to hang out of their mouths at an audacious angle and I didn't even smoke. Some were carrying open bottles of beer at ball games and I didn't even drink. Some were driving cars without a license and I couldn't find it within myself to break the law. Ah, but they didn't tempt me. I preferred to go fishing.

In this year, my father hired a new man, a genius they said, like Jack, at carpentry and wood finishing. His name was Elmo, shortened quickly to "Mo." My father found that he was a dedicated worker; I found that he was a dedicated fisherman. Only four years older than I, he was easier to socialize with than Jack or others who had worked at the shop. Mo had been recently discharged from the Navy and just gotten married. His wife had no interest in fishing and never went with him. He was always looking, he said, to find other enthusiastic anglers like himself. He smoked heavily and drank "whenever he felt like it," and had no religious compunctions whatsoever. We became fast friends.

On his third day of work, Mo suggested we come in at 6 a.m. and quit early enough to get in some evening fishing within an hour away. He would drive. We settled on a place we had heard about, Mountain Dell Creek, which fed the reservoir from which Parleys flowed. I brought along my best grey hackle yellows for the occasion and caught two fish with them. But when I came upon Mo, he had six trout to my two. I watched him carefully on one riffle and noted that he preferred bait to flies, and impaled a worm on the hook in expert wriggle-free fashion. Here was no novice. He looked beneath rocks and used both shrimp and caddis larvae natural to the stream. At dark, he had clearly outfished me. Since the creek was new to both of us, he had no advantage of familiarity. He was, I decided in time, one of the most effective bait fishermen I'd ever meet.

We felt we had made a discovery at Mountain Dell. It was much like Parleys in abundance of trout life, but with less angler competition. Deer were sometimes seen along this creek. One had to be careful not step on a skunk. Dippers frequently bobbed about the rocks. Dippers were a strange bird. They could "fly" underwater and often did, eating insects or perhaps fish, and then drying out on a rock in an incessant "dipping" motion. They were purple in color and inconspicuous against a shadowed background, nearly flying into your face as you crept along the stream.

The fish were less wary than in Parleys, or perhaps I should say, less alert, because they lived in what was nearly virgin water. Half a million people lived 20 minutes away but they seemed not to know about this trout Valhalla. It made the perfect fishing grounds for us as we experimented with various offerings and techniques for small water trout.

In the weeks which followed, we hiked into several Uinta lakes. In the creek below one of them, I noticed a new fish species I'd never seen save in pictures: Arctic grayling. Excitedly, I cast a light cahill fly to the fish in air-clear water. The fish fled. My leader had landed in a coil, plopping far too heavily near his snout. He may have also seen my moving arm or rod tip. On the next bend, I sneaked in low and dropped the fly more delicately. to a finning grayling. He rose to the surface, hesitated…and sipped with all the grace of the queen of England, tasting tea, at the floating hackles. I was ecstatic. In landing the 15-incher I had my first look at a fish with a kaleidoscope of iridescent colors gleaming gold if the sun reflected this way, turquoise that. His dorsal fin topped his wiry frame like a sail, deeply etched in lavender splotched with black. The mouth was so tiny a dime could scarcely pass through. No wonder grayling were mostly fly- feeders. Nature had dictated they be little else.

In Blue Lake beneath pine-studded cliffs, I tossed out a worm behind a water-filled casting bubble to see if I could catch something big. In time, I felt a tug, lifted and was fast to a fish which seemed to have lightning speed. It proved to be a 19-inch grayling, the largest I ever caught or knew of anyone catching in my home state for many years. When records were later kept for the species, this fish (measured by weight) would easily have beaten the initial entry listed at 1 pound 1 ounce. Mo looked at it and I could see he was impressed. Luck…was it really preparation meeting opportunity or was luck just luck?

I was to become infatuated with grayling. Some day I would glean the Earth to catch a world record. Alaska, Great Slave Lake, Yugoslavia, wherever they grew large, I must go.

Mo and I learned much from each other. On one Uinta lake, he badly outfished me by removing a little water from his casting bubble weight and letting the rock roller bait suspend at just the right level above the bottom moss. I had apparently been fishing on bottom in the thick moss and deduced later that my offering could not likely even be seen. First rule of fishing, I decided was that the fish must see what you want them to see.

In the weeks which followed, my father's new right hand man and my closest angling companion took me and my little brother, now six, to a favorite fishing hole his father had taken him to as a boy. It was a brook even smaller than Parleys Creek, one few knew of, for it lay hidden on a dirt road in another state which crossed back into Utah. Few knew it did so. Mo was much more familiar with the creek than the rest of us and outfished all of us two to one. I observed that he knew the precise pockets where the cutthroats would lie in wait for food.

But studying the creek on the second day, it wasn't that complicated. There was little brush as in Parleys and almost no cutbanks. The fish took lies near rocks and in broken riffles where it would appear the water was barren. But cast in, or step in, and there they were. Why did they lie in the open here more so than Parleys? One reason, I decided, was that fishing pressure was light. Trout fed more openly because they were little bothered. One had to have faith that the fish were there and cast well ahead. If you were to see the fish before you cast, chances are they would see you too and be gone.

In the afternoon when action slowed down, Mo played a joke on me. He had caught a 16-inch trout, most respectable for the small rivulet, and had my six-year old brother pretend he subdued the fish in shallow water I had just worked to no avail. "Wow, look what I caught where you've already been!" Doug exclaimed. When I looked properly shocked, Mo emerged from behind a rock laughing.

One price to be paid with someone else owning the only driver's license was that you were at their mercy. Mo liked to quaff a few beers on the way home and with my young brother and myself both being minors, we couldn't even accompany Mo into the taverns he liked to stop at on the way home. Mo always drove directly to the targeted fishing holes, but was not in such a hurry to return home. One trip back was delayed even further while one of Mo's cronies, unsuccessful at catching a trout to show his wife and young children, stopped not only in the taverns but a fish market. He bought three lengthy mackerel and said he would tell his family they were brook trout.

"Brook trout!" I fairly shouted. "If they were brook trout, they would all be world records."

Mo's friend looked at him. "He's right," Mo advised him. "He reads the fishing record books as novels when he goes to bed at night."

"Well, I can't go home and admit I didn't catch anything. My wife will think I went to see my ex-girl friend." He kept the mackerel. And I decided I wanted my driver's license the second I turned 16.

When that time came, I failed the test and had to return for a second try. I had missed seeing a stop sign. The two-week wait was agony. But it was early May and the state's fishing season didn't open until the first

Saturday in June. (Sportsmen would successfully lobby for a year-around season later on, but for the time being, it opened in early summer.) And it was ridiculous. In early June the streams were swollen with snow-melt runoff. The high lakes were still locked in ice. Lowland lakes were a possibility but a boat was usually needed. Water was also often so cold that fish were only marginally hungry.

Nevertheless, I joined the opening day circus along with half a million other anglers. At times there was no way to cast a line into the water without it first striking another line. Water was too roily for fly fishing. With bait or spinner, one had to weight heavily to keep the offering where the fish were, on the bottom of swift flow. But the fish were, if you could find them, far more gullible than at end of the previous season when they'd been hooked and spooked for six months. Meat-seeking fishermen often walked with heavy stringers. Esthetics, however, had fled.

Seeking solitude, I decided to spend more time in the Uintas. With Mo away with his wife on vacation in July, I contacted Deral. We decided to try Alexander Lake where I'd once hooked some nice brook trout. My old car, all that I could afford, refused to negotiate the last mile of the steep road to the Alexander trail head. We carried our tackle the last mile of road plus half mile of trail, pushed off on a rickety log raft and struck the mother lode. Experimenting with various riggings, we decided to use no weight at all but to cast our worms out as if they were flies. This allowed the worm to sink slowly and naturally. Seldom did the offering even have time to reach bottom before the rod tip began dancing. Among the limit of 15 each we caught were a rainbow and a 3-lb. brown trout. How could such anamolies be found in a brook trout fishery? A hatchery worker explained it: sometimes a stray egg gets mixed in with the batch of other trout. In this way, a different species is raised with say, all brook trout and then planted with the others.

The procedure for stocking high lakes was fascinating to me. The fish were netted at the hatchery in the 3-inch "fingerling" stage and placed in a membrane bag, loaded into airplanes and dropped at no higher than 250-300 feet altitudes. Any higher and the fish would die upon impact. The membrane bag disintegrates. It was necessary, biologists said, to stock these high lakes because they were fishless following the Great Ice Age. None would have trout without introduction by state fish and game departments.

Once I had the opportunity to accompany the pilot on his appointed rounds. Flying had to be done by the first light of dawn in order to avoid down drafts when sun-warmed air currents clashed with cold canyon breezes. I had to sign a waiver of liability. "This is dangerous business," Ralph, the pilot, told me. "Those ___ fools in the main office sit there and wonder which lake it would be nice to plant next. But do they care whether I get out alive when a lake is hemmed in by four cliff walls? I have never found any evidence of it." Then he would say, "Watch for the splash. Did you see it?"

"Yes."

"Good. Then I didn't stock them in the trees."

Once I went to Alexander with some guys from the neighborhood. I cast in a worm and soon began fighting a large fish. Two of them said, "It's a carp! It has to be, it's so big!"

"Not at 10,300 feet," I said, and hauled in a deep-bellied, four-pound brook trout. The four of us admired this creature for five minutes. A few minutes later, I repeated with another brookie the same size. For two years, I saw other outsized brooks taken here. Alexander was productive for several years until a construction project nearby working on a dam and tunnel brought in hundreds of workers for the summer. There were rumors of dynamiting fish; trash fish such as dace were introduced; roads into the lake were improved. After that, I never caught a respectable brook trout in Alexander Lake.

It was during that time when I took my second Boy Scout outing to a Uinta lake and where I could entice no strikes just three years before, I now caught 17 trout to unofficially be crowned "top fish catcher for the week." I had worked at it harder as a 12-year old. It helped immensely to know what one was doing.

When I couldn't actually get out fishing, I studied the origins of angling, especially with artificial flies. Aelian, a Greek, was likely the first, but probably the one most publicizing the "Treatise of Fyshying with an Angle" was Dame Juliana Berner way back in the 1490s. Isaac Walton made it more popular to tie feathers on a hook and toss them out on stout poles (no reels) with horsehair leaders to entice brown trout to the surface of English chalk streams. But Walton was tarnished with rumors that he sometimes stooped to catching trout with bait. In America, Theodore Gordon immortalized the sport when he wrote of catching natural brook trout, on flies he tied himself, in the Catskill Mountains of New York.

As for my own heritage, a pioneer fisherman enroute to Utah as early as 1847, namely one Wilford Woodruff, used trout flies brought from England to outwit cutthroat trout in East Fork of Blacks Fork near Ft. Bridger in southwestern Wyoming. Woodruff reported in his diary that he outfished his competitors with their conventional bait, "four to one."

Inspired by this research, I sought to further refine my skills at "fooling fish with fraudulent flies." One serious mistake I made in those early years was to suppose that large trout prefer large flies. Does not a mouthful bring far more calories for growth than miniscule midges? The logic was there but the truth was not. It would be years later before I realized that big trout subsist more on tiny tidbits than moths and caterpillars. The reason is simple: there are far more tiny tidbits.

I was not patient enough then to learn this. When I caught no fish after a while, I turned to more likely methods, often bait. But I drew the line on swill baits when they were legalized, things like cheese, beefsteak, liver, marshmallows. Worms and grasshoppers were one thing; they were natural products. I would fish with cheese if there was a cheese hatch.

Before my 16th summer was finished, Mo and I decided to see what was in a certain lake toward the Great Basin drainage west of town. We baited up 16 hooks with worms one evening and staked them on 50 feet of line to two poles across a small bay. The next day we pulled from both ends and reaped three perch, two small carp, four bluegill, two mudcats and one largemouth black bass. We took only the bass home. So, the lake had bass; well, I would try making bass lures. I experimented with balsa wood and tried to make it look like a frog and painted it green but it still looked mostly like balsa wood.

All right, I would use a spinner for bass. The next week I caught a fish on the spinner but it was a mud cat. What was a mud cat doing chasing a spinner? They were supposed to do nothing but grovel in the mud for slugs and snails. It was proven to me once again that fish do not always do what they are supposed to do. They don't always read the same book fishermen do.

Mo began to be my advocate with the boss, my Dad. Mo could convince my father that we might deliver a refinished piano to some place where the nearby fishing was good…then convince him it would not take long to make a detour there. Such a place was Cottonwood Creek. It was not easy to find, as with most good fishing holes I'd ever experienced. There had to be something formidable and potentially frightening about good fishing holes, else all the fish would be gone. If it was not mosquitoes, it was heavy rain or difficult access, or a long hike or a hidden approach. Cottonwood Creek was all of these things, save a long hike. Well after sundown we drove at highway speed from pavement to a dirt road; a cow corral loomed in front of us. My father slammed on the brakes and we barely avoided collision with a Holstein cow. We groped over back roads late into the night when it began raining. Some roads, of course, don't turn slippery when wet and some do. Clay-based roads always turn slippery. We were, it was obvious, on a clay-based road. After while we heard water gurgling and decided it was a creek, not just an irrigation ditch. We got out map, compass and flashlight and Mo studied it and turned the map around various ways and then announced this "has to be the place."

We put down bedrolls beneath a cloudy sky and cheered when it turned to a star-strewn sky. It had to be an omen of good fortune and in one way it was. We began fishing the next morning at pink light and coaxed out several cutthroats apiece until sunlight illuminated the water. Then we drew blanks. After an hour of futile casting, I felt the weight of a large fish crash my spinner. After fighting my adversary long enough to draw the attention of both Dad and Mo and an old farmer in overalls, I brought the fish to the bank on a short line. Here was the crucial part. I had long realized that beaching a big fish must be done just so; once you begin the swing in, you must keep the rod tip level and smooth. If the fish gets slack on the final sweep, it will pull away and possibly break off.

Perfect. The fish lay on the wet sand, conquered at last. Then I got a closer look. A sucker. There could be no joy in conquering a fish with its mouth on the bottom of the jaw. I kicked at the fish in disgust. My father walked over to console me.

"Don't see a sucker caught on a spinner every day," Mo tried to console me. The farmer turned abruptly and walked off without saying a word. Even he knew that among the fishing kingdom's pecking order, a sucker occupies a most lowly rung. It should have been a trout hitting a spinner like that.

But there is good luck and there is bad luck. I would see more of both.

Chapter Eleven

I suspect my parents thought I would outgrow my zeal for fishing, or at least my total dedication to it. Not so. It became more manifest when I told my father there was a little space behind the garage…could I make it into a fish pond?

"A shallow goldfish pond?"

"No, a deep trout pond. Where I can study them more closely near home. And learn all about growing them."

I could see that this surprised him. But then he surprised me. "Well, not right away son. I took in a horse on a trade from a man who couldn't pay me in cash for the work I've done. It's being delivered tomorrow. The only place we can put it is here behind the garage. I want you to help me put in the fence."

Dad had once taken in 23 bushels of apples for work done. Baskets of apples inundated the back porch and hallway. But never anything like a horse. I'd always wanted one. I'd had opportunities to do much riding when at my grandmother's farm and hiked with friends to a riding academy on the east edge of the city for a single hour's ride. But inside a metropolitan city did not seem the place for a horse.

Nevertheless, the next day we put up a fence and a shaggy looking creature that a neighbor called a "quarter horse" soon filled the space. The day after that we heard honking in front of the house, progressively growing louder down the street.

The horse had knocked down the fence and was dodging cars when we finally got it lassoed with help of a sheriff's deputy. But after we returned the animal to the makeshift corral, it lashed out in fury at the wooden restraints.

"It'll break its legs," my dad said with a tone of compassion and sadness at the same time. "The owner will have to take it back."

But when my father saw me digging a pond later in the week, he said,

"Are you sure you want to do that?" He had been willing to put a horse behind the garage but wasn't sure I should put in a trout pond. But it had to be more than that. He'd hoped some day I would want to take over the family business. And here I was trying to become a trout farmer. That must be it.

Down deep, anytime he saw me take measurements to fill a vacant space on a piano, he had to know I would never be a carpenter. Still, he asked me again a few days later, "Son, are you sure you want to put in a trout pond?"

I soon bought an old pump that pushed water from the garden hose. I fixed it so the water ran over a broken piece of concrete that with some imagination could look like a natural rock, then into the pool. The outtake was more difficult to fit in, but I finally worked it so the water would recirculate. Shortly after that, I put in some small trout I'd caught. The next day I found them dead on the bank. They had apparently jumped out. What would make them do that? Lack of dissolved oxygen? The garden hose water had too much chlorine in it? I could detect no strong taste of chlorine. But just to make sure, I used a neighbor's hose to fill the pond again and restocked it. Same result. More dead trout.

Water temperatures seemed cold enough, almost as bone-chilling cold as Parleys Creek when I'd waded in it. Temperature range for cutthroat trout was about 58-65 degrees according to my fishing books and the house thermometer showed about 65. I deduced the problem must be lack of oxygen.

Later, I put in some mudcats. Caught in a lake 40 miles away and carried in a damp gunny sack for three hours, they vibrated immediately upon feeling the pond water. They then swam to the bottom where they remained for several days. I decided I didn't want mudcats. They were too dull. Nor would they eat any of the insects I tossed in. Finally, I succeeded in catching two largemouth bass and some bluegills, put them in the pond and tossed in some grasshoppers. The surface boiled in a frenzy. Hey, alright! These fish thrived throughout the entire summer in spite of warm water temperatures and the same oxygen supply which killed the trout. Knowing in October that winter would freeze the pond and kill them, the family enjoyed a fish fry.

But I learned something about being a fish farmer. My beloved trout were infinitely more fragile and difficult to grow than warm water species like catfish, bass and bluegill. The experience confirmed to me if I didn't already know it that trout required a much more pristine environment than other species. Trout could not survive in any but perfect conditions, at least regarding water clarity, temperature and available oxygen. They could go without feed for some time but the habitat had to be watched carefully. The fact that trout required near-perfect environment made them all the more admirable to me. They were also more vulnerable.

As bad luck would have it, that very summer I witnessed farmers bulldozing out trees and brush along a favorite trout creek. Without this vegetation to anchor the banks, the latter eroded away with the first rainstorm, badly silting the stream below. I could catch no cutthroats in the creek thereafter, nor did I see any. A fisheries biologist told me something I already knew. With trees and brush, which had anchored and shaded the stream bank, gone, temperatures rose to lethal levels. And if that hadn't killed them, the oxygen-robbing silt pollution likely would have. Silt also clogged the channel, widening it, leaving no pools.

Not only that but the farmers also suffered. Eroded banks cut into the farmers' fields until several rows of crops were missing where they had once grown alfalfa and beets. The name of the stream was to me quite apropos: Lost Creek. I went back for years after that, but the creek channel remained flattened, the flow shallow over a wider terrain, the water lifeless. Lost, indeed.

Not long thereafter, I witnessed a senseless example of stream destruction on a much wider scale. The U.S. Bureau of Reclamation moved heavy machinery into the upper Provo River in the name of flood control, totally gutting out the once vibrant habitat of large brown trout. Where there had been trees and brush lining the water, there was now nothing but a heaped dike of sun-bleached biota and white moss. All that had given life to the river was dead. The bottom was raked and smoothed to make water flow downstream faster; but what would those downstream do with more water flowing faster than before?

To me it was the most wanton waste of all that made life rich and valuable that I had ever seen. The stream lie as barren as a canal sluice, and looked like one. Where was sensitivity and intelligence, any sign of civilized appreciation for what had once flourished without expense to taxpayer or tourist. I was but 16 years old, and would have been thrown out of any meeting of Phd. engineers discussing plans for the project. But their man-made mayhem run amok was inexcusable even to me. I could not reconcile the world of responsible adults doing such carnage.

With the advantage of a driver's license I could explore around the valley and its canyons looking for unsullied signs of natural resources left alone. I concluded that some things were just better the way God made them. I searched for swamps, springs, meadows, woods, rock slides, all that might provide a laboratory to study natural systems. On the edge of the city one day I found Spring Run. I saw two small trout in the stream and persuaded my father to go with me for two hours on a Saturday morning. We enticed nothing to the hook. There must be very few in the stream, and nothing of any appreciable size. Two weeks later, I happened upon a group of people sitting along the bank of Spring Run. They were a university icthyology class with an electro-shocking machine. The latter, said an instructor, would temporarily stun whatever life was in the stream without harming it. I watched and waited, confident they would turn over very little. Within minutes I could not believe my eyes. Two giant trout, one a brown of about 30 inches, perhaps seven pounds and a rainbow slightly smaller, rolled across the surface. They were netted and examined. Both showed the dark and vivid markings of wild trout which had lived most of their lives in deep shadows. When the fish were returned, they finned quickly beneath a lengthy cutbank. I waited a few days and cast for some two hours beneath their now known lairs and could coax neither into hitting. I caught two 13-inch trout elsewhere, and two bluegills, but it was as if the lunkers were no longer there.

Toward end of the summer, a different class was brought to the water's edge and put the electroshockers in place. Immediately, the two oversized trout surfaced, a little larger this time than before. On my return, I crawled carefully along the bank and fished for nearly three hours in vain before giving up. No wonder they had grown so huge next to a well- traveled road! How did they manage to elude the hordes of weekend anglers who descended on this very pool next to well-pounded pavement?

Through that year and the next I did not succeed in catching or even hooking either fish. But every time I drove by I felt a kinship with nature just knowing they were there and imagining them feeding, probably at night or at least in dim light before or after most anglers even showed up. My life was enriched by realizing that wild creatures could abide in the heart of the valley were I lived.

The next year I noticed road crews at work. A new "diagonal" highway was being built through the area, coming within 10 yards of Spring Run. But at least they wouldn't be placing the creek in a tunnel or diverting its flow. Later, however, I noticed crews had straightened the bank where the big fish lived and put in a concrete wall. I contacted the university and inquired when the "fish shocking class" might return to Spring Run.

"It's no use," said the professor. "The fish are gone. We shocked there several days ago and our two friends have either moved out or they are dead. The highways crew destroyed their home.

"Where would they go?" I asked.

"I don't know. But with the banks straightened, there is no remaining habitat. They won't make it for long unless they can locate a home like their old one. I know of none on the entire stream, and even if there any, the highway people have been quite thorough. They are cementing the banks along the entire route."

"Why did they have to do that?"

"The answer they gave me is that they were afraid of snowmelt flooding the new roadway each year."

"But," I said, "I've seen the stream in all seasons for several years. Most of it is spring-fed, not snowmelt. Maybe that's why they call it Spring Run. There hasn't been any flooding."

The voice on the other end said, "Well, that's what they said. We don't have a place to take the class anymore."

I hung up and sat down. Well, there were still the canyon streams. Seven of them coursed into the valley. Starting on the north end, there was City Creek, which the first pioneers entering the valley had diverted on the very day Brigham Young entered, July 24, 1847. They initiated wholesale irrigation which would soon become standard operating procedure throughout the arid West. There were trout in City Creek Canyon, but it was considered critical water supply and closed to the public. On the east rim of the valley was Red Butte Canyon, but the creek was closed to all fishing other than military personnel at Ft. Douglas. Emigration Creek, where the first pioneers actually entered the valley (preceded the year before by the Donner-Reed party), held a few fish; but summer homes dotted the banks and closed most trespass. Next to the south was Parleys Creek, with Mill Creek not far away. Mill Creek was a swift, shallow stream most of the way, harboring mostly hatchery rainbows in and around the four major holidays, Memorial, Fourth of July, Twenty-fourth of July (pioneers entered the valley), and Labor Day.

Towering Mt. Olympus, apparently named for its resemblance to the pantheon of gods written about in ancient Greece, separated Mill Creek from Big Cottonwood Canyon. At the far end of the valley tumbled Little Cottonwood, a well-traveled canyon in winter because the ski resort of Alta graced the upper watershed. The latter was sweetened every summer with hatchery rainbows but also contained brook and cutthroat trout if one took the time to "troubleshoot" away from the road into cracks, crevices and currents that others didn't bother to fish. It was often September before the white water of Little Cottonwood Creek subsided in its steep, waterfall-studded search for peace in the valley. Its canyon of high granite cliffs graced the picturesque backdrop of many local calendars from year to year. I gloried in a 14-inch brook trout caught near the highway on a day when bright gold overwhelmed the canyon's fluttering aspen leaves. A brook trout that size in a stream with food plentiful only one-two months of the year could be a dozen years old. I marveled at the struggles it must have encountered to remain alive and grow on a lean diet of rock rollers and perhaps an occasional meal of snails or beetles, struggling against the current to fill its belly and remaining out of sight all the while from kingfishers and dippers.

But in addition to Parleys, I liked Big Cottonwood best. It held several side creeks with wild rainbows, and a four-mile hike midway up the canyon put one in alpine lakes beneath a giant cirque which reminded me of pictures of British Columbia. At the top of the canyon were ski resorts Brighton and Solitude, with several lakes encircled by trails worked over by summer fishermen. But one could hike a few hundred yards out of sight of roads and resorts and find brook trout

The Jordan River, in upper reaches, held sizeable brown trout, but the esthetics were not there. It coursed through the backyards of industry, with dead animals sometimes bloating the flow and a stench never present in the canyons. Still, the river had potential, biologists said, of being a great brown trout stream if the pollution could be controlled. In a future year, my younger brother, Doug, was to catch a 23-inch brown from the Jordan in the middle of the valley; but it proved to be a fluke and neither of us could figure how it got there or catch any other trout. Carp were in abundance and sometimes threatened to break our rods but they were disdained and avoided. As for presence of the trout, it have been due to a spring or some source of clean water entering the river at that point.

Or I could venture south and fish Hobble Creek, a twisting and brush-laden little stream from which I extracted a 17-inch brown which hit a tiny tidbit of worm after refusing a larger one. Not far away was the Provo River below Deer Creek Dam where it hadn't been channeled or dredged (spot removal of brush and debris). A 20 1/2 lb. whopper brown was caught on a fly from the Provo which won the annual Field and Stream magazine fishing contest. But try as I might, I could not uncover the secret of the Provo River and only years later would I discover that the large trout fed almost exclusively on tiny nymphs, an art which I had not perfected.

There were many outdoor utopias. They couldn't ruin them all. Could they?

During this time, Mo and I explored and hiked into much of the Uintas. Always the work must be done first, but we could fit in 12-hour shifts and go on a Friday-Saturday. A favorite place was Thirteen Lakes Basin on the upper end of the North Fork of the Provo River. Hiking in one day, I stopped and looked about. If everyone could only be here to enjoy it…I decided my life's work might be a writer, that people could see it as I did. But I dismissed that, for I'd seen artists and writers, some within my own family, nearly starve to death in the trying. We would see.

One of the intriguing things about Thirteen Lakes Basin was that while we caught trout amid ospreys and mule deer, there was a "Hidden Lake" we could not find. On our crude map obtained from a sporting goods store, the lake appeared to be two miles south of Duck Lake, on the edge of the known world. The map did not show contours and one day trying to locate a fishing hole, we ran into a thousand-foot surprise. The map showed a lake about a mile from Haystack Mountain but it was half a mile down, the other half up. We spent hours negotiating this "surprise" and then found the lake too shallow for fish to survive. A lake had to be at least 12 feet deep to survive the terrible winters at 10,000 feet, unless fed with inlet flow year around. Otherwise, dissolved oxygen would be snuffed out. There were creatures which lived on the lake bottom, salamanders which remained in the amphibious stage. They were particularly ugly, with big heads and of no value except I'd read they were useful as bass bait. One did, however, have to admire the salamander's tenacity. They burrowed into the mud at end of summer and crawled out eight-nine months later when the lake thawed.

One idiosyncrasy of Uinta nomenclature was that "Lost Lakes" abounded but were easy to find. One Lost Lake was barely out of sight of Utah 150. But Hidden lakes were truly hidden and almost impossible to find.

The Hidden Lake mentioned earlier was well named; there were no nearby landmarks. Most lakes were easy to locate because they lay at the bottom of cliffs and ridges where snowmelt collected in meadows below. But Hidden Lakes had no such geography.

Nevertheless, we set out one day to find Hidden, and did so after wandering about for hours and caught one 17-inch cutthroat from it. We returned exhausted at day's end following the 12-mile hike (including wanderings) but satisfied we knew how to find it again. The next month we set out for Hidden again but failed to find the lake where it had been before. Had they moved it? We checked and rechecked our bearings time and again but returned to Duck Lake with crestfallen spirits.

There was just enough energy left to find Fire Lake, supposedly on the plateau above Duck. We blundered into it on the first try, sat down and began to catch trout as rapidly as we could cast in. Deral caught a limit of 10 and said he would give them away to a man down the lake so he could continue fishing. I cautioned against it, for it was now 1:30 p.m. and I said the fish had gotten their fill. "They quit feeding at 1:30." We did not encourage any more strikes for the next hour and started back for the trailhead.

I had the high country fish figured out, Deral allowed. But why couldn't I find Hidden Lake? In getting outdoors, there was always reason to remain humble. Perhaps that's why it was good for the soul.

One thing that always intrigued me was the solunar tables, a seemingly scientific way to predict best and worst fishing times, based on the size of the moon. It made sense. During a full moon, fish had sufficient light to feed all night. Then, they were not hungry the next morning. But weren't they likely to feel hungry again say, around 1-2 p.m.? This would throw out the 1:30 p.m. corollary I thought I'd proven.

I threw it out, at least partly. I learned alpine fish would feed about an hour or so beyond 1:30 p.m. providing it was a day following a full moon. There was so much to learn. As for the solunar tables, they had one flaw. They did not take into account the fact that fish are opportunists; they feed when food is present, much like people. If an insect hatch occurs during a "down" period, say early morning after a full moon, what is to say they won't stuff themselves while they can? I decided this was true after seeing a 10-inch cutthroat hit my spinner with its gullet filled with a large chub. He could barely get jaw tips around my lure. Or was it territorialism at work…the fish wanted to drive away all competition?

In any event, I didn't pay much attention to the solunar tables. Nor do I now. I fish when I can and I believe fish feed when they can. But if they are only marginally hungry, the angler must give them precisely what they want where they can reach it with the least effort. That is the joy and challenge of fishing.

As for the allure of fishing, I thought then and now that there was something in it which attracted Christ's apostles. Most were fishermen, yet there is no indication in the scriptures that a preponderance of Galileans were fishermen. It does not seem likely that Christ chose people such as Peter for disciples and later apostles because they were poor of spirit. Nay, it would seem they had rich potential. They were alive to the values of the world around them. They had moxy. Well, that may be stretching things too far; but they had whatever they needed, of course, to be disciples and later apostles.

My parents sometimes pointed out scriptures to me. One was "…men are that they might have joy." This was explained to me as a lasting state of mind and spirit, more than pleasure, deeper than fun or temporary happiness. I wanted to believe that. But where was joy without following your inquisitive instincts? There was no doubt where mine lay. Still, tongues clacked in the neighborhood that a "fishing bum" was being nourished in the household of my parents and they would be sorry. To amount to something one had to aspire to be a dentist or something equally as hard, or at least a CPA. Even actors and lawyers were a step ahead of people who went through life having as much fun as fishermen.

I didn't worry much about it. But should I? There was no way of knowing at the age of 16. I pondered it one day and decided to do my thinking in the Uintas. I hiked into Long Pond in the Uintas and caught a 15-inch brook trout which had glutted itself in the seepage inlet below Long Lake. Its stomach contents showed pink freshwater shrimp. Shrimp in the Uintas? Pink instead of the normal green. Why? After that, the original question didn't seem important anymore.

Not long after that, I discovered Arctic grayling in Weir Lake. Some could be seen spawning in the stream above the lake. I dipped my net in a dark hole one day and retrieved an 18-incher. I released it and determined that if they were there, I'd catch one. That month they mostly eluded me, only a few small ones proving enticeable. But Mo and I soon discovered grayling of size in Big Elk Lake in another drainage. The fish would hit a tiny fly drawn slowly across the surface. Across a high ridge we found two lakes with no names showing on our best maps. We named them after ourselves. Later, a more sophisticated map showed them to be South and North Erickson Lakes. What dull names.

Mo liked "Mo Lake" because he caught seven brook trout in it one day which weighed over three pounds apiece. My line broke and when I managed to get it repaired in a steadily blowing snowstorm, the feed was over. Mo had seven huge trout; I had none. I had much better luck on the other lake, hence it took on my name.

About this time we heard rumors that Bigfoot lived in the Uintas. Someone had seen the creature near Mo Lake, and the Cuberant Lakes Basin all in the upper Weber River drainage, where I'd fished several times. What did I make of it, Mo asked. Did we dare return to Mo or the Cuberant lakes? We decided it was merely hearsay, or outright fraud. But a friend who hiked into the latter waters one day in late summer told me he heard something uprooting trees near his tent all night and growling. The next morning, notwithstanding the fact he had hiked 4 1/2 miles to fish the first Cuberant lake, he quickly grabbed his possessions and fled. Later, three more people were to tell me they had witnessed strange happenings in the upper Weber country. One tale came from a hiker I encountered in the Uintas, again in the Cuberant Basin. I ignored it. But yet another similar story came from a retired forest ranger, a man who had been in the wilds most of his life. Had

Improve the World...

he simply seen the hind end of a moose? a fish and game officer asked. There were a few moose known to range this region.

When the ranger insisted it was not, as he had seen moose often in the Targhee terrain west of Yellowstone, the fish and game officer went to investigate. He rode his horse near and around all five Cuberant lakes and found nothing.

Later, the fish and game officer was called to investigate "Bigfoot" prints in the snow along the lower Weber River near the city of Ogden.

"What happened?" I asked.

"I saw Bigfoot all right. The television cameras were there. Bigfoot ran from the river bottoms straight toward me. Then he took off his mask."

A local resident had decided to pull a spoof. Many laughed about it. But had he admitted to being in the Cuberant Lakes Basin…and how could he uproot large trees? The man said he had not been in that area in his life.

I was asked by Dee, who said he had heard trees uprooted around his tent, if I believed in Bigfoot.

I said I did not believe in Bigfoot.

Then, he asked me if I would accompany him into the Cuberant Basin to camp overnight. I thought about it and said no.

"Why?" he wanted to know. "Do you then believe in Bigfoot?"

"No."

"Then why not?"

"Because I wouldn't get any sleep just thinking about it," I answered.

It was not a rational answer. I convinced myself there could be no such animal as Bigfoot, at least not in the Uintas. If so, where was a dead speciman? Why had none been found? Where were they when investigations were launched?

There was another story about a Bear Lake monster which lived in the deep lake on the Utah-Idaho border. "It came out on a misty morning and grabbed a cow of mine and took it back in the lake," a farmer said to newsmen who interviewed him. Then, he admitted it was a story calculated to increase tourism.

Was Bigfoot in this category?

I told myself no. But next trip into the Uintas a fawn deer leaped from beside me on the trail. I was technically in a side branch of the Weber River which drained from the Cuberant Lakes Basin. I leaped higher than the deer.

Chapter Twelve

I soon discovered that Elmo (Mo) was even more of an expert at hunting than fishing. I accompanied him at the age of 15, a year before I could then be legally licensed, on a deer hunt opener to Wolf Creek Pass. Mule deer hunting in Utah was an annual ritual, as in other Rocky Mountain states, and we found ourselves among a Niagara of orange-clad *Homo sapiens* waiting to make left-hand turns out of Heber City. To the east was beyond known civilization.

When we reached the dirt road it wasn't dirt anymore. The skies had begun pouring rain; everywhere, trucks dug out of mud and snow from borrow pits and deep ruts. The first night we stopped at the edge of the Ute Indian Reservation and hunted a place near Blind Stream. The next day we saw only does; the law said hunters could shoot bucks only. Mo said he would not think of shooting an antlerless deer anyway. "Does are for wimps and sissies and novices." But we found no bucks. They were apparently higher this year; we would need to relocate.

The second night we stopped on the steep slope of a mountain in an angry blizzard, just beyond a sign marked "Uinta National Forest." I heard a coyote howling. Not far away was a tent with a fire barely holding its own in a staccato beat of snowflakes. A two-point buck and a large black bear hung from the closest tree. I wanted wild. We had wild.

I was so happy I couldn't sleep. The next day I wished I wasn't so happy. We were out well before dawn and I fought weariness until Mo said, "There. See there?"

I looked and studied the new snow. "Deer tracks!" he said. "They crossed through here during the night." But by late morning we had seen only bald deer and one lonesome porcupine. We sat down to rest. Suddenly, an antlered deer pranced into the opening at our right. I didn't think Mo would ever shoot. He was a "traditional" hunter with a lever action Model

94 Winchester 30-30, no scope. I'd never seen him miss with it on squirrels and varmints. He didn't miss this time either. The buck dropped in its tracks. Almost immediately, several hunters ran toward us. "Where did he come from?" one asked.

I was proud of Mo but the haul back some four miles to camp made me wish we'd sat down sooner. I'd been assigned to write a story about the hunt for my high school newspaper and couldn't decide where to begin. After the story appeared, several people berated me for writing about killing a "defenseless animal." One said, "I thought you were a Christian. Do you think God approves of killing a deer?"

I remembered that my father had seen the Walt Disney movie "Bambi" the evening before he was to go deer hunting. He called his hunting buddies and backed out. My Dad wasn't much for hunting.

But I had read thousands of Bible scriptures about killing birds and animals as sacrifices, without any mention of utilizing meat. "It doesn't appear to me that God worries about birds and animals dying if there is a good reason for it," I said. Besides, I recalled a scripture where a hero prophet was helped by deity in repairing his bow that he might deliver meat to his family.

Still, the conversation got me thinking. I should repent. I had killed song birds on occasion, birds no one would eat, birds that sang their hearts out and hurt no one. I concluded that killing them was, indeed, a sin. Of course, English sparrows, starlings and crows were different. They were honest pests. Had not my own grandmother, as kindly as soul as I'd ever met, advocated killing "chicken hawks"?

As for killing deer, I studied the facts. Deer in the Kaibab National Forest of Arizona were allowed to multiply (no one was allowed to kill mountain lions or other predator in the Kaibab). In a few years a herd of 20,000 reached 50,000. There was then nothing left on the range for them to eat. The deer starved in what must have been painful deaths until there was a herd of less than 10,000. Worse off than before. Where was the logic in that?

Always, it seemed that nature, left alone, sought a balance. Along this line, I was impressed with the wisdom of Aldo Leopold who wrote long letters home describing the birds and animals he observed in the mid- West. Later, as a professional forester, he sought to have wildlife managed wisely, i.e. with the least interference from man, that the latter's experience with nature might be truly enriching. He wrote: "Like winds and sunsets, wild things were taken for granted until progress began to do away with them. Now we face the question whether a still higher 'standard of living' is worth its cost in things natural, wild and free."

Like Leopold, I sought every possible experience to observe the outdoors and gain more insight about the "glue and grit" which held it together. A memory especially cherished was a trip one early September weekend with my father and brother to float the upper Henrys Fork country of eastern Idaho. I had never seen a more pristine stream than the Henrys, save only the Yellowstone. But the Henrys was much smaller and possessed an intimate environment, willows bent over crystalline water as far as one could see. The latter was a problem. As the current pushed our raft gently downstream, giant trout scattered before us. There was no way to beach and cast from shore. Vegetation crowded the bank like a jungle.

The people we stayed with, distant relatives of my mother, told us to fish with beetle grubs, which we gathered from rotted logs near our host's cabin on Lucky Dog Creek. With the grubs, we caught a few pansized rainbows but could not entice the larger fish. Well, I could see why. We spooked everything in sight with the first fling of our rod tips. In addition, we were inexperienced paddlers and with every splashed oar, fish fled. In time, we became more silently proficient and drifted to the Bathtub Hole our host had told us about. Here we could anchor and fish deeper water. My father hoisted the anchor over the raft's neoprene side and lowered it gently to the bottom. I was proud of him. He had not walked trout streams as had I, but he had a certain savvy when it came to boat fishing. I learned later he had done much of it on the Snake River as a lad after becoming encumbered with rheumatic fever. Almost immediately, he caught the largest whitefish I have ever seen, before or since, a specimen measuring 25 1/2 inches. I later discovered the fish would have been a candidate for the state record *Propsopium williamsi*.

The fish, large as it was, came in straight as board, with scarcely a wiggle from its tail. Why so? I had caught a number of whitefish on the Weber and Provo rivers and found them to lack the stamina of a trout in the resistance category; but never had I seen one as sluggish as this from the opening strike. We found its stomach full of snails up to as large as the fish's minute mouth could manage. Perhaps that was it. The fish was weighted down with snails, heavy shell and all. I was never fully satisfied with this answer, but it seemed the only logical one for the moment. Fish with empty stomachs had in all my experience given the most ferocious fight. Years later, I found no reason to alter that conclusion. Fish with lean, empty torsos do the best battle.

Farther down the Bathtub hole I could see chartreuse moss. Just beyond it, the moss turned bright scarlet. We pulled anchor and drifted closer. It was my first encounter with kokanee salmon. All in spawning colors, they formed an electric sight in the clear water. But we could catch none. They had their minds on something other than eating. So, we floated again for trout until entering the Macks Inn area where fishing competition converged before us. If given a choice, never go fishing on Saturday afternoon. Might as well take out.

We had not done very well. The fish were there; we had failed to take them, even with our "secret" beetle bait. But I had spent nearly a day with my father. My younger brother, Doug, now seven, took in all the lore of the float trip as had we. He seemed destined to also become a fisherman.

During my 16th year I had the opportunity of fishing several Wyoming waters. One of them, a tributary of Smiths Fork, named after western explorer Jedediah Smith, was swollen with late spring runoff. But I found a small spring-fed beaver dam and peered over the edge. Six 16-18 inch brown trout finned at the edge of moss. What were they doing here anyway? Even at flood stage the nearby stream poured no water into the dams. The little ponds were isolated, the water barely trickling in from nearby springs. I got excited and stood up to get a better look before casting. And they all vanished in a giant cloud of mud.

I wouldn't get here very often. And I had blown it. Sometimes I wondered if I would ever live up to what I already knew, let alone learn anything else. I went home without any of those big fish, muttering at myself for making such a blunderous mistake. I should have remained below the rim of the dam, casting over the top. It was so difficult it seemed, to cast to something one couldn't see. But if I could see them, it was logical they could see me.

I thought of that later when it came to believing in God. If I had to see Him to believe in him, perhaps I didn't merit His trust. I must build up that trust by taking him at his word and trying Him out. He said in many scriptures to follow His commandments and see if one is not blessed for doing so. It was a homily to me, something which made sense but also something I had difficulty consummating. My parents believed. I would remain a skeptic but at least one who could maintain an open mind. The fish had been there all the time. Maybe He was there all the time. I didn't know. Someday I hoped to find out.

Yet, if believing was so important, why was I failing at so much I had believed in? I loved football and believed I could be a star at it. My football coach thought otherwise. True, I was attending the state's largest high school and at some country prep institution might have been a starter by sheer lack of competition. That would force me to believe in myself. I could take up basketball. But I'd started rather late and didn't even hold a round ball in my hands until the age of nearly 13.

Mo put up a basketball standard on the garage front but with no room to dribble because of cars parked by the workshop. I learned to shoot, at least from the side where there was no power line; but later found I lacked skills to dribble. I hadn't practiced being a guard and was too small to be anything else. I had by now realized I would never be a famous chemist because I couldn't fathom math. I had learned to dance but was tongue-tied near a girl if the music stopped. But when it came to catching fish, I found I believed in myself. Well, I would stay with what I believed in.

There were other aspirations. I saw salesmen at work and decided the challenge of being a salesman was much like trying to catch a fish. I visited my grandfather on my Dad's side and decided he had much to emulate. He was a professional scouter and at times wore the merit badges proudly on his old uniform. He had lost a finger and an eye but he was one of the sharpest men I'd ever known. He also kept bees but I knew I could never be a beekeeper. I didn't know why; I just couldn't. My grandmother was an artist and she smiled and painted all day long in the log cabin he and grandfather lived in. She brushed with a lavish love I did not understand nor seemed capable of duplicating. I admired her but could see I did not seem destined to be an artist. One could become an accountant or businessman but they seemed dreadfully monotonous. And you needed math. There was farming but farmers always complained the government was against them. On my mother's side, my grandfather was a lawyer, the county's prosecuting attorney and had been elected for 28 straight years to that position. I couldn't be a lawyer. They had to read all those dull books bound in black and gold. All around me people were successful. It couldn't be so hard. Could it?

I decided. I would make my living fishing. I didn't know how but if I didn't make a living at it, how could I continue doing what I loved most? I would not back off. It was too rich an experience to abandon. I would be poor if necessary but I had to continue my education in the outdoors. People didn't understand. They said, "Once you catch a fish, isn't it about the same as catching any other of the thousands of other fish you've already caught?"

"This isn't about catching fish!" I'd tell them. "This is about understanding the inner workings of nature, of unlocking its mysteries, of probing into the hidden realm of the Great Unknown. And I'd go off to catch another fish.

No two fish I caught were exactly alike. Every fish I ever caught was unlike all the others, for each one demonstrated a new principle involved in meeting a biological challenge, of unraveling the ball of yarn in a natural system, of fathoming the biorhythm of creatures in another world, of accomplishing something worthwhile that others were unwilling to try because they did not understand, or the price was too high.

To some, of course, I merely caught fish.

Chapter Thirteen

By the time I turned 17 I'd harbored the hope that a scientific breakthrough might be found to replace the Dirty Hand Method. My father said no. The wood stain-filler must still be lovingly rubbed in by hand. And there was still no new scientific technique to make the stuff come out before talking to girls.

At least the fish didn't care what I looked like. Saturday mornings I worked with Mo in the shop and listened to Arthur Godfrey until 10 a.m. and then we talked about places we hadn't been. At noon, we got out maps and studied the white spaces between names of cities and roads, places where there was nothing on the map, places where man had not altered the environment. We focused on places where in all the nothingness of buildings or roads ribbons of blue coursed between outposts of civilization.

Many such places were to be found in or near the Uinta Mountains. Some places had intriguing names: Naturalist Basin, Dead Horse Pass, Rocky Sea, Hell's Kitchen, Crater Lake, Weeping Ledge, Red Castle, One Fish Lake and many more.

Mo wasn't much for long hikes with a pack, so friends and I got together and trekked into the upper Yellowstone Creek drainage on the Uinta south slope. We drove through the night and began hiking at the first ray of light, yet August darkness overtook us still on the trail. Could the map be right? We had only hiked 14 miles in 18 hours? True, the sign said 14 miles but I wondered sometimes if the Forest Service painted those signs in Washington D.C. and then brought them west as an afterthought to some unknown trailhead. Afterall, government signs that said "Deer Crossing" always showed whitetail racks. There were no whitetail deer in my region. Where did the forest service make those signs? And one time I followed signs to a Pinto Lake and found it was two miles farther when I reached the next sign. And further, if the signs were made from actual observation of the terrain, did "sight measurements" take into consideration the rocks you had to sidestep on the trail?

In any event, we made camp by moonlight at the first large lake we reached. Actually, camp wasn't much, since I hadn't brought a tent. The first night at Bluebell Lake I was lucky but the second night it rained. Did I want to share a tent with a few others? No, I had decided to keep my pack light and I would take my medicine. It rained all night and by 3 a.m. I was totally drenched. I had learned long before to keep my raincoat with me in high country no matter what the skies. Why had I not brought my tent "raincoat" with me for nighttime? I suffered, but it was a contented suffering, for I deserved it and I knew I deserved it. The thing I liked best about nature was that it was always impartial. There was no favoritism. All unprepared people were treated equally harsh. I had gambled in not bringing a tent and lost. Fair enough. I had no complaint.

By now I was growing old enough to adapt a philosophy that would help me through many difficult times. No matter what the suffering, I could usually say, "This too shall pass." Sure enough, by 11 a.m. the wind and sun dried out my sleeping bag and pretty much, myself. Temperatures went up when I was actually catching fish. Bluebell was slow angling, but the lake above it, off the trail, yielded beautiful brook trout. Not far away was another lake named "Spider" on the map, for it seemed to have eight legs, or bays, reaching out into a huge rock slide. I loved natural things named after natural things. I would later see the name "Sauerkraut Lake" on a map and detest that label until actually visiting the lake and discovering it was so named because it sprawled out across ravine and lowland exactly like a plate of spilled sauerkraut. Here, indeed, was wisdom.

One of the most endearing things to me about the Uintas were the chartreuse, vivid green meadows. They were anywhere and always seemed interspersed by a divine chamber of commerce to make even the most arduous hike interesting. The mountain range was an old one geologically, bald mountains worn from the top down through eons of wind that reached gale proportions whenever touching peaks and ridges. There seemed to be three elements in the Uintas' makeup: rocks, meadows and water. I sought for the first hint of azure among the lodgepole pines, for it was the color of fishing water. But there was something to admire even in the dry gulches. I was in condition to hike without frequent resting but reflected later in life that most of what I remembered about the Uintas was not when hiking but when stopping.

There were no more lodgpoles or trees of any kind when reaching the high mountain passes about 11,700 feet above sea level. The highlands appeared first as a desert, miles of seemingly barren tundra which stretched to the horizon. But if one looked closely, as in a desert, there were lichens and butterflies, bluebell flowers, and a plethora of life to be witnessed in glory at every looking. The wind was not as cold as it was clean and fresh. I paid homage to Teddy Roosevelt, Gifford Pinchot, Aldo Leopold and all who opened the way for forest and wilderness for the re-creation and enrichment of the soul. I did not want to trammel here for long; it was a privilege merely to be a visitor.

There was one problem with the Uintas. They had not received full status as designated wilderness; they were known as a "primitive area." I wasn't even certain what the difference was between wilderness and primitive but I knew that if wilderness was the higher classification with more protection and higher status, the Uintas deserved it. Some day I would have to see what could be done about that.

Once in a restaurant I heard two people talking, one who called himself an atheist, about the resurrection. He said he would be cremated when dead. "They say we will all be gathered together at the resurrection, every bone and sinew and muscle. Well, I want to make it difficult for them. I plan to be cremated and scattered across five states."

"Awfully expensive," said his friend.

"It'll be worth it if I make them work in the Next Life," he said.

"Who's them?" asked his friend.

"I dunno. Whoever's in charge."

Surely, if I turned out not to be a Christian at my dying I would want to be cremated and have my ashes scattered across the Uintas. But later I read a Christian leader say that cremation was not against Christian protocol. So, it was a decision I could make later. Right now, I was too busy living.

One thing about backpacking. The feeling of putting your home on your back and residing wherever you stop for the night was overwhelming. But first, you had to take everything out of cans and boxes and rewrap them in plastic bags and label them and hope they would be where you wanted them when you needed them. Every ounce made a difference. One also made certain to put things like mosquito repellent, cup, and flashlight where they could be located quickly. As for a rain coat, it remained around my waist, or my shoulders. Rain or hail or even mid-summer snow could seemingly pour from a cloudless sky.

I had heard many scary stories about drinking contaminated water. I learned to avoid all large streams where an animal such as beaver could leave droppings…or die and affect all below. I drank from small springs and seeps, where it was not stagnant, hundreds of times without problems. On one occasion, I did become so thirsty I succumbed to drinking from a lake and contracted trenchmouth. No discipline, no promise.

In those days, there were no fire restrictions, and no sophisticated portable stoves. You relied on building an open fire. Even in a rainstorm, dry wood wasn't difficult to locate beneath logs and in denser stands of conifer. Once a friend and I were rained and snowed on for 27 straight hours and still managed to find wood enough to dry out. By now I always carried a tent. It was the first duty to take care of at each camping stop, for it was the only guarantee of dry clothing and dry sleeping bag. I pitched the tent even before cooking dinner. It was not difficult; I discovered that just about anything became edible when left long enough in a pot of hot water.

Following a map correctly was always the healthiest thing to do. On one occasion, a friend and I were dropped off at Spirit Lake on north slope of the Uintas and at exactly 2:30 p.m. six days later picked up by his mother on the south slope at U-Bar Ranch on the Uinta River. On two occasions a gentle swell was all that divided us from the Whiterocks and the Uinta drainages. Walking slightly left rather than right would have left us cold, lonely and motherless. In all, with a visit to Weeping Ledge Lake, and a tryst for trout in several lakes above timberline, we calculated our expedition with 50-lb. plus packs to cover 55 miles.

In time I decided to explore Wyoming's Wind River Mountains within the Bridger Wilderness Area. The Wind Rivers loomed more imposing in the distance than perhaps even the Uintas, rising to nearly 14,000 feet and showing granite walls some 100 miles away. With two men opening a guide service and inviting me along, we horse packed for 10 hours into a remote lake basin somewhere high in the mountains. The next morning my hosts told me to go fishing while they prepared breakfast.

Hiking around a meadow lake, I saw a young bull moose amble toward me in the traditional shuffle of these huge, black creatures. I leaned my fishing rods against a rock to get a picture. The moose shied away from me and moved toward the rods. I ran to my right to head him off. He lowered his head and charged. I backpedaled 15 yards, then turned to run full speed. He backed off. A bluff charge? No, he simply meant to clear me away. He needed space. If he wanted to trot down the north side of the lake, well, he would do so. When he reached the rock with my rod, I couldn't bear to look. Nearly a ton of beast would surely smash my 3.5 ounce fly rod to pulp. Somehow, he missed. Then I heard the breakfast gong ring and began walking rapidly along the lake. I had been fishing for two hours. Suddenly, there was the moose again. His teenage spike tines lowered toward me.

There was nothing to do but take 45 minutes to walk around the other side of the lake. When I arrived, all the hotcakes had been eaten and only mush remained. "I was charged by a moose," I apologized. My companions eyed me through narrowed eyelids. "I didn't see any moose," said Lou. "Me neither," said Jim.

"Well," I said, "I took pictures. I'll show you later." When we returned home, sure enough, I had three pictures of a moose running directly at me. I had found my calling. I would be a famous photographer. I would take pictures of lions and tigers in Africa and all around the world. But I did not have the money to go to Africa. Alaska? That was it. I would save my money for a trip to Alaska. Some day.

During this same trip, a pounding near my tent woke me at dawn. It turned out to be a fully-grown black bear. What did the book say to do…play dead? No, he hadn't attacked me yet. I yelled. The bear panicked and fled. i went back to sleep. He returned. I yelled. He ran again. Well, I was getting pretty good at this sort of thing. But, so was the bear.

Would he return again? I looked around. What had attracted him here? Our camp was relatively clean with no garbage dumped nearby. Then, I found the problem. Someone outside our party, previous campers, had thrown out hotcakes and syrup near my tent. I moved the dirt-saturated syrup well away from camp. We had no more trouble with the bear. Another night, I saw deer return to a spot where leftover noodles had been discarded. I moved them farther away. So much for the idea that it is all right to toss out biodegradable leftovers.

If it hadn't been bears attracted in, it might have been skunks. I'd discovered on previous outings that they were small enough and brave enough to find their way inside a tent flap as they followed food odors. There was never any opening after that for a skunk to get into. A bear, of course, might not even look for an opening. I could not believe the story I read that the first camper killed in Yellowstone had used a side of ham for a pillow. It was the last thing he ever knew. Were such stories apocryphal? I didn't know. The lesson would be the same nevertheless.

At the top of the Wind Rivers, I beheld one of the grandest sights I'd ever seen. At the outlet end of a large glacial lake, a fish two feet long finned where the water flow slowly gathered speed. There was no bush to hide behind, for the elevation was nearly 12,000 feet. I got down on my stomach and crawled forward. I could see bright gold-orange on slab sides with a streak of crimson down the belly. Golden trout! It had to be!

My cast was perfect. My black woolly worm fly landed directly in front of gaping jaws. The fly drifted down perfectly. The fish looked neither left nor right. I'd try a different fly. The lake ought to have caddis larvae in it, so I'd feed him a yellow nymph. No interest. I changed to a spinner. Nothing. Back to a fly. No different. Was it a statue out there? An apparition? No, the fins waved gently. I beckoned my associates over. They also saw it. Proof. But no luck.

There could be only one reason why a fish would depart the depths and move to such a conspicuous place. Food. But what? The fish would budge for nothing. Yet, the torpedo shape occasionally opened its mouth for something. It was the early days on Parleys Creek all over again, only with a larger fish the stakes were higher. Many Parleys cutthroats were six inches long; this specimen was possibly six pounds. Throughout the day, I returned to study the fish. But it would have nothing to do with me. Finally, I caught a 14-inch fish in a pond below and it turned out, sure enough, to be a golden. If other trout were exquisite, this was nature's most spectacular effort. The scarlet and orange, even more than the gold, were so bright they almost hurt the eyes.

The fish had struck a small Adams on the surface. I tried the artificial on the levithian at the outlet but it simply moved to one side. Uplake, the fly drew no interest. I tried a spinner. No coaxable fish. Then I put the first fly back on and three fish rushed up from the bottom. They swam at least 10 feet in the clear water to make contact. What was this? Expending 100 calories to take in two? What was the energy efficient logic in that? And what motivated them to ignore me one minute and with precisely the same offering, gang tackle me?

If fishing was so good from shore, it must be great from a raft. Jim got it out from the packs, pumped it up, paddled to the middle in what appeared to be hundreds of feet of water and returned without a strike. The food it seemed, was along the shoreline. So were the goldens.

My cohorts and I discovered a strange thing about goldens. They struck on whim. What they didn't want, they suddenly did. Was there any science to it? Were they suddenly hungry, then they weren't? We could not decide; but if one cast long enough to a single fish, easily visible with their brilliant colors, it might eventually turn and take. Before departing, we lay several of the fish, brilliantly hued against the snowbanks, to take color pictures. But the giant golden in the outlet refused to cooperate. Last I looked, it was still there when we had to head for camp in a hailstorm.

Had God made golden trout to keep mankind learning? Or at least the fishermen among them?

At camp, we hung the fish on a line in the trees, high above the heads of any wandering bears. I pondered the ways of golden trout. Would I ever be able to figure them out? The next morning, we discovered there were other things we needed to figure out. Our outdoor education was not yet complete. The heads of all the fish were eaten, the remainder hanging by a thread of skin. Later, I read that pine martens had to be the culprits. They liked to eat fish heads and were quite adept at climbing trees. In fact, they preferred to run on logs and remain in trees rather than walk on the ground.

There was much more high country to explore. Utah had Manti Mountain, Boulder Mountain, Thousand Lake Mountain, among others. The latter was a misnomer, for it was Boulder with the myriad lakes while "Thousand Lake Mountain" had about 25 of them. The explanation given to me was that a map-maker got mixed up between the two mountains and when the mistake was made known, he wouldn't admit it. Nevertheless, there were many lakes yet to be explored among these highlands. I decided to look at the Manti first among them, and drove up alone when a friend who said he would go backed out in a drizzling rainstorm. An hour later, the rain was gone. I drove past a small pond by the road and saw no surface activity. I looked back 10 minutes later and the surface was alive with splashing fish. Dry flies? No, only the dorsals were breaking water. They were taking something just beneath the surface. I tied on a scud and immediately began hooking 12-13 inch rainbows. Sure enough, I opened the first fish and it was filled with fresh water shrimp. I had guessed right on the first try. Around me were dozens of bait fishermen catching nothing. That figured. There was an "outbreak" of scuds for some reason and that was all the fish wanted for now.

Several trout later, I drove to another lake. Here too, fish were working the surface. These fish were *on the surface*. I tried four dry patterns and drew a blank. Just two miles away and a completely different breed of trout.

I would try some streams. Below a lake was a roadless creek. The fish were there by the score the farther away from crowds and cars that I walked. But what did they want in the July heat? I tried several patterns that might match grasshoppers. The cutthroats came up and looked and went back down. Too big a fly? I tied on an elk hair caddis that might simulate a small 'hopper and caught every fish I saw. My major challenge was not to strike too quickly, for the trout inched up slowly to check it out and then inhaled like a baby slurping milk from a tight nipple. If I became too anxious, I pulled it from their lips.

Improve the World...

Later, I explored a different creek and found that it emerged from a tunnel. Water users had diverted the flow from a lake on top into a creek coursing down the west slope. I could catch nothing from the stream. I cast up into the tunnel darkness itself. Jackpot. Fish were congregated there where they could feed without being exposed to danger. Yes, I liked Manti Mountain.

Ego satisfaction it may have been pure and simple, but I loved the mountain and felt good about myself. By now I had begun to return many of the fish I caught and felt a wave of euphoria that I could return, or someone else, to catch them more than once.

While I did not have the equipment to explore the rough back roads of Boulder Mountain, I did spend much time with the streams at base of the mountain. The Fremont River, I was to discover, was one of the West's great trout streams. I found brown trout to six pounds in this stream as it coursed through a maze of swamps known as Bicknell Bottoms. The fish seemed slow to hit a fly but would eagerly attack a spinner retrieved downstream if simulating a wounded minnow at mercy of the current.

Catching a six-pound brown came about by sheer accident. Because the river's flow was swift and turbid, I placed a large sinker on the line above the No. 3 silver Mepps spinner. After the fifth fruitless cast, I was about to move on when suddenly a large rainbow trout appeared from the roily flow and chased a minnow into a clearwater spring at my right. The rainbow swallowed the minnow and vanished back into the muddy water. If the trout wanted a minnow, why hadn't it struck my own minnow imitation spinner? Afterall, I'd given the hungry trout five chances. I tossed out three more times just to make certain the trout saw my spinner. Nothing. I sat down to figure this mystery out.

What was the key here? The minnow swam in a spurting and bouncy manner that looked real. It was real. My spinner must not have looked like the real thing. That was the only possible answer. The trout had to see my lure's flashing blades. They just didn't resemble a minnow.

I removed the sinker and made a cast. With no weight on the line to stifle action, the freely-rotating blades now "fluttered" slowly toward me. I kept my rod tip above the spinner, reeling in slack line to avoid snagging bottom. Suddenly, I felt a tremendous jolt. I didn't get the spinner back until landing a 27-inch brown trout nearly one hundred yards downstream. The fish entirely filled my landing net. It was a great, blackish brute with a big belly. A chub larger than my thumb fell from its gullet. Obviously, it had focused on forage fish and thought my offering looked like one more.

After that, I returned to the little point of land near the spring where I'd seen the rainbow, and on the next cast, landed the arm-long rainbow as well. I reflected then that many anglers live in a different world than the quarry they pursue. If I'd not witnessed the minnow being chased and noted how it appeared in the water, I'd likely have continued casting in vain. Fish simply do the natural thing. If fishermen don't, they don't catch fish.

Using the weightless spinner concept with downstream retrieve, I caught many other large brown and rainbow trout on the Fremont. While I had in the past concentrated on fighting brush and willows to reach hidden hotspots, the Fremont's largest trout proved to be in a vast swampland where there were many submerged ledges and hidden cutbanks. One section appeared to flow evenly through moss beds but ledges not readily seen from the bank harbored slab-sided browns. One had to look closely to see the likeliest lairs. Polaroid glasses helped remove glare from the surface and see the secret hiding places. If the lure moved near their feeding stations, the trout struck. If the fish had to move more than half a foot, they would not budge. Most likely, the reason was pure laziness. Feed was everywhere. Put it where they could reach it with little trouble and they wanted it. Reading the stream correctly was everything. One day a friend fished alongside me and caught nothing. He was tossing out the same spinner as I. Putting the spinner to the fish, I caught 13 browns, all of respectable size.

But seasonal timing had to be just right. In summer, the water turned warm and the fish seemed to feed very little. In early spring, the fish were lethargic. The perfect time was when a tinge of mud began to flow down the stream but before it became swollen. That was usually mid-April.

It didn't matter then whether the snow spit in your eyes or the sun shone in them. Air temperatures mattered little. A five degree temperature drop in the air might take several days to affect the water. The fish were hungry and cruising for minnows. Year after year, the oversized trout were there to be taken. But one spring day, I found the channel filled with silt. A flood had raged off the mountain and choked both the stream and its two main tributaries. The water, 30 yards wide, was only inches deep. There was no habitat left for fish or waterfowl or much of anything else. "An act of God," stated the U.S. Bureau of Land Management official on other end of the line.

"But what caused the flood?" I queried. "There have been heavy snow pack in years past as well."

There was no forthcoming answer. I suspected overgrazing and so did professional biologists I talked with. One told me he had been trying to reduce the number of livestock and big game animals on the above mountain for years. The ungulates had eaten out the vegetative root system. No root system, nothing to hold back the water.

Act of God? Why blame it on Him?

Chapter Fourteen

One observation I made in my youth was that north slopes of anything were greener and more jungled. It figured, for the sun's rays were scarce on north slopes and water lingered longer. Englemann spruce grew broader, lodgepole taller and straighter, with lusher grass and more ponds. Snowbanks lay longer in purple shadows. Such was the scene on the north slope of the Uintas which stretched for nearly 100 miles across Summit and Daggett counties nearly to the Green River on the Colorado border.

I loved this land at first sight. There was no place I'd rather be, from Bear River on the far west across Blacks and Smiths Fork to Beaver Creek along the Henrys and Burnt Fork drainages to the eastern end. I had hiked much of it by now, watching for new wildlife, having a bull moose glare at me until acknowledging it was his domain, not mine, making my way to Hell Hole Lake and exploring up the verdant Stillwater Fork of the Bear to lush springs where elk looked at me in bewilderment. One of the most beautiful places in the entire Uintas was the upper West Fork of Blacks where peaks converged in a spirited battle to see which could rise higher than the others, Amethyst Lake watching to see who won the right to cast its shadow upon her.

Some of the best fishing was in obscure places. I once caught nothing in Dead Horse Lake but enticed cutthroats almost at will with a rock roller nymph imitation in the feeder stream. There was an unnamed lake nearby with levithian cutthroats but I could not find what they wanted. They defied me to catch them and I left crestfallen. But there was too much to see and do here to remain downcast for long. I wanted to live here for an entire summer, envying a fisheries crew I met mapping and checking trout survival in the high lakes. I couldn't think of a better way to spend a summer. And get paid for it.

On one trip to the north slope, the Forest Service taught me how to tie a horse down in tundra swept clean of all vegetation. They looped a knot around the fetters so that the animal couldn't lift its leg. The mount remained while one glassed the country. Seeing nothing, I moved on to look for outsized bucks which I'd heard lived here near timberline. Ironically, such a buck crashed through our pack string one day, reached the edge of a chasm just beyond, and barged through the horses once again. I had thought wild animals had their terrain memorized; this one must have forgotten.

Some of my most vivid memories from the region were of giant deer, antlers towering above their heads. Not all were in the back country. One day when Mo and I drove at dawn toward Mill Creek, a giant mule deer buck stepped from a line of aspens at the left into our path. Mo braked to a halt and we marveled at the rack. It was as if an aspen grew from the deer's head. We had no rifle; it was not hunting season. We simply gaped, jaws slack. Half a century later, I remembered the moment as if it was yesterday.

In the winter, Uinta mule deer herds were quickly pushed by autumn storms into the flatlands below the mountains. The only mountains in the continental United States ranging east and west, the lofty peaks straddled the Wyoming-Utah border. Once pushed by deep snow to the high plains of Wyoming, deer found little to eat. They migrated some 70 miles to the lower country along the Green River, believed to be one of (if not the) longest mule deer migration in the Lower 48.

One year, I found a fawn they left behind. I was walking a small but deep stream when my eye caught something, a look…a live something look in the water. I walked closer. A fawn was barely treading water at edge of matted willows. Its head lay on the willows but they were beginning to droop with the fawn's weight. The hapless creature had no energy remaining to struggle and was gasping for breath. I had on my fishing boots and walked over to cradle it in my arms. Then, the idea hit me that even though barely 40 lbs., this animal could lash out with a single sharp hoof and blind me in either eye. Nevertheless, I carried the creature to a high bank and deposited it there. As it turned out, the fawn did not move a muscle save for two blinking eyes. Both seemed grateful. I patted it on the head and said goodbye. Returning an hour later, I was relieved to see it gone. Quite likely, a doe giving up its young for lost returned and moved the yearling to join others on the long migration trail.

I did not think it ironic that three days later I passed through here to join others in opening the state deer season. Such is the flexible heart of the big game hunter. Both actions seemed entirely congruous to me.

The north slope stream trout were small. Cutthroats, or an occasional brook trout, seldom measured more than 10 inches. Many, in the short growing season, barely reached 8 or 9. The Bear River was a prime example. Rushing on its roundabout way to a rendezvous with Great Salt Lake, the Bear traveled 595 miles to die 95 miles away. It coursed through a plethora of pines and luxurious grass meadows that would add splendor to any calendar scene. But the Bear's water was nearly barren of life. Turn over a rock and caddis or stone fly larvae were scarce. Trout took on no size. Still, it was a magnetic scene which I photographed one winter to make my own Christmas cards.

There was, however, a certain magnetism about these small trout. They bore the colorful markings, gold, orange and oft-times deep scarlet, of wild and born-free trout. They were naive, unsophisticated to the ways of man and unlike the Parleys cutts, accepted almost any reasonable offering. Drop a small renegade fly on the water and they competed to see who might get there first, a phenomenon I'd seen elsewhere only in the Grand Canyon of the Yellowstone. There was something in the eagerness of these north slope trout to be first that gladdened the heart of any angler.

The north slope lakes held larger fish. One day Deral and I were asked to help a boy scout troop at Camp Steiner, where I'd enjoyed a week's stay at ages 12 and 15. I said yes, I'd help out. I owed them. But after taking the scouts fishing on the first morning, I returned them too late for breakfast. The scoutmaster kicked me from camp. He was obviously angry. I said nothing. I was wrong. There was nothing to be said.

Deral and I had planned on three days' outing, so we hiked across the ridge to Ruth and Naomi lakes. We packed sleeping bags but had no food. Well, we would live off the land. We each caught a fat brook trout and proceeded to cook them on hot rocks. I had brought no aluminum foil with me, which would have simplified matters, cooking 10 minutes on each side in hot ashes. We placed flat rocks in the fire and lay the filets on the rocks. An hour later, Deral said he would rather eat the ashes than the raw fish. We waited two hours. Not much difference. Then the fire went out.

We didn't dare eat berries along edge of the lake because we couldn't positively identify them. We went to bed hungry that night after eating only a few bites of semi-cooked fish. Deral said he had seen something in a movie about cooking fish on hot rocks but allowed now that it didn't work.

I allowed that he was right.

The next morning we were awakened by a spike buck snorting along the lake's edge a few feet away. We caught some more brook trout but were at a loss to determine how to cook them. Then we saw several boys approaching. More mouths to feed. But they were boys from the camp and they brought food, glorious, contraband soup and chili. They also brought can openers. We had a hot meal in minutes.

When we got into town, Deral bought a whole shelf of cookies and got sick. He could barely make it to the car. I waited for three hamburgers. Then we drove to Beaver Creek below town where I hooked a large rainbow but it got away. When I returned to the car, Deral was still sick. That ended our efforts to live wholly off the land. I never tried it again. I doubt Deral did either.

The following Sunday I saw the scoutmaster. He apologized for losing his temper at me. But he had been right. I shouldn't have returned the scouts late for breakfast. It's just that I hadn't guided them into any fish and I didn't want to admit failure.

That one was a mental mistake. Not long thereafter, Mo and I committed physical failure and again it was in the Uintas. We had rented horses at the Moon Lake Lodge to ride into the upper Lake Fork Drainage. It seemed logical enough to push the horses directly up the trail alongside the stream. We went about five miles when we found ourselves in a deep box canyon. The trail dissipated. We thought we might be able to push the horses out over the south side and locate the real trail, wherever it might be. But the terrain was too steep and rocky. The pack string refused to go any farther. We had no choice but to back down and return to the trailhead near the Moon Lake Lodge. We had lost half a day when we headed our mounts up the trail. There was even a sign, out of sight from the lodge, which said "Kidney Lake, 13 miles." That was our destination. We barely made it before nightfall.

The next morning I took my fishing rod to Kidney, a water seemingly more than a mile long, and drew a complete blank. Late in the morning, none of us had felt a single strike. The fish had to be there. The lake looked impressive. The third day, just before we had to leave, we finally fished some little nondescript ponds previously ignored. They were choked with lily pads and appeared more like a swamp than a lake. We began immediately catching cutthroat trout. I thought all the way back about how many mistakes we had made on this trip. We hadn't used our heads. When we were exploring we should have been following the status quo. And when we did the latter, we should have been experimenting.

On another expedition into Lake Fork, I caught dozens of cutts from a deep crater-like lake which appeared to have no fish. For three hours I cast in vain with a small spinner. When it began to rain, I managed to catch a single cutt. Opening it up, I found dozens of small red ants. I grabbed my fly rod and tied on a small royal coachman, the closest thing I had to a red ant.

Trout hurtled up off the bottom by the score to crash into my "red ant." Now, at last, I was using my head.

Not far away I caught an 18-inch cutt from a lake I found by following a topo map. The fish swam eagerly to my first cast with a ginger quill which imitated the caddis flies flitting about. Two others struck but eluded me. When I returned, I learned of a five-pound trout caught from a lake I decided I didn't have time to fish. I was kicked myself for not taking time to try that particular lake.

My father took me one day to fish the Uinta streams. Four of them headwatered from the Mirror Lake area, Duchesne to south, Bear to north, Weber to west and Provo to the southwest. We caught some browns in the Provo but only in the few miles where it hadn't been channeled or diverted. Bulldozing and drying up one of the nation's great trout streams hardly seemed intelligent, let alone a respectful way to treat it. Maybe it could be excused. Maybe those who let it happen had never taken Biology 101 in high school.

One day on another stream, I attempted to stop a bulldozer operator from gouging out the river bottom. He was dumping all the insect-laden moss in a pile by the river. He called it flood control.

"But don't worry," he said. "We're just making the stream deeper for the trout."

After the Provo was ruined, we turned to the Weber. It coursed north toward Echo Reservoir and then flowed into the Wasatch Front community of Ogden. The Weber had been spared channelization because it didn't flood as many homes. People had more sense not to build in the natural flood plain. The Weber yet carried life in its currents. One could still hook into respectable brown trout. Chalk Creek ambled down from the Uintas to the Weber and produced some fine pansize trout fishing. But it ran through banks of red clay. If a few drops of rain fell, the stream turned opaque. I never did like to fish water where I couldn't see beyond the surface. Much of the time the stream ran red and I had to give up on it. The only other stream in the state which turned to mud as quickly was the Duchesne. It seemed that even a cloud passing overhead made the Duchesne unfishable.

A stream didn't have to be perfectly clear, however, for like the Henrys Fork, that would make fish more spooky. Yet, esthetics were always important. I had great admiration for the watershed managers in places like Idaho's Henrys Fork where the water ran clear.

One peculiar thing about Chalk Creek was that when the water was clear, fish spread out and fed from almost anywhere, tree roots, small rocks, grassy overhangs, everywhere. One didn't look for places to fish but assumed trout were there and cast slowly ahead with measured steps.

One day I was fishing the Logan River when I saw a class of students by the stream. They had been electroshocking and turned over several large brown trout. "You should have been with us yesterday," said the professor. "We shocked a brown in the Blacksmith Fork [a tributary of the Logan] which we weighed at 32 lbs."

Since that would have been a world record, I asked the professor to reweigh the fish next time they shocked it. The next year, he told me the fish now weighed 34 lbs. Since a brown weighing 36 3/4 lbs. had been caught on the Logan drainage, it didn't seem impossible. But that was in 1937. This was in modern times. How could it have grown so big?

"I dunno," said the prof. "But two hatchery rainbows fell out of its mouth when we netted it. A lot of hatchery rainbows go in there because there's a campground nearby. Fish and Game says they'd like somebody to catch the fish because it's wrecking havoc with their local planting program" The fish was shocked and weighed the next year at 34 1/2 lbs. But it was not seen nor heard about again. So far as I learned, no one ever bragged of catching it. And I was sure if someone did, they would.

I received a photo of the fish, broad across the back and deep in the belly, like a boat paddle. How did the fish manage to live for some 15 years among heavy angling pressure alongside a paved road? Size? Food was plentiful. A small reservoir was nearby if drought conditions ever struck. The fish had a deep cutbank where it could remain out of sight during daylight hours, most likely stalking the water for unsuspecting prey at night. The prof said he envisioned the monster not only attacking planter trout but frogs, mice, ducklings, baby muskrats, even snakes. I'd killed a four-foot rattlesnake once in Logan Canyon while fishing—I almost put my hand on it—but the prof said he meant small watersnakes.

It fired my imagination to visualize such a mighty fish. Think of casting along casually, say at dusk or after dark and hooking such a monster! You'd tell your companion it must have weighed at least 10 lbs. and he would jibe you about telling a fisherman's fib. Who knows if some of the whopper stories anglers tell wide-eyed youngsters around Saturday evening campfires aren't about such giant trout?

There were many wild places for me to fish or hunt within half a day. One was the Book Cliffs "a great mass of nothingness" as one county commissioner told me, which encompassed nearly 10,000 square miles in Uintah and Grand counties. The region appeared from paved roads to be only sand and sparse cedars but 30 miles farther south it gave way to thick cedars, then aspen mixed with pines. The region was well named, for hundreds of ridges ran in all directions, seemingly like the edge of a book with the pages partly open. The few road signs were as wild as the country: "Cat Canyon, 65 miles; Wild Horse Mesa, 80; PR Springs, 95; U.S. 6, 120 miles." Distances were rounded off because they were estimates. I doubt anyone ever measured the miles on a speedometer because there were so many of them. I was to later explore this vast hinterland on dozens of excursions and find one of the most amazing fishing holes anywhere. Trout grew at stupendous rates in Towave Reservoir. It grew cutthroat trout even faster than Yellowstone. The first year they were 11 inches, then 16, the following summer, 2-3 lbs. By the fourth year, we caught a seemingly endless number of four pounders. These cutthroats pounced on any large lure, metal, wood or plastic. My most ecstatic moment came in catching one on a fly. I watched a 19-incher finning in front of me pounce on my black leech streamer. I lost that one only to cast again and catch the first trout's twin.

Of course, one must pay a price to get in; 51 miles of back roads which, when muddy, allowed only the most ambitious driver through, providing he/she has chained up all four tires and is lucky.

To get all this in, I had to juggle school and work. I often worked in my father's shop until late Friday night, then drove with Mo or Deral from 2 a.m. until dawn to reach our destination. We fished until early afternoon, then took a fast nap and returned home Saturday night. I did this the entire summer between junior and senior years of high school and into the following autumn. Heavy snow and ice usually closed Uinta access by early October at the latest, but fish normally slowed their feeding by late September. It was just too cold to feel hunger in the higher elevations after that. Mid September was the perfect time for fly fishing because night time cold killed insects and dropped them in windrows on the lake surface. They washed ashore and fish followed them. If you could match these insects falling to the water you might hook dozens of trout in a short time. With experimentation I found that a Siberian wood-ant, yellow, jointed body, size 12-14, would fetch so many strikes that an angler's arm might begin to ache after a while from fighting even small fish. The strange thing was that I could never find a real wood-ant. They were nowhere to be found. Was there such a creature? There had to be, else what did the trout think they were eating? One day, years later, I cleaned a 15-inch cutthroat from a Montana lake with what appeared to be in its stomach a jointed yellow body wood-ant. It was the only real wood-ant I was to ever see. There were none drawn in any English language books on aquatic insects. Maybe in Siberia? Seldom did I find them for sale in angling shops. Yet, they had to be out there, in my native America, in numbers. Most likely they were a nymph, dwelling on the bottom of lakes, which were hard to find and hatched into a caddis fly of some kind. Whatever, the fish loved them,

I resolved the problem by accident. Selling advertising space during one summer, I talked to a sporting goods shop owner who tied his own flies. He had wood-ants. I took in lieu of money, 375 Siberian wood-ants. In time I used them all. But after the sporting goods dealer died, I found no one selling them. I had to learn how to tie my own. My fingers didn't seem delicate enough to handle such tiny materials. My fingertip dwarfed the hook itself, let alone the minute thread. I decided I couldn't do it. But if I wanted Siberians, I would have to do it. The process didn't turn out to be as difficult as I thought. Making the final loop was the most difficult thing and I fumbled through the first half dozen flies. Then, seemingly through no extra thought or effort, my fingers glided into place. There was nothing like repetition for getting it right. Nothing at all.

At high school graduation, I had compiled a respectable grade point average, except for math. I took Latin because teachers said chemistry labels were written in Latin. I had drawn good grades from my chemistry teacher and decided I might have a future in it afterall. In art class, a peculiar thing happened. My teacher came around and saw me struggling with a drawing of a great blue heron ("Your heron's neck looks like the grass around it") and he showed me how to do it, painting over my shoulder. He did the same a week later with a picture of a waterfall scene. To me, painting water, especially if reflecting sunlight as I'd seen in nature, seemed the most difficult task in all art. My teacher showed me how to do it in watercolors with a deft and light touch of the brush. "Think it out ahead before proceeding," he said. Before long, he became so engrossed in the challenge he couldn't lay the brush down.

When I handed in my art work, he said, "I couldn't do it better myself!" and marked a large "A" on the corner of the picture.

My history teacher droned on and on about the military strategy of the civil war; I could barely remain awake. Why were they fighting? Not just over slavery you say? Economics? Just money? Years later, I was so fascinated by history that I took a number of college graduate courses in the subject. And I was so enamored of the Civil War, specifically, that I drove hundreds of miles out of my way to see Gettysburg.

Zoology was an easy "A" so long as the focus was on taxonomy or ecological relationships. Function of pancreas and esophagus of a mongoose or inner workings of the mandible in a monkey provoked a mild crisis. In botany I had trouble keeping my pistils separated from my photosynthesis. But I realized that anything worthwhile rarely came easy. I'd witnessed that from the first days on Parleys Creek.

When graduation night came in late May, I realized I had paid almost no attention to social matters. There was no one I could invite to the Graduation Dance. Many of my peers were going steady and it was said he or she "belonged" to the mate in hand. As I saw couples strolling about the halls, they seemed inseparable. When did they find time for study? It was obvious to me that love, like beauty, was in the eyes of the beholder. What attracted one to the other? Opposites? Alikes? I could find nothing whatsoever scientific or logical in the process.

Such couples were oblivious to the rest of the world. We were not there. It must be wonderful, I thought, to live in such bliss. But it was not for me. There was too much to do, and if I had to do it alone, I would. To be sure, I'd gone to some neighborhood dances, usually just before they ended, giving a girl a ride home. But it was carefully calculated to avoid any relationship. I wanted to keep my life untangled emotionally. Or something like that. I could never quite figure it out myself.

Chapter Fifteen

The fact that I was a high school graduate didn't seem to make much difference. I felt a little older but not much smarter. The trouble is, I was now expected to be smarter. I was a high school graduate. I would continue to work in the refinishing shop but it was understood at end of the summer I would enroll in college. My major: chemistry.

My first chemistry test required memorization of chemical elements; no math. I got a very high score. The one after that contained math. I got a very low score. I was required to take algebra and after two weeks, I quit. I was three weeks behind. What was it with math anyway?

I talked to a professor and poured out my woes. He listened with great sympathy and then advised me to change majors. I'd been tip-toeing down a primrose path that led to an impossible chasm. It had been my life's dream to be a famous chemist. Where would I go now?

I would go fishing, that's where. On the following Saturday I drove alone to Wyoming's Hams Fork. I'd heard there were big rainbows in the stream. They weren't difficult to find. They finned near the surface and slurped no-see-um somethings as if they had been fasting the week before. I tried various fly patterns, large and small, bright, dull, winged, non-winged, nymphs, dries, wets, streamers, bucktails, bare hooks. None worked. Finally, I cast out a spinner and caught five respectable rainbows in almost as many casts. I couldn't figure it out. The fly had to be perfect but one didn't have to match a spinner hatch. Any large spinner would do. So long as it was retrieved downstream like a wounded minnow.

These trout were willing to suddenly switch from flies to minnows. They were opportunists. Not all were like that. Next trip proved it. They were feeding on something, nymphs or emergers, well below the surface and they would not touch spinners or anything else. I rigged with two flies at once and went through several until casting out a size 6, shiny-bodied stone fly nymph. They went wild. Eighteen to 20 inch rainbows, their crimson stripes crashing from the water, dug into the moss beds until I waded in and worked them loose. In this I used an old trick learned on Idaho's Blackfoot, giving the fish slack line until they thought they were free and swam into open water by themselves. Eventually, I caught and released half a dozen. I went home on a cloud.

And I knew I could make it. I didn't know which of a hundred subjects would become my new major. But somehow, I would decide what to do with my life. I would not worry about it. I would take more classes and keep an open mind. There was psychology. Did everyone who graduated in psychology do so just to know more about themselves? Well, that was a legitimate reason. Wasn't it?

I soon returned to Hams Fork. This time, I brought my younger brother along, eager to learn. It was October and very cold in this part of Wyoming. We had to wear gloves and skull caps during the early morning. Fishing with gloves was awkward but one could clip the glove off at the index finger. To start fishing, I tied on a medium-sized captain that appeared to resemble a hatched stone fly. Voila! I couldn't keep the big trout off my hook. Thirteen fell victim in two hours. Doug also caught fish. He experimented and caught them on a large crane fly larvae. I bragged to Doug that I could go back after lunch and catch another 13.

Humility was not long in coming. The fish had focused on something else. I looked on in frustration at sunset as the trout dined daintily on Unknowns across the golden surface glow. Oh, that I could press my left wrist and turn into a fish, swim among them and ask them what they were eating and re- emerge as an angler and give them what they wanted!

Yet, all I could do was watch them play leapfrog in a frenzied feeding spree, then trudge back to the truck with coat collar pulled tight. There were still things, obviously, that I didn't understand. Another secret of nature to unravel. Another mysterious ecological system at work to be understood before calling oneself a fisherman.

This was the last of the fishing for the year. November was upon the world and with it days of battleship grey skies in which trout seemed to slip into semi-hibernation. I, too, went into a cocoon. There were advantages. I found my homework much easier to do. But in the last of the semester, two friends and I decided we would withdraw from school and go south for the winter. By mid January, I told my parents goodbye. While they watched wistfully, they knew their son must see more of the world. Jack and Ephraim and I drove toward the warming sun, stopping when we reached Phoenix.

We found a place to stay in the YMCA. The room held two thin beds but by pushing them together, three could sleep in one room. Two days later, we were discovered and evicted.

Jack found a job in a plush resort as a bus boy, Eph in a brick yard and I in a chemical warehouse. The foreman confronted me rather gruffly. "We had to fire the last warehouseman. He was too small. Let's see you pick up that 100 lb. sack over there and put it at my feet." I did so. "You're hired," he said. "So long as you can do that all day."

During this time I was helped daily by a foreman, a black man whose name was George Washington Jones. He woke me up one day at 1:20 p.m., asleep in the sun, and when he saw my surprised look rushing back to work, laughed uproariously. If I needed help on anything, he gave it, although he knew full well I was a "snowbird" who wouldn't be around come the heat of summer. A man needed friends, I concluded, wherever he went.

When early spring arrived, I made some local friends who fished. They took me to Roosevelt Lake and proceeded to catch several 3-4 lb. largemouth bass. I didn't have enough money to buy a fishing license and could only look on. It was difficult not to cast with them, but I could learn by watching. I was impressed with the strike of the "bucketmouths" as they called them. First, huge jaws extended around a plug skipped over the surface; then the water exploded in a spray of foam while their fishing rods plummeted. Some day, I would learn to catch big bass.

By late March, Jack and Eph ran out of money and had to return home. I remained until receiving a telephone call from my father. "You've been drafted," he said. "You're to report to Ft. Douglas Thursday of next week." I had ignored the war in Korea, or "conflict" as they called it, since Congress had not officially declared war. I had registered as required and remained legal. I couldn't honestly claim to be a "conscientious objector." And now my time had run out.

I returned home by bus and read the notice. "Greetings, your friends and neighbors have selected you..." Dad and Mother said, "You love a challenge. Here is a new one, son. Like you do when fishing, remember all you've learned." My father took me aside, "We'll miss you in the shop, son. We had just trained you in the Dirty Hand Method and now the government has found out and wants you."

The following Saturday I stood in a soldier uniform at Ft. Ord, Calif. There must have been a thousand of us standing in formation, all looking precisely alike, except that some yet sported long hair. Mostly it was drab green fatigues and glum faces. As we stood there, it began raining but it made no difference to the sergeants. They called it "California dew."

Six soldiers were needed for KP that night. What were the odds of me being selected among a thousand others in the same color uniform? Good, I found out.

"You," he pointed. "Get over here." What had attracted the attention? I felt my hat brim. It was turned up, in some sick, subconscious effort to retain individuality. Eighteen hours later, I got off KP. I stood in formation an hour later and made certain my hat brim was turned down. It made no difference. "You," he said. "Get over here." Another eighteen hours KP. I had read cartoons about sergeants being funny, but by some coincidence, none of them were here.

We were advised that we were to become "professional killers." Yet, the Army seemed in no hurry to make the transformation. We spent nearly four days aiming M-l rifles at make-believe targets with no ammunition, aiming and saying "Bang." Then a comrade pushed our shoulder in simulation of rifle recoil. I had spent hours on the rifle range with Mo preparing for deer hunting. Now, we spent nearly four days with simulated rifle kick. In addition, we were only allowed an average of four hours' sleep per night. The biggest "kick" we got was when we fell asleep and a non-commissioned officer klunked us on the head.

The days were spent in blazing summer sun, many on the Camp Roberts parade field, learning little about using firearms, spending most of the time learning to march in step. If sent to battle, how would looking good while we marched help our side win? I didn't get it.

One day I received a telegram. My grandmother had died. I called home. My grandfather couldn't be consoled. He would leave all the paintings exactly where she left them. And I tried to forget everything at home in order to survive. We were merely bodies carrying weapons. We must not forget why we were here. To defend America. Only that could provide the incentive to remain motivated.

We were sent to bivouac in the mountains, spending two weeks camping out. I couldn't have been happier to get out of the spit and polish barracks, where we were advised that somehow, keeping the building spotlessly clean would help win the war. One day we were given a demonstration on how to kill everything on a hillside. Machine gun fire splashed dust from left to right, top to bottom. "That's how to dispose of the enemy," the sergeant said. But when the firing stopped and he looked away, I saw something stand up from behind a bush. It was a doe and fawn deer. They walked off as if they had been inconvenienced by all the noise.

The next day we were hiking along a creek when we came to a cavernous pool. Against the far cliff wall, in the dim shadows, I saw a faint stirring. It was a long, lean rainbow trout gliding along almost effortlessly in the shallow water. The sight of it was an inspiration. I participated in war games that evening with special gusto. I put in such an enthusiastic effort to save our hill from the enemy "Aggressors" that a major put his hand on my head and labeled me "Audie Murphy." Whatever.

Then came the day our captain called us to attention and announced he was sorry to say we wouldn't be going to war afterall. At least not the one in Korea. An armistice had been signed. He had so wanted to personally lead us into battle. We smiled inappropriately. Now, we would probably be going to Europe to help the occupation army over there.

I was, indeed, assigned to Germany. My family came to fetch me from Basic Training. I was a person again. After spending 10 days at home, including a day fishing with Mo on Mountain Dell Creek and another in the Uintas, I reported to New Jersey to ship out. By October I was in Patton Barracks, Heidelberg, Germany. It was a beautiful place on the Neckar River where it emerged from the Black Forest. Although it had only been nine years since end of World War II, there were no signs here of conflict. Twelve miles away, however, Mannheim stood in stark reminder of those terrible years. Its sheered-off buildings looked like brick ghosts about to crash.

After a month, a fellow private showed me four brown trout he had caught on a nearby stream. I had an opportunity as a soldier to fish for them without buying a license or going through red tape. There were some perks here. Then, too, I could visit Paris and Rome and the Isle of Capri and the places I'd only read about. I marveled at the seemingly groomed hills of Austria. But most of all, I admired Switzerland. I sat in awe of the Grindelwald Glacier. The Eiger intrigued me, although I had never gotten into mountain climbing with piton and rope. If I was to risk my life it should be for a fish or deer, or in meeting some biological challenge. For hours I walked beyond the alpine village of Zermatt, taking photographs of the Matterhorn, although no matter how far I walked, it seemed I never got any closer.

A guide asked me if I wanted to climb it. I should, of course. But I declined. It would take two days. I had only one and a half. I felt relieved that there was not time. I could not meet every challenge in life. I would have to prioritize.

My job in the 4th Base Office was to sort airmail and bundle it in destinations by end of each day. I had declined a job in the stamp windows because I didn't want to meet people all day. After memorizing the addresses in Long Island, Jamaica, etc., I was put in charge of air mail.

It was customary at day's end to recruit half a dozen privates to help carry sacks at the Bahnhoff to meet train deadlines. Most of the sacks had heavy eight-day clocks inside. No one liked the task and a game was played every evening as soldiers gave excuses to get out of the job. One evening I was tabbed for the unwelcome duty. I gave my excuse. "I'll go with you," I said, "But if I do, I refuse to be responsible for getting the air mail out on time."

The sergeant conferred with a Lt. Jackson. "He has a point," said the lieutenant. "Better keep him here." The other privates noticed. I was a hero after that, and for a reason I could never fathom. I simply did as my father taught me. "If you are to do any task, son, do it well."

The sergeant voiced it around that I was a tough kid no one could fluster. The officers thought of me as one who got the work done without showing negative emotion.

After several weeks, the same sergeant called me away from my work and handed me a telegram. I opened it slowly. My father was dead.

I sat down with my head in my hands and wept openly in front of the sergeant.

I called home. My father had gone deer hunting with Mo, a sport he seldom participated in, and caught cold. The cold turned to pneumonia. He was thought to be recovering in the hospital. But with his weak heart, he didn't make it.

There had not been many opportunities to become better acquainted with my father. He had been busy in the shop. But there were the times while fishing I could have said, "Dad, how did you do as a kid in math? Tell me about yourself. Tell me about your boyhood, your dreams, your aspirations. How am I doing as your son? I could have told him I loved him. I didn't because…then he would know. There were so many times. So many, many, many times.

I lay there that night thinking of all he had taught, all he stood for. There was the time when he said, "See that truck in front of us, with one tire in the gravel? No one can see for blocks behind him. Some people go through life that way, blinding the way for all behind." My Dad pulled over and waited for the dust to clear. It was subtle. But I knew he was not giving me a lesson in driving. There were many times like that. And now he was gone.

Chapter Sixteen

The Army agreed, upon a report from my mother, that I was essential to my family's business. For that reason, the Army would pay my way home and consider a "compassionate discharge" to work in my father's place. I took a train to Frankfurt and waited for a Military Transport to fly me home. But the plane was delayed three days and I did not arrive home in time to attend my father's funeral.

Mo told me he never attended funerals. He did my father's. I read the talks given. All praised him for his honesty and sincerity. I visited the cemetery, ground locked in January cold, the trees leafless, the ground barren. I vowed to never die in January.

Mo could manage the shop without my services. He said it would not be the same working in the shop without my father. He had lost his best friend. "You're a very close friend, too," he said, "but…"

"I understand," I said.

Mo received offers of much higher pay from cabinet and carpentry shops across the city. But he would stay where he was. Mother was assured of that and so was I. He could run the shop single-handed if he had to.

I returned to Camp Carson, Colo., then crossed the Atlantic in a troop ship for the third time, bound back to Germany. A sign the length of Patton Barracks, some 80 feet long and 15 feet high, welcomed me back. It was not the Army which hung it but the 18 other soldiers in my squad room. The Army noticed. The next week when we had an inspection from Col. Pyrtle, I was one of two ordered to stand inspection. Sgt. Mackay and myself. The colonel had a reputation for cracking down hard on military installations and soldiers which didn't adhere to the colonel's form of discipline and rigid decorum. The troops said that Sgt. Mackay, a veteran soldier of 27 years, was chosen as an honor, because of his many spotless years of service in

Korea and World War 11. Me? No one was sure. I had been back to the States, in effect, a civilian, and now, I must prove myself capable of military discipline once more. Yes. They were determined to make me into a soldier. That was it.

Col. Pyrtle looked us over, Sgt. Mackay and myself, standing at full attention. He spoke to me first. "You," he said, "are in excellent condition. You have a look about you that must come from physical activity. We could send you into combat immediately." He asked me to open my locker. "Bar bells. Football. Golf clubs. Tennis racquet. Fishing pole. Is this how you stay in shape?"

"Yes sir."

"You have one hanger turned the wrong way, soldier. Would you please see that it hangs the same direction as the others?"

I straightened the damage.

"And you sergeant," he said, standing back several feet. "You are badly overweight. Did you know that?"

"Yes sir." Col. Pyrtle himself was a skinny man, one might even say wiry, no ounce of surplus flesh. The sergeant glanced at him apprehensively, but remained silent.

"I admire your service record, Sgt. Mackay. But you've become flabby. When it happens physically, it happens mentally. You need some physical hobby. I would suggest you eat less and exercise more. That is an order. Do I make myself clear?"

"Yes sir."

Afterward, soldiers rushed into the room. One of them was Lt. Jackson, the officer we called "Stonewall." "What did he tell you?" Jackson asked Sgt. Mackay.

"He told me to do more fishing," the sergeant replied.

"More fishing?" retorted Jackson. "What?"

I said nothing. But from that time on, I decided the Army was more intelligent than I had given it credit for.

A few months later, I learned that a soldier could leave the Army three months before his two-year tour of duty if signing up for college. I signed up and returned to the States. After several weeks of fetching coffee for officers at Camp Carson, I was on a plane home. It was Christmas Eve. But there was too much fog over the Rocky Mountains. The plane would have to fly on to Los Angeles. We could catch a plane back the day after Christmas if we were lucky. At the last second, an opening appeared in the fog and we touched down in familiar territory. By 9 p.m. Christmas Eve I was home with mother, brother and sister.

I would not remain home for more than one semester of college. I had in my last few months in the Army become convinced I was in danger of drifting. The military discipline had not been comfortable but it had been directive. I taught a class to church youth during that last few months wherein we talked about the need to making strong moral commitment. I said I felt sorry for anyone who didn't have a cause more important than themselves. I thought about career, something without math... but that wasn't it. The challenge was attitude. Someone said attitude determined altitude. A lofty expression perhaps...but true. I knew little about the Bible or official tenets of the religion I'd grown up with. My religion had been the trout stream. I had, indeed, learned much from every moment spent beside rushing water. Flat water. Any kind of water with fish in it.

I'd heard the phrase, "I can get as much spirituality on Sundays from going outdoors and looking at the trees and skies. I can worship and feel as close to God in the outdoors as inside a church." I mulled that over. It was a ready-made excuse and I liked it. But...was there any service in it, any accomplishment in behalf of others? Is that what my Dad would advise? I weighed it and it became more weighty the more I pondered it.

At the end of the month, I decided to go on a mission for my church. I would be an ordained minister for two years, paying my own way, with help from my mother and sister, and go wherever I was sent. I was sent to Illinois, Nebraska and Iowa. Eventually, I asked to work with the Indians of Wisconsin on the Oneida Indian Reservation 10 miles west of Green Bay and was sent there. I was now 22 years old, and hadn't decided what I wanted to be when I grew up.

After serving an apprenticeship with a more experienced missionary, I was told I was now in charge. During the week, my companion and I, always working in pairs like the FBI, knocked on doors and met with strangers and explained the Christian principles of our church. At one of the first doors, my companion said, "We are ministers and calling on all the good Christian people of this neighborhood."

She said, "Well, we are Jewish."

He fumbled and finally managed to come up with the truth, "We are meeting with everyone."

"Go away," she said.

Improve the World...

My job description included being Scoutmaster on Saturdays. We had a troop of about 25 boys, all Oneida Indians. Would I help them learn the skills necessary to become Eagle Scouts, take them out camping, fire building and cooking and help them learn about nature and birds, perhaps take them fishing?

I said I would try.

The boys and I built fishing rods from bamboo, not split bamboo but real, raw, ramrod straight, heavy bamboo. There was no money to buy sophisticated fishing rods. We did the best we could with materials found in homes of the boys. We took an outing to the Oconto River and caught brown trout on hellgramites (stone flies) I showed them beneath dark, flat rocks. This was, indeed, heavenly service. Soon, the boys began receiving tenderfoot, second and first class awards. They were the first in several years.

One day I told the boys rather ceremoniously that we would learn how to build a cooking fire without paper and no more than two matches. I shaved fine kindling spunk off branches and stacked it carefully, adding heavier wood, making room for oxygen to take hold. Finally, at just the right moment, I put a match beneath it and was rewarded with a bright orange puff. "Where's the hot dogs?" I asked one of the Scouts.

"John has 'em," said the closest boy.

"In fact, John has 'em cooked," said John. He had a roaring blaze going. Several boys were cooking hot dogs over John's fire.

"So much for fire building instruction," I said.

A boy commiserated with me. "You taught us about fishing," he said. "We teach you about fire building." I learned that these boys built a fire in their homes almost every day except mid-summer. All their homes had wood or coal stoves rather than central heating. I concluded that a little adversity was a good thing. The boys amazed me, too, at how fast they learned to catch brook trout in nearby Lyndhurst Creek and local streams. Lyndhust reminded me of Parleys Creek. I yearned to visit once more the stream of my boyhood.

In the meantime, there was much to learn in the Wisconsin woods. In the fall, families we met with invited my companion and I to hunt whitetail deer. I marveled at how these creatures could live at the edge of civilization, seemingly vanishing when you looked for them, re-appearing the day after hunting season ended.

I also learned more about the New Testament, amazed at the fact Jesus chose mostly fishermen (and one despised tax collector just to keep the ledger balanced) for his top disciples, they who would later become his Twelve Apostles. I found wisdom and strength for daily living in the scriptures which I had never supposed to be there. Now that I was nearly 23, my father and mother were much smarter.

My main duties dealt with people, not nature; but I took every opportunity to learn truth from all sources. Truth came in many forms.

Deer did not enter blindly into swamp or thicket until testing what lie ahead with all available senses. Beavers and squirrels prepared for possible adversity months ahead. Trees grew their thickest bark on the side bracing into the northern cold. Bees helped flowers cross-pollinate by visiting more than one. When birds perched, they always faced into the wind. People did best when they faced squarely to their problems. The deeper secrets of nature were rarely ascertained upon first glance. That of greatest value usually required greater focus to understand and even more work to attain.

Upon completion of my mission, I rejoiced once more to meet with Mo and my companions from so many memorable outdoor excursions. Mo had done much more work in the shop, he admitted, since I was gone. We spent one day hiking into Blue Lake and I was relieved to find a grayling there. Just one. But a grayling. It was like part of Alaska or British Columbia even yet here, less than two hours from my home. It was good talking to Mo. He now had an adolescent son and daughter. But he was divorced now and didn't see them very often. "Be careful who you marry," he told me. I'd heard that advice before, especially from fishermen.

I had also written to a girl during my mission who sent letters saying "Happiness is like potato salad. Share it and you have a picnic." After several days at home, I asked her for a date, something I had not been allowed to do for two years. Jessica accepted. "Where would we go?"

"On a picnic. Fishing to be exact," I said matter-of-factly.

"I'll bring the potato salad," she said.

On a beautiful morning in late September, we drove to East Canyon Reservoir. September was, we agreed, the most beautiful time of year. We spread a blanket by the still water and I hesitated long enough to cast out a salmon egg bait, lay down my pole and turned to talk. We looked at one another. She had exquisite eyes. She reminded me of Liz Taylor. She had sent me a photo of herself with an Italian hairdo which I yet could not get out of my mind. It reminded me of a movie I'd seen Liz in. Her dark hair fell lightly against her neck. We drew closer. I looked at her lips, she at mine. She closed her eyes. I had almost closed mine, when I noticed something from the corner of my eye. My rod tip was bouncing almost into the water.

"Excuse me," I said. Picking up the rod, something bucked and cavorted on the other end. A large rainbow trout catapulted from the water, silhouetted against the cloud and pine-studded backdrop across the blue-green water. A few minutes later, I hefted an 18-inch rainbow for my new found girl friend to see.

"A great welcome home!" I almost shouted.

I saw she was not impressed. "I had something else in mind," she said.

"But I...I put bait on thinking that we wouldn't be disturbed... I... we..."

"They told me you were a good fisherman," she said coldly. "I think you knew exactly what you were doing. And even if you didn't, you could have ignored the fish; you could have...oh, never mind."

The mood was clearly gone. I looked at the fish and I looked at her.

"I could have ignored the fish...ignored...no."

We drove home in partial silence. "Did you have a good time?" I asked. "Almost," she said.

"I'll make it up to you," I promised. "I'll take you to Cocoanut Grove."

We went to Cocoanut Grove and after dancing twice, a fellow rushed over and pumped my hand. "Deral," I said. "How are you..."

"Hey, I went up to Alexander Lake yesterday and..."

I realized there was no way to escape it. When you are a good fisherman, everyone wants to talk to you.

In a few days I had time to drive alone around the valley. What had happened in my nearly four years' absence? The foothills where I'd watched deer and elk was filled with houses on stilts. Spring Run was channeled into a near-ditch, shopping malls encroaching the stream's edge on the opposite side of the highway, leaving no cutbanks whatsoever. At a place we once called "Pheasant Run," a condo now stood, named appropriately enough, I suppose, "Pheasant Run." Another housing development labeled "Willowbrook" had replaced both willows and brook. Mill Creek was diverted at mouth of the canyon into an irrigation ditch. Big Cottonwood was diverted at mouth of the canyon into a power plant. Little Cottonwood had no water at all until driving far into the canyon. Access was denied at mouth of City Creek Canyon and housing on Emigration Canyon forbade any trespass. The Jordan had been dredged and channeled into a barren sluiceway.

Last of all, I visited Parleys Creek.

It was not there.

In the canyon, a highway of wall-to-wall concrete replaced the creek. I looked for the pool where I had caught my first crimson-tinged brook trout. The pool was nowhere to be seen. Nor the roadside tree where I'd talked with the tourist fisherman. Water yet flowed from the Wasatch Mountains, of course, but in a pipe beneath I-80.

Downstream in Parleys Gully, I found no sign of the riffles and holes where I'd tossed a fly to finning cutthroats. None of the greenery by the creek where I'd observed quail and pondered my life's dreams. To be sure, the waterfall spillway was still there. The stream bed above and below were dry. The golf course was still there, and in places a muddy flow was allowed above ground as a water hazard. But everything was fenced off to the public. A cop no longer need search for fishermen. There were none.

I was told that some current could be witnessed during spring runoff at Sugarhouse Park. At other times, the stream bed was dry.

Mountain Dell Creek, too, was gone, buried beneath a water storage reservoir. There were no trees, scarcely a blade of grass in the little valley where I had found solitude so many times as a young man. The tall cottonwood tree where I'd parked my car in the shade and listened to the cooing of a mourning dove was now a high chain link fence.

The homes where "Crazy Mary" and "Old Ed" lived were gone. Perhaps they had died. Only the gravel pit remained.

Only visible remnant of the old Parleys Creek itself was a sector just below Suicide Rock, placed in public ownership, some day perhaps to be preserved as "Parleys Gully Park." At least they allowed for that. Would it again support orange-hued cutthroat trout plucking minute may flies from the surface?

No one knew.

I sat down. Were the vivid memories of my boyhood real? Or had I just been dreaming?

I sat there for more than an hour wondering.

Chapter Seventeen

A few days later, I arranged with Mo to take the company truck and drive by myself into the Uintas. There were many new side roads to explore. I had no idea at all where they led. One took me half a mile to a gravel pit. Another looped toward Beaver Creek but stopped and served no useful purpose I could see other than providing a turn-around. Why so many meaningless roads? Do people just like to build roads?

Once I had found a U.S. Bureau of Land Management sign on Diamond Mountain, at the other end of the Uintas, which read "Vernal, 14 miles," while another stated, "Vernal, 9 miles." They were 150 yards apart and pointed in the same direction. Such erratica made driving more interesting. I looked for such unique signs on this day but other than one which read "Nudist Colony Ahead" just before entering the Wasatch National Forest marker, I found no more unusual signs.

I did find some I'd never seen before. "Upper Setting Road." I had to see where this went. It went, in fact, nowhere. It switchbacked up the north side of the canyon, leading to no lake or stream. I returned to the highway and began searching for nostalgia. There. This was where I parked the car, rode with a Boy Scout troop to the Thirteen Lakes trailhead, and guided them in.

I wanted to do something for Scouting. I had by now nearly earned my Eagle badge, lifesaving being the only merit badge lacking. (I was, for some reason, a strong hiker but weak swimmer.) So, I helped the scoutmaster organize camp at Cutthroat Lake, then turned to hike out where I'd left my car. It would be some 11 or 12 miles. At mid-afternoon, there would barely be time to fish my way down the North Fork of the Provo before dark. One hitch. Nathan, one of the leaders, decided he wanted to go with me.

"Can you hike fast?" I asked, looking at the extra weight he packed around his middle. "This is rugged terrain. We'll have to work down those cliffs ahead and drop 4,000 feet through a narrow canyon." I'd never been there before, but one could see from the rim this would be no picnic. He assured me he was in good shape.

An hour later, I knew we were in trouble. He had to stop and rest, he said. Several small canyon flows had by now converged to make a sizeable creek. I indulged myself for an hour catching small cutthroat and brook trout on a black barberpole pattern, size 14. Since rain had begun to fall, I chewed the fly's wings down to resemble a bedraggled insect caught in the downpour. The trout had probably never been fooled before and were eager hitters. Nathan remained at my elbow, ambling along slowly, occasionally catching a few fish himself. Then, heavier clouds moved over us from a western ridge. Fine; I always carried a rain coat in high country. But Nathan didn't.

The rain increased. Thunder and lightning filled the sky. Nathan began to grow wet and cold. His eyes puffed up. He was, he said, walking too fast. Then the bombshell: he'd had trouble with asthma. If he overdid, the doctor told him, it could trigger a heart attack. He would have to slow down. We rested. We walked 100 yards and rested again.

I was growing nervous. I hadn't brought a flashlight, hadn't seen any need for one, and light was growing dim. I estimated we had traveled only four or five miles, not even halfway there, when total darkness overwhelmed the two of us. There was no trail. We proceeded by lightning flashes down the only opening in the jungle-like forest that we had, the stream bed itself. In one place, as Nathan held my hand, I stumbled into waist-deep water.

There was spectacular beauty in the lightning. I stopped for a second to admire it. Nature had never been more violently beautiful.

"Water is a conductor of electricity, is it not?" Nathan asked.

"The best," I said.

My companion looked ashen. He saved his energy to put forth one more foot in front of the other. Finally, we sat under a tree. When he felt strong enough, we proceeded downhill once more, waiting for the lightning to see where we were going down the stream bed. When we reached a waterfall, I took Nathan's hand and commenced to feel my way around a rocky ridge. Suddenly, his hand wrenched from mine and we fell into a black hole. I heard Nathan call my name but could not see him. The storm continued its fascinating and fearful fury.

In my right hand I carried my favorite fly rod. I had two choices. I could fling the rod aside and never see it again, or I could hang on and hope to catch myself with my left hand. But alas, my foot had twisted on the muddy ground and I fell to the right. I'd caught many trout with the rod. I could not risk parting with it. Yet, if I did not get my right hand out to break the fall, my chin might be first to crash into a tree stump. In the next instant, my chin hit what felt like a tree stump. I felt around with my free hand. A tree stump.

Nathan was calling me. I groped in the direction of his moaning and found he was lucky. He had fallen into a bog and seemingly sustained no injury. I felt blood oozing from my chin. More importantly, I felt to my fly rod. Yes, the same two pieces were there as before. No more. Everything seemed all right. But Nathan crawled under a large pine and he did not move for a long time.

An hour later, he said he felt faint. I pondered our situation. It was well after midnight. There was not a single dry spot on my body. Nor probably his. I felt my innermost underwear. Nothing dry there either. I tried to get some sleep. I may have actually dozed off for a few minutes; I couldn't be sure.

Finally, I asked Nathan if he thought he could try once more to move, even only to crawl. "It's cold here," I said without needing to. "We would be better off to…"

"I might find a little more energy…if you could pray for us."

As a missionary, I'd prayed for many people, including myself. The daily routine was to walk along a row of houses, knock on each door and ask if we could leave a thought and a prayer. Sometimes people let us in.

I said a prayer for Nathan. After finishing, Nathan looked out from beneath the tree. It had protected us from the rain. Now we would have to face the deluge once again. I crawled ahead first and motioned Nathan to follow. He was close behind. I didn't know which way to go, the vines and brush were so thick. Then, my hand touched a bare spot in the grass. I felt again several feet farther on. Another opening in the grass. A tire track! Nathan felt the track too and we both rejoiced.

With the first hint of purple illuminating the pate of Mt. Baldy, we found the car. I went to the doctor and had pine gum removed from my eyes and reported to work on time that morning. Nathan went to the doctor and was given a clean bill of health.

I stopped now at the precise spot where I'd parked the car and gazed up the canyon of the North Fork of the Provo. It looked tame enough. True, up there was the most miserable night I'd ever spent; but it was over and we had survived. No harm done. An experience. Another valuable experience.

Another dozen miles up Highway 150, I came upon a sign which said, "Slate Canyon." I gazed into its bowels. On my first trip into these mountains with my father, Slate Canyon was the first place we began fishing. We knew nothing about what might be down in the canyon some 500 yards below but Dad said he was game to try. At the time I thought that fish live in water, this is water and fish could be here anywhere Afterall, this was water. As I studied the flow, I could see it was far too swift for trout in the main current where we'd cast for some two hours. I cast a fly into the first slack eddy and immediately caught a nice cutthroat. On my first cast. How I wished that Dad or I knew something about fishing then and that we could have shared success on that outing. Well, if he was watching, I thought, "I've learned how to do it, Dad. Here's one for the two of us…"

I hiked back up the steep ledges of Slate Gorge and recalled how I'd had to pull my father to help get him back to the rim. He gave it what he had. Some day I would have a 12-year old boy to bring here and would see to it that we shared a successful angling experience together.

At the end of the climb, I began to wonder. Would my son even care if he caught a fish here, or anywhere…Maybe it would be too much work. Maybe he would want me to take him to museums or drag races. I hated drag races.

Near Haystack Lake, I remembered how Mo and Deral and I had carried the rubber life raft into a June snowstorm, caught nothing at the lake, and nearly frozen, became lost. Each of us said nothing but shielded our faces and headed somewhere toward the east. Or so we thought. When reaching a split in the sparse game trail, each of us began walking up a different gully. Each thought we were right and the others would soon notice and soon follow. In a few minutes, I called through the blizzard. "Mo! Deral!" No answer! Before long, with each path apparently angling sharply away from the other, I could not locate them, nor them me. Well, the highway was out there somewhere beyond the horizon. We would find it. When I reached pavement, I saw Mo half a mile down the highway. Then Deral far below him. The truck was nowhere to be seen. We were all wrong. Surely, each of us insisted at once, the others had moved it. Mo sounded like a father-figure. "I think," he said, "there's a lesson in there somewhere."

There were many other priceless memories at nearly every bend of the road, every lake, creek and meadow. Too many. They came in a flood tide. I should have spread them out over a longer period of time. I walked toward the decaying smell of moss and watched a flicker and a kingfisher dart away before me. At the river's edge, there was my old friend, the dipper. I sat and listened to the sound of wind in the trees and the onslaught of the water, ever probing for lower ground. I decided that Nature hates uphill. Everything uphill is always trying to get downhill.

On the way back, I stopped by Pass Lake. There were orange-hued fish there slurping something from the surface. I went through six fly changes but could not find what they wanted. Lighter leader. Smaller patterns. Larger. More careful stalking. Midges. Just below the surface. Ah! At last I caught one of the mystery fish. On closer examination it was one I'd seen only in picture books. An albino rainbow. A few skimming the surface were yellowish, almost white. But the one in my hand was bright orange.

I somewhat resented the fish. It looked like a goldfish. But this was nature, not a backyard pond. Still, it was, in a way, a resplendent looking creature. A family down the bank from me came running to see it. "Pretty. Oh my! Pretty!" said one of the children. Mother and Father agreed.

Chances for an albino's survival must be slim. It could be seen by a flying bird half a mile away. But fishermen like to see the quarry they seek. It must be fun for the kids…for successful or not, they could always know it was there.

I left Pass Lake and drove homeward. I couldn't decide for sure what I thought about albino trout. Nature had compromised them. They seemed especially vulnerable in the water wearing a neon sign. On the other hand, they were highly suspicious of the first six flies I threw at them. I decided they were challenging enough to be respected.

Near town, I stopped at the fish hatchery. There were millions of albino rainbows here. The fish were given hand-fed pellets. A few years before, it had been ground horsemeat. The pellets were less messy. But the fish learned to later subsist somehow on minnows, snails, scuds, insects. The problem was that they were lazy. I watched them lay there in the concrete runway, almost morose. Couldn't they be forced to fight current, thereby developing muscle structure? By having things so easy, they grew up flaccid and lazy. Adversity. That was it. They needed more adversity.

From the off-road terrace at the mouth of Parleys Canyon, I could look out on the entire city. The freeway wound like a snake down Parleys Gully, obliterating most of it, save a little greenery at fringes of the country club. Indeed the pavement also carried thousands of restless motorists who did not want to be where they were now. There on the middle right was Sugarhouse. There was no ribbon of water where it should be. I could see no water whatsoever.

At the far west end of the valley sunlight shimmered from Great Salt Lake. To the south, one could see the ugly scar of a hill behind the Copper Smelter. Between the smelter and the Great Salt Lake was a giant lake of mud and water known as the Magna Tailings Pond. One man single-handedly was trying even now, so the *Salt Lake Tribune* said, to revegetate the barren land behind the sulfur dioxide-spewing smelter; but at times like now, it seemed a losing battle. The story before me was one that I had witnessed over and over in my life: humankind seeks survival. But if it is all that *Homo sapiens* seek, the species is little better off than the animals.

The next day, after dark, I brought Jessica to see the valley's lights. Many times at night I had driven here for a dozen miles through canyon blackness. Then in an instant, a vast panorama of lights sprang up across the level Great Basin as far as the eye could see.

"It is," said Jessica, "an inspiring sight."

"Much of it is different now," I said.

"Well, you've been gone for four years! Things happen in that much time. You have to expect it."

"Why?" I said.

"Because...because...of progress."

"Some things, yes," I allowed. "The old highway through the canyon was inadequate. They had to widen it. But did they need to destroy it all?

Some things are done through design, some through carelessness. Roads, flood control, diversions, dams, pollution, politics. There's a conspiracy to get rid of everything—or put it under concrete. Why does man's ego suppose nothing is right until he puts his hand to it?"

She was silent.

"I'm sorry," I said. "I won't bring the subject up rest of the night."

"No...I like talking to you about what's important to you."

"You're a very sweet girl," I said.

She looked at me somewhat special and I leaned over and kissed her and she pulled me tighter. "That's... that's for the one I didn't give you at the reservoir," I said.

She hugged me even tighter, then looked at me. "I have a confession to make," she said. "Once, when everyone else at Deer Creek was catching perch, I caught a trout. The only trout."

"I knew you were special," I said.

"There's one question I'd also like to ask you," she said seriously.

"Yes..." I said, not daring to guess what it might be.

"Would you...would you...take my little brother fishing? I mean he's nuts about it...and he's having problems, you see...and you..."

"Sure," I said. "How old is he?"

"Twelve."

"That's a good age to begin learning how to fish."

"Good. I'll tell him you can take him...next week?"

"I'll take him along with my younger brother," I answered.

"But I should tell you...Delbert is...a little difficult...he won't mind any one, parents or teachers. He's rebellious and he might..."

"I get the picture," I said. "Let me find out the rest for myself so I don't get any advance bias."

"Wonderful idea," she said. "You take him, so you can talk and tell me what you think. I don't want to prejudice you further." And we drove home.

I didn't see Jessica again for several weeks. One reason was college. I had decided to major in journalism. It included a statistics class. It proved to be all math. The teacher talked about not having a "math anxiety." I made an appointment to meet him at his office. "What's wrong, young man?" he asked.

"I have a math anxiety," I told him. "How come two numbers side by side are automatically multiplied? How do you know it isn't a double digit number instead of two single digits to be multiplied against each other?"

He looked at me. "We need to send you to the math lab," he said. "You better go down soon. And I would say, often."

I tried to do that. It left little time to see Jessica because I had to work the math lab in at night. When there, one might have to wait 20 minutes to get help. I did manage to cut the time down by bribing one of the assistants. I found he loved apples. I brought some with me each time. Still, there was so little time for doing what I really wanted.

To fit in my college classes, Mo lined up work around my rag-tag schedule. Mo was still good ole Mo. Some things never changed. We talked fishing. We talked everything. "When you get your degree and start writing," he said, "what are you going to write about?"

"What is happening," I said. "I'll write about what is happening."

"The destruction of Parleys Creek?" he asked.

"The destruction of natural systems," I said. "All of them. Quality of life. What people hold important in the enriching of their lives."

He suddenly stopped puffing on his cigarette. "You ought to go into finishing. You've gained a feeling for wood. You've learned to 'love' the filler into the wood rather than merely rubbing it on. When you love wood like you do trout streams, you could make one hell of a refinisher."

"I never noticed," I said.

"At least you're not afraid now of getting filler on your hands."

I thought about it. "No. This is your field, Mo. I've been like a visitor in the wilderness. I'll hike out and leave it to you." I hesitated. "But Jessica does seem tolerant of it. She looks for the real person underneath. She doesn't care about fancy cars and glib talk. She has…depth of character. She understands my dirty hands and she understands my fishing."

Mo lit up and then said casually, "Don't bet on that. Women pretend to go along with men until they get them hooked. Once their man is landed, they put him in the deep freeze to look at him once in a while. Worse, they try to change him. It's in a woman's nature." He took a long drag and blew a funnel of acrid smoke. "They just can't help it."

"Jessica is different," I said. "In fact, I'll prove it next Saturday by taking her fishing. You'll see."

Chapter Eighteen

"We'd have to leave at 2 a.m.," I told Jessica. "It's a five-mile hike to the lake and we want to be there by dawn. That's after driving a seven-mile back road to reach the trailhead."

"Sounds like an unusual date," she said.

I allowed that she was correct. "Bring a raincoat. I'll bring mosquito repellent."

"Well, O.K. It could be fun, I guess."

"Good. I'll be there in the truck at 2."

I hadn't mentioned the food. When I arrived, we discovered that we brought two bologna sandwiches and a can of root beer apiece.

"No potato salad," she said. "It would be difficult to backpack."

"You're a thinking outdoorswoman," I said.

"Have you…have you ever had a girl…friend before," she asked.

"Once," I said thoughtfully. "It didn't work out."

"She didn't go fishing?"

"It didn't reach that advanced stage," I answered, and she looked at me strangely.

Niceties over, we headed east. I hadn't been to the Erickson Lakes for five years. They were the ones Mo and I called after our own names, but after seeing "Erickson" appear on a map for the second time, we decided the duller names were legitimate. North and South Erickson Lakes they would be. Pointing the truck lights up the narrow road, it seemed the dropoff on the right side was steeper than I'd remembered. Jess, as I was beginning to call her now, pretended not to notice.

We reached the trailhead a little later than I'd planned, at 4 a.m. We would have to hike rapidly to reach even Big Elk Lake by first light.

We shouldered the day packs. I carried the fishing rods. She had bought a fishing license special for this occasion. Mo didn't know that. I would have to tell him. "Let's go," I waved the flashlight toward the trail and started out. Fifteen minutes later, Jess was not in sight.

"Over here," I waved the light. We're going to have to hurry…"

I heard a crash. "Wave the light over here," she shouted. "I think I've stumbled into a swamp." I walked back and helped extricate her. I forged ahead and held up the light so she could see where I was going. She stumbled over a log and received a bruise. I applied some triple biotic ointment and patted her on the back. She was a good sport. A mile and a half later, I saw Norway Meadows in the morning mist. We yet had the steep ridge to Big Elk, then the ridge above that.

But where was Jessica? I called. Her answer was faint. Well, she had a little daylight now. I would call and steer her in the right direction. When she showed, she was swatting at something. That's right, I had the bug dope. I walked back. She had several red welts on her hands and face. Then, it began to rain. Her rain coat was a torn poncho and it was in the bottom of the pack.

"Don't look at my hair," she said. "It's wet. It's…" she pulled out a purse mirror. "It's a mess."

"I won't look," I promised. "I'll just look at the lake. Let's see if any fish are jumping." There were not as many as I'd expected. Big Elk had foot prints all around And litter. Soda pop cans and beer bottles. Candy wrappers and even an empty can of fruit cocktail. "

It looks like Liberty Park after a Sunday picnic," I muttered.

"How can fishermen be so lazy?" she asked.

"Oh, these are the swillbait fishermen," I replied. "Not the fly fishermen."

"I see," she said.

We could entice no fish in Big Elk. I did not have to be Sherlock Holmes to deduce that the lake had been discovered by the masses.

"We used to catch big grayling in here," I told her. "But it looks like the riff-raff has found it. Well, let's hurry over to the Ericksons."

It was full light now but seeing the trail made little difference. Jess was almost too tired to take the first uphill step. "I've never been on a hike this steep," she said.

"Well, this is the Uintas," I enjoined. "They're all like this."

"I don't think I like the Uintas so much," she said.

"Don't make any hasty judgments," I responded. "Anyway, not while you're still going uphill."

When we reached the Ericksons, fish were jumping all over. I baited a worm for her and pointed out how it must be threaded so that the ends were free to wriggle. "See that," I said. "It's important."

"Very well," she responded. I let her toss out but she forgot to let go of the line and it wound around her neck. We tried again and she let go too soon. It landed on the rockslide behind us. The casting bubble, filled with water for weight, burst on a boulder. I tied on another. She said that I must think she was a ninkinpoop.

"These are hard rocks up here," I tried to sound as it didn't really matter. "We'll just try again. I'll put the first cast out for you." When it landed well out, I retrieved several feet of line and explained. "Now you reel in a little so that the bait is not near the line. That would spook the fish away."

"Spook the fish away?"

"Yes. The line doesn't look natural. You want to keep the bait away from the line because the line doesn't look like it belongs out there."

Before I could toss out my own rig, her rod tip began jumping. She jerked. She missed. Somehow, she timed the next three strikes wrong and missed them all.

I tried to sound encouraging. But she soon tired of trying to catch fish and began trying to catch a small orange butterfly. Meantime, I caught several beautiful brook trout and lay them on the rock nearby for her to see. She glanced at them. "So, we can stay here?"

"No, let's try Mo Lake...North Erickson," I suggested.

"Why? We're catching them here!"

"Well, that's the reason. I know we can catch them here. Let's see if we can catch them at the next lake."

We arrived at Mo just before noon. I told her how Mo had caught seven large brook trout here in a snowstorm while my line kept breaking. But I don't think she heard me. She had started to examine some bright green moss in a side bay. She wandered down the lake and I caught several more trout.

Soon it was late afternoon and time to start for home. "I think fishing is fun," she said on the downhill trail. "I get a hint now what you see in it."

I had been right. I couldn't wait to tell Mo.

I had timed our departure to reach the truck just before dark. We walked down the road a mile but someone had moved the truck. Or I was...on the wrong road. There had only been one road five years before. Now, roads seem to be everywhere. I hadn't seen them all on the way up because it was dark. "I thought you were the great outdoorsman," she said, a touch of sarcasm in her voice.

"I'm not lost lost," I protested. "Lost is not finding the road at all."

"Oh."

Soon it was dark. Jessica looked at me nervously. "What if we have to spend the night here...just the two of us...I mean you and me and..." She stopped. "You don't look nervous at all. Say, did you plan it this way?"

"No, no. I'm nervous. Very nervous. Look at me; I'm sweating... I..."

"Well, you don't look nervous enough to me." She stood there, hands on hips. I cast the flashlight about. "We outdoor types try not to panic," I said. "We try to at least look calm."

"You are calm. Can't you panic or something?"

I knew I had to sound reassuring. "There's shelter in those logs over there," I heard myself exclaim. "It'll be warmer in there for you..."

"I'm so tired I could lie down anywhere," she said. " No, no, I didn't mean that. Cross it out. I'm wide awake."

"Let's try one more thing," I suggested. "I think this is the wrong road entirely. Let's look on the ledge below this one. I walked to the rim. Nothing at first. I peered more intently. There...there! There below us!"

She perked up quickly. "Lucky for you, buster!" she muttered. "Lucky for you."

Back on the highway, she asked, "So do you admit being lost?"

It was difficult to admit. Very difficult. "Yes, you could almost say I was lost. For the very first time in my life...I, well, I guess I was...lost."

"All right then if you were lost. Otherwise, I'm mad at you."

I couldn't decide what to tell Mo. Was Jess an outdoor girl or not? I decided it would take one more outing. This time I took her to Buckeye Lake. The walk from road's end was 200 yards. We could depart at daybreak. I positioned her at an inlet with dozens of trout milling around. I returned after catching several fat brookies and noted she had caught nothing. "I had one hooked," she said. "But it broke off." She held up the rod to show leader flapping in the breeze. Then she began crying.

I sat down beside her. I had rigged her with 6-lb. test leader and the biggest known trout in Buckeye Lake had never been over 13 inches, perhaps three-quarters of a pound if pleasingly plump. How could she break a line on something as small as that? I tried logic. "Jessica, you couldn't really…"

"I don't want you to tell me what I should have done!" she said. "I just wanted you to listen to me."

"Oh."

A few minutes later, it was if nothing amiss had happened. On the way home, I asked her if she liked going fishing with me. "With you," she answered. "I think so."

"What do you like about it?"

"I don't know."

"Well, I guess that's not important. But if we are going to go together, I hope you like fishing."

"Why?" she asked blankly.

I was taken aback. "Well, I don't know…"

Then, we're even."

"Yes…I guess we're even."

Two days later, I called and asked Jessica if Delbert would like to go fishing with Doug and me the following Saturday.

"Are you taking him to the Uintas?"

"Yes but we don't have to…"

"Take him where you took me…or somewhere like it. Wear him out. I told him what we did and he said he wants a rugged experience like that. Don't you dare take him somewhere easier."

Doug, now 15 years old, no driver's license, said that was fine with him. "Wherever you can take me and there are fish." He had a good attitude.

Delbert did not. When we arrived, he was up but hadn't made his lunch. If you are going to be a fisherman, I told him, you'll need to plan ahead. He mumbled something and as I understood it, he was blaming his mother.

"Why, is Jessica's mother going fishing with us?"

"No."

"Then why should she put up a lunch if she isn't even going?"

"It's her job."

"Do you also want her to catch the fish for you?"

It was not a good start and it got worse.

Mo needed the truck for the day, so I took the old Chevy I'd just bought. I had owned a sleek 1940 Ford convertible, had it painted metallic black cherry, leaded in the trunk and had the back shocks removed to make it look underslung. At last it resembled the "passion wagon" of a friend.

It wasn't me. I got rid of it. The older Chevy would do just fine, provided it ran at all. In the brief time I had the car, it seemed to go anywhere; it just wouldn't come back. This time was different.

We started a little before dawn and got as far as Parleys Canyon. As I rounded a corner near a steep incline, the lights went out. Not only the lights but everything, including the engine. The entire electrical system. I could see nothing but applied the brakes and steered the car in the direction the road led at the edge of a chasm. Or so I hoped. Now, with no lights, we were sitting ducks for anyone coming along and hitting us. We had to get out of the way. I got out a flashlight and told Delbert to hold it while Doug and I pushed the car around. We began coasting down the canyon, picking up speed.

"Keep that flashlight shining out the window," I told Delbert. "So people can see us. We'll see what you're made of. Do your part and we might make it." He scowled but did as he was told.

As we approached a red light, I had a decision to make. If we kept our speed, we could make it down 21st South to Sugarhouse and find a garage to solve our problem. I looked both ways, saw no cars, and glided through. Unfortunately, there was one car I didn't see. A police car. It was parked at one side. Flashing lights motioned me over. "Three counts," one of the officers said. "Driving without lights, speeding and running a red light."

I explained the situation. "And if you had let me go, I could have coasted far enough to get help. Now, I'm stuck. I can't even get the car started so I can go get the lights fixed. I was trying to take these two boys fishing. You can see how disappointed they are."

The two officers looked in the car and walked to one side. I could hear them talking in low whispers. One told me to get in my car. "We'll give you a push and follow to make sure you get to Sugarhouse," he said.

An hour and a half later, we were on our way once more. I had not received a ticket. Praise be for two cops who didn't go by the book. If I had actually endangered anyone's life…well…praise be.

It was a late start. The fishing would be over within four hours and we had a long hike to make. But at least we were outdoors. We set out on a trail from Trial Lake toward Notch Mountain and upper Weber River basin.

At the base of a steep slope, we saw a monster mule deer buck. It appeared as a bush standing up."Makes the trip worthwhile already," I said.

"Not for me," said Delbert. "We're came to catch fish. And we better catch them. And it isn't Trial Lake, it's Trail Lake."

Doug got out a map and showed him.

"The map's got it wrong," he insisted.

In another hour, we skirted the edge of Clyde Lake. Delbert began to cast. "Not here," I said. "No feed. Fish are too small."

"I'm tired," he said. "I want to fish here."

So we let him fish here. After 20 minutes, he had watched several four-inch cutthroats follow his spinner but none were large enough to get their mouths around the lure. "Too small here," he said. "Let's move on."

We had lost valuable time. Now, Delbert wanted to stop at the three Divide lakes. "The fastest fishing is at North Twin and the biggest fish are in Little Hidden," I explained. "Which do we want?"

Delbert trudged alongside and I could see that he was willing to go wherever I decided. Good, now we could get something going. I opted for Little Hidden and we veered slightly east. There we encountered Peter and John lakes. "No fish," I cautioned. "Too shallow." We continued to the summit and half a mile down the north slope. Two casts with a large spinner into Little Elk and I felt a mammoth hit. Two-pound brook trout. Turquoise, edged in purple, orange belly, emerald and green body, fins etched in black, white and scarlet. Delbert's eyes nearly fell out. "Show me," he said, "how to catch a fish like that and I'll follow you anywhere."

Good. I had his attention. I rigged him with a large spinner and after some miscasts, he landed the blades at the edge of a dark hole near some lily pads. He reeled in quickly.

"Cast there again," I advised. "Let the lure sink. Reel in very slowly. Tantalize them. Like that." Almost instantly, his rod tip plummeted. But he tried to horse the fish in too quickly. As the fish pulled left, he jerked right. The line went slack. Yet, he'd seen the fish; his adrenaline was up. I left him to see how Doug was doing. He had learned the consummate skills of a worm fisherman. Half a nightcrawler, ends wiggling. He cast out, lifting and reeling slowly to make the worm appear as if washing toward shore. He caught several pansize brook trout. He was on track. For worms.

I would focus on Delbert. He had been cussing and complaining mightily; but I saw that deep down, as Jess had said, her little brother had the heart of a fisherman. He had seen the possibilities and now he cast relentlessly into the shifting wind. Unfortunately, the fish didn't seem to cooperate. Then I noticed a hatch of what appeared to be caddis flies. Looking closely, one could see slurping motions in the near cove. The fish had shifted their feeding as the day warmed to concentrate on the caddis hatch. That was the way they were. Opportunists. They had the minows with them any time, but had to take advantage of the insects during the short time they were available.

"Delbert, would you like to learn how to fly fish?" He said yes. I let him use my fly rod. At first he made the mistake of all novice fly casters. He didn't allow the line to straighten out behind him before he attempted to cast it out in front of him. The line landed in a heap at his feet.

"Patience," I said. "Let the rod tip do the work. Far more energy per square inch than your wrists. Make a great back cast and you have a great forward cast. No, stop your rod tip at 11 'O Clock. Don't let your line drop too low behind you or you can't cast it out front. I demonstrated.

In time, he got the line out and even stopped the rod at the 1 O'Clock to let the fly flutter down gently. "Golf and tennis require days to learn," I said. "Fly casting can be learned in half an hour. If you know what to do."

A few minutes later, I saw a quiet swirl near Delbert's fly. He was looking at something else. "You had a strike there, Del. Now, be ready."

He cast again. There. Pull." He was too late. Too late twice.

Five minutes later, I saw a small fish fly over my head. "Terrific, Del. Now you're a fisherman." Doug looked over. "No, you're not supposed to…"

"Shhh," I whispered. "He just walked on Mars. He needn't run yet."

"My first trout!" Delbert said happily. "And on a fly!" Good, he'd been reading the same magazines I had as a 12-year old. I couldn't get my fly rod back from Del for the next hour. I nestled down on my back in the spongy grass and admired an afternoon's white fleece of clouds. A perfect day.

Chapter Nineteen

"What did you and Delbert do?" Jess wanted to know next time I called her. "He's still...got a long way to go...but he seems...more at peace with himself. He well, he suddenly treats us all like human beings again. Even Mom and Dad mentioned it.

"Just took him fishing."

"Nothing more?"

"And talked."

"Well, I hope you can take him out again."

The following Saturday I took Jessica and her little brother to Crystal and Washington Lakes near road's end in the western Uintas. It was now late summer, and I knew Washington would be low. The latter was an ugly, heavily drawn-down mud flat reservoir by August, with no more snow- melt coming in. But the feed was there; it held fat rainbows. The fish would be concentrated and easier to find. As for Crystal, it was a totally different kind of spring-fed natural lake with boggy bottom and lily pads changing little from month to month. It harbored brook trout.

They were alike in that rock rollers or caddis flies abounded in each. The perfect imitation I'd found was my standard size 14 Siberian wood-ant. I never knew the Siberians with the jointed body not to work in either lake. One could always count on it.

As soon as we got out of the car, Jess commented on how she liked the smell of pine cones, the fresh, cool wind. I wanted to give her a peck on the cheek or more right there but Delbert headed down the wrong trail toward Long Lake. I had to hurry after him and face him sharply southwest.

We started out at Washington. I rigged Jess with a worm so she wouldn't have to keep casting and Delbert with a fly rod and wood-ant.

I could have done it so he might be lazy, with a water-filled casting bubble and fly tied on behind. But the fly rod was more entertaining. Some anglers I knew claimed just the action of wafting a fly rod, whether fish are present or not, is a mesmerizing and satisfying activity. As a matter of fact, I had seen full-grown men on many waters cast for hours without enticing a single strike. Someone catching fish right next door bothered them not all. They remained with the charismatic, magnetic, life-fulfilling fly rod.

However, walking down the shoreline, Delbert found half a box of cheese. He wanted to try that. "No cheese," I told him. The statement came out sounding a little harsh, I suppose.

Jess looked at me. "Why not?"

"Because no one who rides with me fishes with cheese."

"Why?" Delbert wanted to know.

"It's all right during a cheese hatch," I allowed. "Look around. Do you see any cheese hatching?"

Pause. "I think that's ridiculous," Jess said, her eyes round and perplexed.

Delbert quickly tied on a bait hook and began wadding Velveeta around the barb. I stopped him.

"But you use worms," Delbert protested.

"Worms are different. Worms are natural bait. People who use cheese and marshmallows and liverwurst and corn for trout are degrading their lives. And the trout. It isn't worthy of their lofty status. People who use swill baits for trout become perverts, dissipates, apostates; they lose their self-esteem and and become debased. They lose hair on their heads and grow it on their palms. Some studies even indicate they tend toward pornography. Preliminary results show it's the first step."

"You're weird." Jessica stepped back to look at me.

Delbert said I hadn't been like this last time.

"Well, you didn't try to use cheese," I reminded him.

"Do trout eat cheese?" Jess wanted to know.

"Those with no self-respect," I allowed.

"Then, I want to catch those kind," Delbert announced.

"Yes, if they can be caught that way, what's wrong with it?" Jess echoed.

"They can be taken by dynamite too. Shall we use dynamite?"

Delbert continued to wad on the cheese.

"All right, but I'm going to fish down the lake from you," I said.

In a few minutes, Delbert caught a rainbow on the cheese. From where I stood, it looked like a recent hatchery plant, although it did seem to have all fins intact. Jess walked over. She stood defiant. Silent. Clearly, she expected me to say something. So I said something. "I just wanted Del to be the very finest person he can be," I said. "Isn't that what you want for him too?"

"Didn't you ever use anything like cheese?"

"Spaghetti once. On carp and catfish."

"A 12-year old doesn't care how he catches a fish. He just wants to…"

"I thought he might some day be my brother-in-law."

She sat down. There was a blush to her cheek. But she did not smile.

"Jess, I want a brother in law that I can fully respect."

"You're toying with me now, aren't you?"

"Not really. But Delbert did seem interested in learning to fly fish. Like I did at his age. I just wanted him to learn how to enjoy the sport to the fullest and sharpen his skills and…"

"Doesn't it take skills to catch fish on cheese."

"Well, see, it's this way. You're pandering to their basest instincts. They eat meat pellets in the hatchery. After stocking, they don't have pellets and learn to find natural food. If we don't use natural food, we persuade them to return to baser instincts. You're supposed to fool the trout, not defraud them. It's like feeding pablum to an adult."

"A matter of principle?"

"Exactly. If one doesn't hold firm to values and principles in fishing, one could backslide in life as well."

She pondered for a full minute. "But you've made a friend in Delbert. Now, I'm afraid he…"

I looked back. Delbert had picked up his fly rod and was casting with it. We walked over. "This is more fun," he said. "I just wanted to see if I could catch one on the cheese." He cast again, letting the line straighten out behind before thrusting his arm forward. The line sailed out like I'd taught him at Little Hidden.

Thus was disaster averted.

At Crystal Jess said she would like to learn to fly fish like Delbert. She learned to cast reasonably well but still didn't catch any fish. Yet, it didn't bother her. I decided that she didn't really care about fishing. But she did like to be outdoors and talked about how she loved camping. Her family had gone once in a while to Yellowstone. She had also been camping director for her neighborhood girls' group.

Had she passed the test? No...Yes. It wasn't something I could tell Mo about but she had passed the test. Had I passed the test with her? I had revealed to her, it would seem, a deep bias in my mental makeup. Not everyone viewed cheese fishermen as I did. I must remember that. There were probably many fine people who used cheese on trout. I just hadn't met any yet.

"Sit down," she said. "I brought along potato salad. And root beer."

We ate hungrily, especially Delbert. "Fishing like a true sportsman makes me hungry," he said. Before long, he was fishing again. I could learn to like this boy.

"I think you've created a Frankenstein," Jess said. But she was smiling. Oh, how I loved it when Jessica smiled. I decided she didn't look like Liz Taylor at all. Liz Taylor looked like Jessica.

In a few minutes, Del walked over. "The wood-ants don't work any more," he said. "I've put them in front of several brook trout and they turn away. They're eating something else."

This was, indeed, a crisis. These trout had always dined on wood-ants. I looked at my watch. Twelve fifteen. The heart of the mid-day feed. What was wrong here? Delbert sounded casual and relaxed. "You always know what do do," he said. "Just give me the word."

"Panic," I said, but too low for either of them to hear. Indeed, I didn't know. Sooner or later, I figured my angling luck with Delbert would wane. But not now. He was counting on me. Later, he would be on his own. What other patterns had worked here? I'd never had to use anything else. I stood there trying to think...when a stiff breeze blew past. We had to grab the napkins and empty paper cups from blowing off the picnic blanket. One cup tumbled 10 feet before I could retrieve it.

Suddenly, Jess called. There was trauma in her voice. "Something's on the back of my neck! A whole bunch! Get 'em off! Are they spiders. I..."

"I know," I said. "You hate spiders. Naw. Just ants. Black ants." I examined one in my hand. I held it up for a better look. "Say Delbert, did that wind just barely come up...or has it been blowing around the other side of the lake. I've been sitting here talking...and I didn't notice."

"Blowing all around. Why?"

I looked on the ground. Then I heard Jessica's voice. "Hey, are you going to get the rest of the ants off me or not?" There was some excitement in her voice. Ants all over? And the wind is blowing in several places from shore to lake...

"I've got it, Del. Here, try this." I dug a pattern from my box of artificials. He tied it and hooked a trout on his first cast.

"What did you give him?" Jess wanted to know.

"A black ant," I said. "Size 14."

I rigged up. Terrestrials. The trout were gorging on terrestrials! When that happens, trout can abandon all caution. And all other food. I left Jessica to join Delbert. We caught seven in almost as many casts. Delbert shook my right hand and then my other hand. His faith had obviously been restored in me.

Enroute to the car, Jess pulled me aside. "I appreciate you're taking my brother fishing," she said. "But next time I'd like just the two of us. I want to do some talking. Back and forth." She looked at me hard. "Yes, you can take your fly rod...I can see you'd be lost without it. But promise me one thing. You'll spend at least half an hour where you can't even see the water."

I took a deep breath. And I promised.

Chapter Twenty

"What would you like to talk about?"

"Something besides fish."

We were sitting on a log overlooking Moosehorn Lake. I chose Moosehorn because it is visible from pavement, receives heavy fishing pressure and would thus tempt me less. At the same time, it was an emerald-sheened natural water surrounded by purple-flowered meadows, with jagged, nearly 13,000 foot-high snow-plumed Hayden Peak for a backdrop. On the far mountain to the south one could see the first oak turning to scarlet, the aspens showing gold. It was a nice place to sit and look. Or talk.

"I have no knowledge of anything else."

"I bet you do. I hope you do."

"Mmmmm. Can't think of anything."

"What about books. What great books have you read that have influenced your life? Other than those on fishing, I mean."

"Well…I like Mark Twain for humorous fiction. But I don't think he left me with any particular inspiration. One book that made an impression on me was Norman Vincent Peale's *Power of Positive Thinking*. In the field of novels about the Mountain West, I like Vardis Fisher's way of saying it. In poetry, Robert Frost's *Stopping by the Woods on a Snowy Evening*. But Shakespeare was the best story-teller. The Bible has some intriguing plots and characters. I dunno'."

"Go on." She sat forward with her chin on her hand.

"Time to learn about you. Tell me what you like to do besides go fishing."

She winced but soon turned to think. "Mostly I've read books about art, sculpture, Monet, Rembrandt, de Vinci. Leonardo was a master, you know, in drawing the human figure. Most difficult of all things to draw…" Suddenly, she seemed to feel self-conscious, as if sounding too stuffy. "Like that."

"So in our old age I would be fishing or writing about it and you would be painting. Did you bring any watercolors?"

"No, just paper and pencil. But I could sketch a Uinta landscape. Or those kids playing with the ball by the campground." She went back to the car and emerged with the tools needed and in a few minutes finished a drawing of Hayden Peak with a man in the foreground looking at it. The man stood not as one passive, but with muscles tensed as if he was about to begin walking toward the mountain, only fully realizing how far away it was. The mountain itself was draped in fog, so as to make it look higher than it really was, yet nothing was out of proportion.

She sat there, legs crossed in blue pedal pushers, lacy but not overly dressy black blouse, pearl earrings, just right red lipstick, dark hair flipping casually in a light breeze. It was her smile I noticed most. She smiled whenever she glanced up and I looked forward to every time she did. "You been drawing your whole life?" I asked.

She nodded.

Half an hour later, she said she wanted to sketch me fishing. I obediently began casting a fly from the nearby meadow. I could see a few fish slurping but they didn't want my first four offerings. One thing I had never done was make a switch quickly. Each knot had to be just right. Jess noticed.

"Why don't they just eat what you have?" She sounded a little impatient. "I'm waiting to catch the expression on your face while you catch a fish. Why do they need to be so fussy?"

"Well," I started off didactively, "more than one million five hundred thousand species…that's species mind you…of insects have been classified. Insects occupy almost eighty per cent of the species of the entire animal kingdom. That gives the fish a lot to choose from. Sometimes they see a whole bunch of one kind and that's what they focus on. When they do that, they won't take anything else."

"So I have to wait for you to try another one million and four hundred ninety nine thousand insects?"

"I could get lucky," I said. "The main thing is to determine whether they're feeding on nymphs or larvae or the adult insect."

She looked perplexed. "You've told me about dry and wet flies. What's this about larvae and nymphs?"

"Nymph is the Greek word meaning bride or maiden. According to legend, they went through a metamorphosis before emerging from an ugly duckling to a swan. In nymphs the wings develop early on the exterior of the body. In larvae, the Latin word for mask, the insect has no trace of wings. Like a caterpillar turning into a butterfly."

"Where do you get all these details?"

"From a class I'm taking in college on immature insects. I have to collect 50 species of *Trichoptera* alone."

"Class in immature insects? A whole class on it?" She didn't wait for me to answer. "Tri…what"

"Rock rollers."

"Oh."

"Do you want to go with me to collect some?"

"How many do you have now?"

"Six."

"Forty-four more? OK. How do you do it?"

"These vials." I pulled one from my pocket. "We could go look for some now in that little creek."

She went with me and we turned over rocks. "See there's one now I don't have. Only 43 to go. The fish love this one, big fat and yellow. But I don't think the trout are focused on them right now. Looks like most have hatched and gone. Not enough to interest the fish for the present."

"Well, I want to sketch you at it. Go try again." I tried several flies and could not match the one they were taking. After another hour, I tied on a spinner and immediately caught a 10-inch albino rainbow. Jess began sketching. But she could see the look of defeat on my face. "Look happy," she said. "I can't sketch you looking sad and frustrated."

"Well, I…"

"You can't find the right fly out of the one and a half million?"

"No."

"Discouraged?"

"Not really. That's why I love fly fishing," I said. "Matthew 5:48. Perfection is a never-ending quest. One lifetime can't master it. That's why I think there must be trout in Heaven. And insects." She frowned.

"But they don't bite or sting. One must be constantly searching for answers when fly fishing. I'm glad the fish fool me sometimes. It just makes for a bigger challenge. And greater determination."

"You're weird," she said matter-of-factly. "Now look happy so I can get a decent picture out of this."

In the end she put a hint of a smile on my face, compromise enough to satisfy us both. When she finished, she got out the potato salad, we ate and began driving home. "What do you dislike doing most in the whole world, besides math?" she asked.

"Public speaking."

"Why, I've won half a dozen speech contests. There's nothing to it."

"A matter of attitude, I suppose."

"You just focus on what you want to say. Rather than yourself," she explained.

"I suppose."

"Didn't you have to give many public speeches when you were a minister in Wisconsin?"

"And conduct a funeral. A person can do many things if he or she has to. Still, I can have my druthers."

She snuggled up to my shoulder and I drove one-handed. "About druthers, which you just mentioned. My folks and friends…they…"

"Wonder if I'll ever ask you to marry me?" She gave a slight nod.

I stopped the car by the Provo River. "This isn't something I can talk about while driving. I took her hand and she followed me, her eyes serious. Probably, too, were mine. We sat on a flat rock. "Would you be happy married to a…a…someone…well a fisherman?"

She put her arms around me and I felt it to my deepest consciousness. "Does that worry you?" She pulled back suddenly and looked into my eyes.

"Jess, I've seen some…problems among people I know. Love burns brightly at the wedding. All weddings. And then…something happens. Especially to my friends who are fly fishermen. I don't want something ephemeral. I want it be like…like two streams, their currents flowing together. Forever. No, that's corny."

"No, no," she insisted. "It isn't."

A squirrel somewhere chastened us for infringing on his forest. A flicker, it's yellow-shafted wings flashing, flew toward a low line of cliffs. Soon they were gone. But the sound of river before us did not abate.

"Jess, we've talked before about one aspect of marriage. We both know people who make shallow commitments. They say one thing and do another. They have a road map that shows only the local neighborhood…"

"I know, Bill was like that."

"What did you like about him and what didn't you?"

"He was…a popular guy. A lot of the girls were chasing him even after high school. He was flashy. I mean, not just clothes and car…but he could make you laugh and he…"

"Sounds like the perfect catch."

"No. Couldn't trust him. Not being a wolf, going after the girls physically, I mean. He seemed to change his mind and he said he'd meet you somewhere and he would…not show up. I don't think a promise meant much to him at all. Now, what about the girls you've gone with?"

"Becky. She made commitment two minutes at a time. I don't think marriage vows would mean anything to her. And Dolores. She had her own agenda. A boy would fit in part of the time. When she tuned him out, he should disappear. She was very affectionate, however, when she…"

"No," Jess said. "I don't want to hear about that."

"I wasn't going into any details."

"What does your mother think of me?"

"She said I should spend more time with you. Pay more attention to you. She was right."

"So you thought it over carefully before inviting me out anywhere. To your most sacred fishing holes, I mean."

"Yes."

"That's good. I think."

"Another thing, Jess. The rest of our lives is a long, long time. I've had cold feet…yes…about jumping in water over my head. I want to be sure I can swim in it. Some people don't look first. I believe marriage is…I believe it's forever. Eternal. I don't like that part, 'until death do we part'."

"Yes. Why should love cease just because we're dead? I mean…"

We sat there for several minutes saying nothing. I tried but could think of nothing to say. I started to open my mouth but closed it and remained quiet. She made no effort to speak.

I peered at the water. There were colorful golden-hued rocks in the stream bed where it eddied against a broken pine bough. A small cutthroat trout finned in a side riffle less than 15 feet away. A cutthroat trout. It was feeding. On the surface. I strove mightily and ignored it.

After a while, we began to get up. "Well," she said. "Aren't you going to try to catch it?"

"Jessica," I said. "You and I were meant for each other."

I walked back to the stream and took another look. "No. It's too small."

She looked at me close and personal. "Too small?"

"Yes. Too small."

We got in the car and drove home in an aura of silence. Only one time did I break it. "I suppose your family and friends have wondered. But I have to be sure you can accept me as I am. Too many friends have…"

"I know, " she said. "Every wife tries to change her man. That syndrome. I can't promise there. But I know fish and the natural world are your life. Just always remember to include me in it. As you do now."

"We could wait another year," I said as we reached the street where she lived. "Amass more money. Have more time…"

But when I walked to her to the door, we both knew it would be soon. "In September," she said. "It's my favorite time of year. I'd like to celebrate our Golden Wedding anniversary in September."

"And beyond?" I queried.

"And beyond."

Chapter Twenty-one

Jessica and her mother did a wonderful job on the wedding. Everyone I had invited was there, except Mo. He told me simply, "I don't do weddings." I understood.

Where would Jess and I go on our honeymoon? Montana. Jess was aware this was fishing country but I promised I wouldn't take a fishing rod along. And I didn't. I did scout out some possible future fishing holes on the Madison, Jefferson and Gallatin, where the Three Forks come together to form the Missouri. But these were scenic spots that Jess said she also enjoyed seeing. We picnicked along the Madison but I kept my eyes from the water. Jess said that now we were married, she thought I'd want to give up fishing. "Just kidding," she added quickly.

We had one week before I had to start school again and of course, to find a job. Money. Two might live as cheaply as one but now we were the ones paying for it. I managed to land work at a newspaper writing about… the outdoors. I told Jess it was preparation meeting opportunity but it was also a fortuitous stroke of luck.

One of my first on-the-job assignments was to attend and write about a meeting on flood control. Mill Creek had leaped its banks in one place just below mouth of the canyon. I drove over to examine it. Someone had built a home too close to the stream, it seemed to me. They hadn't allowed for a normal flood plain, or even the right of water to move where it had always coursed for eons of time.

At the meeting, the U.S. Army Corps of Engineers officer from San Francisco recommended placing the entire stream in a metal pipe where it ran near the homes and into a concrete sluiceway farther out into the valley. Essentially, the same thing that had happened to Parleys Creek.

The meeting continued for nearly an hour discussing designs and costs.

There were several men, in uniform, placed at maps and charts, with pointers pinpointing the problem areas mentioned by the colonel at the podium. Words and precision pointers droned on. They talked about the importance of preparing for 50-year floods and 100-year floods and if we were wise, we would prepare for the very worst kind. Finally I raised my hand. "I know this creek," I said. "It is only about five feet wide and floods to seven feet wide every spring. People can allow for it when they build. The creek makes for beautiful back yards and a trout fishing stream. Why do we have to destroy it like we did Parleys Creek?" Several people in the back rose up and echoed my comments.

"Five feet wide?" said the colonel in amazement. "From the size of the flood described to me, I thought it was a stream of 50 or 60 feet wide, and worse when it floods. We have a Mill Creek like that in California."

"No," came a chorus from the audience.

"Then this meeting is adjourned," he said. "I'm going back to San Francisco."

That was the last anyone said about putting Mill Creek in a pipe.

Soon thereafter I attended a hearing on a stream known as the "Wild Strawberry" that was to be reduced in flow. The creek had been set aside as a "fly fishing only" water, the first of its kind in the state. The government wanted to reduce it from 24 cubic feet per second guaranteed flow to 6 cfs, or about three feet wide and one foot deep. The remainder would be held in the reservoir for irrigation water to be diverted elsewhere into a tunnel. The public was told that a special outlet spigot would be placed on the dam so that water flowed forth more oxygenated.

"So you want us to rejoice even though it has been decreased by 75 per cent," I wrote in the newspaper, checking my math. "It's nothing but a cruel hoax this spigot business. I know that stream; I've fished the length of it several times. It barely carried enough water in the first place to support a trout population. What difference will it make if the fish are all dead?"

The world was hung up on math and I'd managed to find a use for it.

At the hearing, a man stood up and said he was concerned about reducing the flow by so much. "This is an environmental age," he said. "We are engineers but we are also responsible to lend an ear to the public and see what ecological concerns they have. If not, we are just busy beavers plugging everything in sight."

"Who is that?" I heard someone say.

"The project engineer. Mr Crandall."

He motioned me aside after the meeting. "I wasn't told all the facts, he said. "I'll take this back to Washington with me tomorrow and we'll see what we can do." The stream was left at 15 cfs.

I showed my stories to Jessica and told her what happened. "I love my job," I said. "Everything I learned as a kid on Parleys Creek is…well…it's proving useful to me. I don't have the formal training of a Phd biologist but there are some things a person can learn by observation and from there, just use common sense."

"You better be careful," she said quietly. "You've got a great job. You don't want to lose it. Not now. "

"You're not pregnant are you."

"I don't think so. But we still need the money."

"Sure. But I have to tell it the way I see it."

A week later I was sent by the boss to do a story on the upper Provo River, to see if fish life was returning after the destruction of a decade before. I began walking out of the house with my fishing rod. Jess asked where I was going.

"To work," I said.

After fishing two miles of the Provo and taking pictures of the carnage which had been wreaked there, most of which remained, I had my story, subjective though it might be. I had never fished through this sector in the fall, when the brown trout became more active due to spawning, without catching at least two or three brown trout 16 inches or better. This time, a few rainbows, planters, showed. I peered beneath rocks. Barren. The feed hadn't returned. Therefore, the fish hadn't.

When April finally arrived, I decided to do a feature story on the Fremont River. I'd long had a love affair with this stream, for I'd fished it every spring since I was a teenager and taken brown trout to six pounds.

On one occasion, Doug and I had started on the upper end of Bicknell Bottoms, hooked and landed several monster rainbow and brown trout, watched the mallards and pintails fly into the sunset and arrived at the bottom of the marshes four miles later with a problem. We'd had such a good time we hadn't thought about how we'd get back. Now, that it was dark we could never make it safely back through the swamp without stepping in sink holes or quicksand mud. It was difficult enough to get through during daylight hours. Besides, we had no energy remaining. We walked to a farmhouse and threw ourselves on the mercy of the man inside. For 10 bucks we said, would he drive us the 10 miles back around where we'd left our truck?

"Why didn't you take getting back into consideration?" he wanted to know.

"We have a very easy answer for that, sir. We lost our heads." Doug agreed. He drove us around and wouldn't take the money. "You're lucky my husband does a little fishing himself," said his wife from the kitchen. "Or we'd take you two for those stupid city slickers."

I took Jess with me this time to the Fremont but carefully kept her out of the swamp. We would go downstream. The fishing was as good as ever…so good that I stayed away most of the morning. Jess complained on my return. I'd been having fun, she said, even if it was my work and I'd abandoned her.

I much preferred wading a stream to lake fishing. Each bend of a stream was a whole new world of natural wonder; but a lake was more sociable, in that you could see each other at all times and usually be within talking distance. I would have to figure out something if I was going to stream fish. Here was a minor crisis.

Was she willing to try stream fishing? She said she'd give it a go and I made certain I didn't leave her more than a few minutes from hole to hole. One time she saw me strike back on a good fish and grabbed the camera, taking four pictures which could be used later in the newspaper. Excellent composition. Her art talent showed. And good sport. I owed her.

But before we left the Fremont, she was in tears. While I was downstream, she tossed a worm into a large pool, felt a heavy tug and fought a giant fish for some five minutes. Then it broke her off around a half-submerged tree she hadn't seen. This was the second time a fish had busted the line on her since I'd taken her fishing. "I wanted to show you I could do it," she sobbed.

She had tried so hard. "Let's dress up and go to dinner," I suggested.

While we were dining, Jess said that I had never actually asked her to marry me. Another crisis. I asked over chicken-fried steaks. She accepted. It seemed to me we were bonded before that trip was over, even more than when we repeated wedding vows.

When summer arrived, Jessica's parents invited us to Yellowstone with them. Delbert would be there. Jess suggested I let him know that since we were married now, I couldn't spend as much time with him. He seemed to understand and there were no problems. Jessica's father turned to me at one point and made one of the most profound statements I'd heard. "I read somewhere that a judge of some 15 years said he had counseled hundreds of boys during that time, but never had one appear before him who was a fisherman."

He suggested I teach the family how to fly fish. "But we've always used worms and found them completely effective. I don't know if we'd could ever convert over to fly fishing."

The next morning when we arrived at our first fishing destination, I yanked my rod from the van and cast to Sylvan Lake while yet a distance away. The fly landed barely on the water along the shoreline next to a log. Instantly, I saw the strike and set the hook. As the entourage arrived at the lake, I was fighting a plump cutthroat. I released the fish and heard Jess's mother say, "Don't you ever throw them back! We want some for dinner!"

"He'll catch you another one," Del said matter-of-factly.

Jess's Dad hadn't yet cast in. "One can, indeed, catch them fast on flies," he allowed. "Faster than I can bait my hook."

Jess looked at me proudly as he asked how it was done. I explained I had noticed the fish dimple the surface as we were approaching the lake. Luckily, an Adams was what the fish wanted.

Before long, the entire family was gathering around to observe a demonstration on fly fishing. A little while later even Jess's mother was waving a fishing wand at the fish and everyone seemed content to put the bait away.

Actually, I had nothing against worm fishing. It was a good way to start. Fly fishing should be a natural skill attainment after learning the rudiments of fishing with bait. After all, every beginner must receive some encouragement or it was only human nature to quit. Jess soon impaled her own bait on the hook and practiced casting until she could reach the river currents where the fish faced the current looking for food. She learned to hold the rod tip high so the bait would drift past the fish rather than getting lost on the bottom. Soon she caught her first golden- bright cutthroat trout while all of us applauded.

But there were problems in Paradise. The fish limit in the park was five cutthroats and the garbage cans were filled with them. A family could daily haul out dozens of fish from the river, often on a long stick, take them home, eat two, find them smelly, and throw the rest away. That would bring on the bears and cause another problem, for when people and bears clashed, the bears always lost sooner or later. A ranger told us about a grizzly which frightened some campers and was relocated but upon getting into trouble again, was destroyed. Another man used a large ham as a pillow inside his tent. The bear didn't know a man was sleeping on it. The man died and so did the grizzly, for merely following its nose to food. So it went. A little bit of nature dying every time it encountered *Homo sapiens*.

Another dismaying thing was that where I had seen trout in the park as a teenager, they were now scarce. The habitat was still there; the Yellowstone River still ran by as pristine as ever, and the lake from which it was born remained as beautiful a lake as I'd ever seen. Where I'd witnessed fish alongside the highway, they were now nowhere to be seen.

Some other changes had taken place. Fishing Bridge was "Non-Fishing Bridge." A ranger said the trumpeter swans had returned since giving fishermen the boot. Another said an angler on the bridge had stepped back with his fish, and "walked smack in front of a car. We had to do something to stop the circus."

Still, I remembered the good times visitors had on the bridge, casting to fish they could see and shouting excitedly. I'd stood by the bridge one afternoon. and observed a may fly hatch in progress and taken three big cutts by matching the hatch. The larger 14s wouldn't do. One had to match it perfectly with size 18s. The drift had to be dragless. I'd released the three fish but watched the people next to me kill nine trout and proudly hoist them over their shoulder for the triumphant journey home. It would seem the resource was limitless. No one need worry about it. There would always be nine trout for every family to kill and carry home.

Catch and release. "It's the only possible way to save the resource,"

I told Jess. But for now, there was nothing anyone could do about it. Except maybe write about it. I did, but there was no way of knowing if anyone who could make a difference ever read it.

We returned through Jackson Hole and visited the art galleries. I had always marveled at the mix of rugged and sophisticated West on display. Nature was chic, haute couture. Jess could have spent a full day looking and more. A favorite painting of mine was two elk hunters reining their mounts across a flooding mountain stream by lighting flashes. A large bull elk rack sat high on a pack horse. The rain drizzled down their faces. And they were smiling.

That summer I received an invitation to spend a week in Canada's Northwest Territories as a guest of Frontier Lodge on the remote eastern shore of Great Slave Lake. As the float plane flew away from Yellowknife, the territorial capital, I could see that if it went down, there was no way for a survivor to walk more than a quarter mile without encountering water. I could see lakes with islands themselves on islands. Wilderness. It had always seemed harsh in a friendly way. It would mean death if stranded down there, but it looked much more inviting than the time our shuttle plane winged over the ghetto suburb of a large eastern city.

The plane arrived at the lodge in mid-morning. Guests were supposed to wait until after lunch to be assigned a guide and boat but I walked a mile and a half to the Stark River and caught several 20-inch Arctic grayling. These were much heavier than the *Thymallus arcticus* I'd caught near home. They fought like fury. But that afternoon, they wouldn't touch the same dry ginger quill caddis imitation which had worked earlier. I could see the ghost-like bluish forms of the grayling feeding voraciously just below the surface. They were definitely taking something not winged. I went to the lodge manager and asked if the Chippewyan Indians over at the village of Snowdrift caught grayling in their nets. They did. I managed a ride to the village with a guide who lived there and made an offer: if they would let me, I'd like to clean all the grayling in their nets. There were 46. I cleaned them all and closely examined the stomach contents. I found many beetles, dark brown, no wings, shellback, about size 14. I found an artificial in my fly box which might make the match, except that I had to chew down some of the fluffy hackle. It seems some artificials are made more for the fisherman than the fish.

The manager's son, Drew, agreed to guide me up the river for the evening's fishing, which, in late July, would last until nearly midnight. While we were talking at suppertime, some other anglers heard us and laughed. "You don't need to go to all that work."

"What," my young guide inquired, "will you use for tonight's fishing?"

"Oh, just our brook trout flies. No need to make a problem out of it."

That evening we anchored at the outlet of Stark Lake and I caught 13 grayling 19 inches or more. When we came in, Drew asked our "brook trout friends" how they'd done. "One measly 13-incher," the angler said. Drew threw his nose in the air and walked away.

The next day I made a mistake. I'd been casting for 5-12 lb. lake trout in a bay when something swirled not far from the boat. Figuring it to be an oversized grayling, I took off the lure I'd been using and tied on a fly. But I continued to use the same spin rod as before. With it, I hooked a heavy fish which soon split the horizon near the bow of the boat. A grayling and a big one. When I landed and weighed the fish, it tallied 4 lbs. 1 oz., 15 ounces shy of the world record. Drew's father became excited about the fish being a record for the lake and possibly more. It did, in fact, win the annual Field and Stream angling contest, the largest fly-caught grayling entered. But it did not win the fly division because while it was caught on a fly, it was not taken on a fly rod.

A few days later, I hooked some Northern pike on my fly rod. The guide took me to a place called "Bay of Death," so named because there were no ducks on it. "If there were, it would prove there were no pike," he said matter-of-factly. I skittered a large, gaudy artificial over the surface. Almost immediately a Northern rose like an alligator to intercept it. The violence was repeated on nearly every cast which landed near structure such as moss beds or logs. But I soon learned it was easier to hook these fish than hold them. Their sharp teeth cut through the leader on the first or second lunge. The guide produced wire tippets. I landed some on them. That was exciting but I could take little pride in it. To really outwit them I'd have to learn how to subdue them without the wire. I knew that would also be required to establish a valid record of any kind.

I also learned to set the hook quickly. If I hesitated, the fly would become engulfed too deeply in the pike's throat. It was then easier for the teeth to slash the leader. I wanted the hook caught in the jaw only.

I returned from this trip, however, with just the grayling record. On the next trip to Great Slave, I would land a 31-inch pike on 6-lb. test leader, no wire, which I photographed and had witnessed before releasing it. The fish was declared a world record in the 6-lb. line test category for the National Fresh Water Fishing Hall of Fame. I'd done it. I slept that night dreaming how difficult it had been to catch my first 6-inch trout on Parleys Creek. Things you persist doing, I told myself, just become easier with the repetition.

At home, several old friends mentioned how lucky I'd been. I was simply filling a vow made as a 12-year old trying desperately to catch my first trout.

The next summer, I was invited to spend a week as a guest of Alaska River Safaris in the Togiak Wilderness of south-central Alaska. I was frustrated for several hours with trout and salmon ignoring my flies. Finally, I tied on a muddler minnow streamer and fished as a minnow imitation, enticed nothing. My attention was diverted by what appeared to be giant grizzly tracks a few minutes later and I let the muddler drift across the surface. When I picked up to cast again and sink it right, I had a 5-1b. rainbow aboard. The muddler on top. The rainbows loved it. But I could find no logical explanation for it. Was it really fishing to catch them without understanding the theory behind it?

Then, the lodge manager showed me his collection of artificial mice. When retrieved in short jerks, the tail wagged across the surface. A large rainbow rose to smash the "fly." This I understood, for frequently I saw mice scurrying through the alders. It figured one would fall in the water on occasion. And there was always the possibility that artificial lemmings would work. There was just no end to learning in this fly fishing business.

That afternoon I found a pod of scarlet sockeye salmon milling at the edge of an eddy. I cast a silver-tinseled Mylar fly among them and one struck savagely. I wasn't prepared. The fly flew over my head. More strikes and more misses. Then, I hit solid flesh and the fish headed for the comfort of the ocean from which it had reluctantly yielded to the spawning urge. The only trouble was that the salt water of Bristol Bay was 35 miles away. I found myself stuck to the waist in mud and couldn't move my chest waders fast enough to catch up. Soon, even my line backing was stripped to the reel metal. Goodbye to all my fly line.

The next day I returned with new fly line and beached a nearly 13-lb. sockeye half a mile downstream. The guide examined the Mylar to make certain the fish was not foul-hooked and then eagerly shook my hand. My fellow angler, who lived in Anchorage, said he had never witnessed a battle quite like that.

What a wonderful lifestyle, fishing. How could anyone want to steal, or lie or do drugs if they could get hooked on enjoying natural surroundings? Matching wits with one of nature's offspring? Or more specifically, one of its favorites, the fish.

Chapter Twenty-two

In the years that followed, Jessica never again held a fishing rod in her hands. In time, it no longer seemed important. We understood our separate roles, and in fact, cherished the differences between us. But she did share an abiding love of nature and for a time moved to Wyoming where we lived on a ranch. Sandhill cranes, Canada geese and even a moose were seldom far away.

Meantime, we had seven children.

I tried to interest them in fishing but while deep curiosity was there about the natural world via hiking and camping, specific interest in trout fishing was marginal. I learned to live with that. The youngest girl did take up fly fishing; the oldest boy would say I left him alone too long on a stream bank with instructions to "stay there, I'll be right back. Only you didn't come right back." He was likely correct.

I took the young ones on outings near home where we might combine easy fishing with a picnic or nature stroll. Yet I also yearned for more rugged activities, like exploring the remote reaches of Lake Powell, a day's boat ride from the nearest marina, doing what I had vowed I'd do as a young man. I'd never seen a more beautiful artificial lake than Powell, not in Europe, Canada, or North America. Rainbow trout, the "popular fish," were planted enmasse in this new lake astraddle the Arizona-Utah line, but it simply wasn't suited for trout. Ninety five per cent of the fish caught were warm water species like largemouth black bass. The trout bunched in cold water at the bottom of the lake some 400 feet down, leaving the shoreline to bass. I discovered our kids loved going out on a houseboat where all of us could enjoy a different water activity. They liked swimming best but I managed to gather them all on a sandbar one morning to catch spawning bluegills with a fly rod. The fish showed little restraint. Cathy squealed with delight each time a bluegill swam near her bare toes.

I also learned something startling in the experience at Powell concerning fish and hunger. I had caught a few bass at daylight, but enticed no strikes for hours. Since I had nothing better to do, I kept casting in the warm sun to several bass I could see near a submerged tree. They completely ignored me, apparently not the least interested in the spinner I was throwing at them. The concept in bassing had always been to make a perfect cast to fish near structure, for they wouldn't move far away from cover or ambush. Nothing moved and I began to lift my lure from the water. Suddenly, a bass catapulted from the submerged tree and propelled directly to my feet, hitting the blades just as I began the lift from the water. I caught the bass, but why? I sat down to figure it out. The only answer I could come up with…why one had and the others hadn't, was sheer hunger. The "look" of the lure had been the same for all the fish. One fish was hungry and the others simply weren't. So, it made no difference if a dozen fish ignored me. I wasn't fishing for the stubborn ones, anyway.

I also discovered casting and trolling for monster brown trout on Flaming Gorge Reservoir. The latter required launching a boat in April or November at 4 a.m. and being on the right "run" before daylight. When the latter approached, one didn't even need look at a watch to know it was nigh. Well before the first lemon hue, winds blew in from the north and seeped through my pad of clothing topped by a snowmobile suit. It was easily the coldest time of day. On successive mornings I felt as as if being born and reborn, plucked from the womb of night and thrust into the cold and painful reality of daylight.

But it was also when the giant brown trout struck. About the third morning out, I'd barely let out line into the faintly-lit water when my rod tip plummeted. I didn't get back my size 11 Rapala plug until landing a brown of just over 11 lbs.

It was a lake of violence, I decided, where one must be careful not to make a mistake, run out of gas while losing one's way, or remain out in heavy windstorms. But it was also a lake of violence in another way, of predator feeding on unsuspecting prey. One day a chub, or rather half a chub, floated to the surface near the boat. The other half, teeth-scarred at the mid-section, also floated to the surface. It was a lake of monsters and down in the depths I visualized the carnage being wreaked on the weak and unsuspecting. It was no place to be small.

The lake finally yielded a brown trout of 33 lb. 14 ounces, a world record, and North America's third largest lake trout at 51 1/2 lbs. I marveled at the size of these fish. But even more impressive to me was a nearly 28-lb.

rainbow trout caught on a blustery March evening on a fly and fly rod. The angler had been fishing only 45 minutes. But reading about the accomplishment, it was clear he had spent a lifetime casting large flies into cold wind. How seldom, I thought, does a truly unprepared person blunder into good luck. What is luck? It would seem the more time spent at it, the "luckier" one got.

Below Flaming Gorge Dam was the new and improved, air-clear Green River. The former load of heavy silt dumped at top of the lake. Rainbow trout were soon stocked and seemed to flourish. I made my way down the steep west bank of the gorge, where there was no road or competition, and caught a dozen 11-13 inch fish. The fly didn't seem to matter. Later, when the trout grew larger and looked at more angler's wares, they became finicky. I spent two hours finding the right fly. It happened one day when my son, Ben, called to me, "Daddy, I just saw a big fish come up and swallow something black floating down over there." I cast down over there with a black cicada and instantly hooked a respectable rainbow, then another until the barb broke off and I couldn't find another fly the fish wanted. I went strikeless until late that afternoon when the fish decided to take a midge the size of a pinhead. The only trouble now was that it took me much more time to tie on a size 22 artificial. After several switches, even with magnifyers, my eyes began to water. That had never happened on Parleys Creek. Walking several miles along the stream, my legs also began to tire. That had never happened in the Uintas.

I soon realized I would never again be able to hike with a full pack into the farthest reaches of the primitive area. But I might preserve it for others who could. I was invited to go with a local conservation group to Washington D. C. to testify in behalf of the "High Uintas Wilderness Area," giving it more protected status than with the old designation of "Primitive," and with wider boundaries. I showed the chairman of the House Subcommittee on Interior Affairs a picture I'd taken in the Henrys Fork area when climbing Kings Peak, highest mountain in Utah at 13,528 feet, with blue lakes between emerald meadows and crimson cliffs. The picture passed among the Congressmen several times. The measure later passed in House and Senate and on the next map, the Uintas proudly wore the new designation of official wilderness. I was proud for an old friend.

When I returned, I found my sister, Shari, had died of cancer, leaving a young family. It was January and once again, the family mourned a casket placed in frozen ground. The winter was not a pleasant one.

In the spring, I took our children to visit an aunt who lived in suburbia.

Two of the girls somehow found a pond and returned with tadpoles and frogs in their pockets. Their aunt was shocked when they brought the creatures inside the house. I led them out. Then we took a closer look. The tadpoles we put in a ditch where they came to life again, the frogs in a tuft of grass. For nearly an hour, the kids fed them worms, left from a rain. The children shamed a definite liking to nature. I was proud of them. When it was time to go, Jess asked, "Where were you?" Catherine answered, "We've been attending school." Becky added, "and today it was fun."

During this period, Todd and Ben also got jobs floating and guiding in the Grand Canyon of the Colorado. They told me about the beauty of the area. The next spring, Todd, Ben, and I hiked into the Grand Canyon. We got the necessary permits, wound our way to the Colorado River at dusk and next day caught 20-inch rainbow trout on any foppish black fly. The fish must have taken them for horse flies, although we saw no horses. Burros… now that was a possibility.

Maj. Powell had named it correctly. The canyon in any light was magnificent. But it was hot, so hot in the June sun that we left for the rim well before dawn. Even then we would have perished for lack of water if making a single wrong turn. It was not as easy to find the way back. Heading toward the river, one need only go downhill. Returning, one must find the one and only trail leading to the rim. We studied the terrain very closely, determined precisely where we had entered the gully we were in and found familiar landmarks. Nearly to the top, we vacated our packs, clawed our way from the canyon, found a ranch, and stood for 15 minutes beneath a hose of water. Then, we found the energy to return for our packs.

The following summer Ben took me aside to say that while he had enjoyed the Grand Canyon trek, I'd taken his older brother to climb Kings Peak. Ben, now 14, wanted a "faraway adventure as special" as I'd taken with Todd. He paused. "How about driving to Alaska?"

As we headed into Idaho, toward Alaska, Benjamin asked, "Why had I taken five days to climb Kings Peak when there were no trout up there."

"We almost didn't," I told him. "After backpacking 17 miles to the top of the Henrys Fork drainage, we woke up in the morning to so much fog we could scarcely see. I thought this released me from hiking to the top. But I'd promised so…we walked blindly by a contour map until we came to a place where we could go no higher. Looking down, we saw a sign that said "In honor of Clarence King." Only then did we realize we'd done it. All the way back sliding down a glacier and for days afterward, we had such an exhilarating feeling of triumph "that we couldn't describe it."

"That's the way I want to feel with this trip," he said.

Somewhere in Montana, I called home to tell Jess where her son and I were. "A sign says 40 miles from Glacier National Park," I told her. After driving across Going-to-the-Sun Highway, we emerged on the Alberta border, and drove all day to Calgary. Then we fished through Banff and Jasper National Parks and saw a black bear waiting by a "School Bus" sign until the bus arrived and scared the bear away. We drove through Prince George, British Columbia to the Skeena, Babine and Kispiox rivers. But it wasn't steelhead fishing season and we proceeded north from Kitwanga over gravel roads until reaching a clear stream south of Dease Lake. This was not the original and famous Alaska Highway but we would connect with it near Watson, Yukon Territory. I had studied the geography of this region by the light of a winter fireplace and now it seemed euphoric to know we were finally here.

On the Tanzanilla River near Dease Lake we caught Dolly Varden and grayling on flies. Or at least I did. Ben didn't connect for some reason and I could see he was downhearted. Through the Cassiar Mountains we saw stone sheep, a moose and a wolf. We spent the night at Whitehorse and reached the Alaskan border by next evening where Ben took out the "Alaska or Bust" sign and tore it up. North of Tok we stopped at Jan Lake where some kind of fish was tearing off the surface. Here was the perfect place for Ben to learn fly fishing. The fish proved to be small rainbow trout and before the Midnight Sun stole off into the night, Ben caught his first four trout on flies. He had caught as many trout in his first day of fishing as I had my first year.. When I told him this, he beamed.

We looked at grizzlies and moose in Mt. McKinley or Denali (Indian for the Big One) National Park, and camped for the night at the Kasilof River. Some locals were catching 25-30 lb. salmon on long-shank red "Coho" flies. I tossed out, hooked one that took me 300 yards downstream and lost him on a boulder in the middle of the river. Seventeen pound monofilament seemed gossamer. I retied to 25. Ben shouted that he had a fish on and with his light line, the fish caromed out of control, snagging other lines and fishing boots. When I finally put the net beneath Ben's fish and swung the contents onto a gravel bar, everyone for a quarter of a mile up and down the river let out a giant cheer. They were happy for the lad and perhaps even more that we were out of their way. The net was a shambles by then and we had to take even longer to land them by hand. No use fooling around with these fish. I tied us both to 30 lb. test.

We hooked and lost some king salmon on the Kenai River and headed back toward Canada. Ben began fishing for trout in a nameless stream, but hooked a huge salmon with his tiny gear. We had a dilemma on our hands. He couldn't land it and I couldn't reach out far enough to get a hand on it. Finally, I tossed a rock behind the fish and it swam close enough for me to grab. In so doing, I knew how powerful and slippery it might be. But Ben had worn it down enough for me to hang on the gill plate.

On the way home, we rode the Inland Passage Ferry from Haines to Prince Rupert, B. C., looking at whales and killer sharks. On the road, it rained for six straight days but we talked about all the things on our "Father and Sons Outing" that we never seemed to have time for at home.

Later as a Christmas gift, Ben carved out a map on a wooden plaque which showed our 7,300-mile route to Alaska and presented it to me. It read: "The Last Frontier…I was confused, looking for strength and discovered from this voyage of length… that mountains may have stood in our way, yet with patient struggle we conquered…now I can see what has happened to me…you showed me my future…it is you I want to be. Your Son."

I was reminded again of what a powerful experience it is to meet an outdoor challenge, especially when accompanied by a mentoring companion. I thought of those who had made a difference in my own lifetime. At the earliest, there was my father. And Mo, who now owned the refinishing shop and kept my father's last name on it, "because of his reputation for honesty and good work." In spite of many lifestyle differences, Mo had been a powerful influence on me because he possessed skills of great value to me in and out of the shop…and was willing to share them. But in visiting him one day, I learned he could not fish or hunt with me as before. "I can't walk uphill anymore," he said. I don't have the energy." Years of smoking had taken their toll. In my youth I would have followed him to the ends of the planet while sleuthing out deer and bobcat tracks on hard ground, or solving other mysteries of nature. Now our outdoor adventures were finished.

I had learned many valuable lessons of outdoors and life from spending time with people like Tom, the Ute Indian game warden. Tom was hard of hearing and so self-conscious about it that while he wore a hearing aid, either it didn't work, or he didn't bother to turn it on. He read lips to fully understand what you were saying. I tried to be certain I was facing him when talking and one day shared my lunch with him. He smiled and took me to a beaver dam on Rock Creek he said he had "shown no white man." He said it "held the biggest brook trout east of Strawberry Divide." I soon found he was right.

Since becoming an outdoor writer, I'd also had the opportunity of getting out with conservation officers of the State Fish and Game Dept., soon to receive the more sophisticated label of "Wildlife Resources." These "CO's", dedicated to protecting the resources in their assigned territory, often worked 65-70 hours a week, patrolling the hinterlands so often they knew the path of every porcupine, mule deer and kit fox, or so it seemed.

Over many miles of lonely roads and trails they maintained vigil for the wildlife they vowed to protect against dishonest sportsmen. (no, they were not worthy of that name "sportsman"). The CO's watched over it, tallying doe-to-fawn ratios, measuring how much browse had been eaten during a tough winter, monitoring the balance of nature, browse and grass to ungulate, ungulate to predator. They came to love the land and water in their bailiwick and all that called it home. Yet, the government would every so often threaten to have someone else patrol it, a directive from some city supervisor who hadn't stepped outside his office in 10 years. And at the last minute, common sense would prevail and the edict would come down that perhaps those who knew the wild creatures best should continue to manage them. How long, I wondered, would common sense prevail?

Many hours were spent under the tutelage of professional outdoor people like Casey and Arnold, the former a man who grew up "on the back side" of Boulder Mountain and participated as a boy with the local Indians in killing deer for sustenance, before the days of fish and game laws. The Piutes let Casey and his father do the shooting because they were "so accurate with a rifle," while the Indians were content to dress out and convert the venison to a year's supply of jerky. Casey grew up with grizzlies and timber wolves and other wild things; he could tell stories around a campfire that made one envy the old pioneers. Yet, the most amazing thing of all was that if you told him in which ravine or gully you planned to camp somewhere in the state, he could tell you exactly where the nearest seeps and springs were located. Or you could make a "dry camp."

When Casey died, a little of me died with him.

When Arnold explained a thing, he held back nothing. He pushed his skeptical bosses into letting him go to Colorado to bring back opossum shrimp to "fill in the gap" on Fish Lake "between the 10-lb. lake trout and the 10-inch rainbow trout. "I think it's working," he said as he pulled on a rope to loosen a boat from its moorings. "I'll take you out and show you." The rope broke suddenly and he fell into 20 feet of water, full uniform and all. He changed clothes and took me out to catch a 3-lb. rainbow.

There were also LaVar and Ken. They took me onto the Manti Mountain where we listened to the eerie and magnificent bugling of bull elk.

Many people heard such sounds only from a Walt Disney movie, if that. There was something special in hearing up close and personal the challenging call of wapiti, as the Shoshones call them, challenging and fighting over their harems. Jack London's call of the wild indeed, but here and now, somehow more real than anyone could have imagined it.

I owed my outdoor education to many. Even my uncle who killed the cow and bit off the watersnake's head had taught me there is a limit to physical excess. He was, "too tough to die," he said, but the doctors told him he would if he continued drinking. He had haunted the bars until it was an ingrained habit. But he made the choice to live.

There was my mother who had fought on courageously after death of her husband, continuing on in a man's business, encouraging me to "gain an education outdoors," though she personally cared little for the "bugs and mud and discomforts" which "naturally followed."

I thought of my own kids and how they had, perhaps without realizing it while very young, gained many insights and valuable experiences being beneath sun or clouds rather than merely walls and ceilings. There was the time I hooked a 30-lb. carp on 40-lb test line and handed the rod to Todd who at the time also weighed about 30 lbs. I stood there with knife in hand ready to cut the connection should fish prevail. The fight seed and sawed. Finally, Todd began to win out and I helped him land the fish. We "planted" the beast in the family raspberry patch and it seemed the bushes grew a foot overnight. But most of all, self-esteem had been planted in the boy, a commodity I noticed was of all things most lacking in juveniles I'd witnessed among street gangs and in detention centers.

Jessica had by now revealed her true identity, a mother. She did not wish to accompany me on "outings" if it interfered with maternal instincts in looking after the children. But I was grateful for the day I hadn't kissed her at the reservoir and made up for it later. We took each other for granted in a way we both approved. And eagerly returned to each other's arms.

Although lonely at times, I perceived that solitude in the outdoors was a powerful teacher in itself. There were days I was most content to be entirely alone, for I talked less then and paid more attention to the hushed whisperings of the wild.

I returned in earnest to the Provo River where it had been destroyed 30 years before, catching a 21-inch brown trout, cause for joy that the stream was alive once more. At first I cast a dozen times in vain to a deep pool but noticing a submerged and neglected boulder near current, made one more cast. The fish struck boldly, showing all the signs of health, small head, deep color. I sat down and said a silent thank you to nature that she had held no grudges against man and saw fit to heal his mistake.

There were to follow some comical and humbling experiences such as the time I fished the Weber fruitlessly, stumbling upon a camp of men dressed in white, all holding fishing rods…one without a line. An attendant rushed over to explain these were mental patients. I turned to leave when one of them asked me if I'd caught anything. I told the truth and suggested he ought to put some line on his rod so he might. "Why should I?" he asked in perfect logic. "You're using line but you haven't caught anything."

I thought of the days I foolishly risked my life on the Uinta River. When looking down from a ledge, I saw a brook trout of at least 19 or 20 inches. Such a fish, deep-bellied as with most brookies, could weigh some four pounds, larger even than the monsters of Alexander Lake. I inched along the ledge and made several casts slightly behind the fish. He ignored them. I pushed closer and found myself starting to fall. My hand-hold on soft shale gave way. I now resigned myself to falling straight down 40 feet where I would break both legs in the rocks. Then, somehow, I managed to throw my rod back overhead, gain a new grip on the cliff face and extricate myself straight up and out of danger.

I reflected on the resource pluses and minuses I had recently encountered. On my last trip to the Fremont River, the stream was on its death bed. Giant floods of the year before had silted in most of the channel, including the Pine Creek tributary. Who was in charge of the watershed on the nearby national forest and was supposed to protect it? Later, a private hatchery on the system was discovered to have whirling disease which spread to the Fremont itself. The hatchery survived. The river didn't.

One "plus" was Yellowstone. Biologists there finally grasped the problem of wasted and dead fish, invoking catch-and-release regulations. Two years following, cutthroats were again dramatically plentiful. On a return to Great Slave Lake, I could see that even that remote water benefitted from catch-and- release. Truly a game fish "was too valuable to catch only once." Yet, I couldn't of myself gloat, for the one thing which Jess said most chronicled the years in the lives of our children were the pictures I'd taken of them holding up fish from the different trips we'd enjoyed. I'd made a mistake—not of photographing the young ones, but of photographing them smiling at a limited resource their father had killed. I could as well have had them smile at a live puppy, or even at each other.

But the malady was ubiquitous. I'd found a lake full of tiger trout and blessed the fisheries biologist who had stocked them there three years before. I took Doug with me and we caught and released within a few weeks on dry flies more than a hundred tiger trout. Being a hybrid brook X brown trout, the fish couldn't reproduce. Yet regulations allowed eight fish, any size every day. Within a year, the larger tiger trout were gone and soon, most of the smaller ones. Those who could have controlled it knew what was at stake but "feared political pressure" if managing the resource properly with sound biology. Thus, greedy anglers were allowed to kill the goose that laid the golden eggs and all suffered equally.

As for Doug, he was beginning to show a distinct sensitivity to the art of fly fishing. He noticed that emerging midges released from their stone cages on the stream bottom sought the surface with head elevated. Watching trout intercepted the midges just as they slowed slightly beneath the surface. By then the insect had begun to probe with legs and head for the new life to be encountered in the world of air beyond. In so doing, they held their heads higher. A watchful Doug dabbed some floatant on the head of the artificial midges to more accurately match the "sight picture" of the real thing and quadrupled his catch rate. The latter observation greatly increased our fishing success on the lower Provo where oversized brown trout had eluded us for years. Thus was the mystery solved.

I had taught him well. Or had he learned this all by himself?

I experienced some firsts, including catching a respectable rainbow at Strawberry Resevoir on a tiny midge I'd tied myself. I landed a 48-lb. king salmon on Alaska's Kenai River. The years of frustrations, asking questions and seeking answers in the outdoors was beginning to pay off. The rewards were a long way, it seemed to me from the simple beginings on Parley Creek. But it was Parley which had launched the quest now being fulfilled.

On New Mexico's San Juan, I caught and released some 20 respectable trout in one evening. A sophisticatedly dressed angler from New York, who said he left his profession often as a druggist to fish the now famous San Juan, called over to ask what I was using. I answered honestly that it was a size 20 caddis emerging from the shell, black "head" over gold body. He said he had one but an hour later, still held a limp fly rod, while mine continued to dance. He walked over at dark in the parking lot to compare flies. "But that's exactly what I was using!" he said.

He hadn't paid enough attention to one detail. The nymph had to be held at a level about one foot below the surface. I managed to do that by tying the nymph one foot beneath a dry fly. The fish ignored that but while floating, it held the nymph where the gorging trout wanted it. And were looking. If this angler had paid as much intimate attention to fly fishing as he did filling a prescription, he might have succeeded in both endeavors.

Details. I thought of the woman with a young boy one Sunday in Montana trying to teach him how to cast a fly on the Madison River. As I approached, she whipped the rod until exhausted, the line piling on each cast like a bird's nest. She sat down on a rock and flung the fishing stick aside. The boy had a scowl on his face. The mother looked at me and implored, "Do you know how to use this thing? The clerk at Ennis had to know. I was a dumb widow spending her last dollar." I picked up the rod. It felt balanced in my hands, the line obviously weight forward, the leader delicately tapered. I cast to a dark place against the far bank. The fly landed perfectly. The boy jumped to pick up the rod now as if it was a magic wand.

"No, he did right by you," I said. "It is a superb match, rod to line and leader. You just need to let the line lay out completely behind you before beginning the forward cast. Done right, nothing could be easier." As I left, the lad was getting the feel of it, the line playing out smoothly. The mother glanced back over her shoulders in an unspoken "thank you" which for me, spoke volumes.

I had often asked myself how much devotion I should pay to fishing and the outdoors. It was not my panacea, my object of worship, for clearly two matters came first, feality to deity and family. But I remember what a Wyoming old-timer once said about his favorite stream, the Salt River. "Don't even mention the words without reverence in your voice."

I knew whereof he spoke, for I had seen the natural jewel of Star Valley shining from beneath the mist of a September morning and felt the same way. I had placed myself before the shrine of many other trout-filled waters. But all must be kept in perspective. There were many other pursuits important to the human race. But if the word recreate meant to literally re-create one's spirit and soul, I knew of nothing more meaningful than learning at the feet of a masterful teacher, nature. The same was so valuable because it was created not by man but by the same being who created man.

I thought how I was sometimes in need of repentance, cussing or swearing at departing fish, usually one with my broken leader in its mouth. I'd have to be more careful about that. But never had I been tempted outdoors to speak lightly of sacred matters. It didn't seem fitting. I remembered the story of a famous baseball player[1] who said within my hearing that a batter

---

1. *The name of the pitcher was Vernon Law, for many years an award-winning pitcher for the pennant-winning Pittsburgh Pirates.*

he was pitching to in practice began cursing names from the Bible. The pitcher began throwing faster and closer to the batter's body. "Why are you doing that?" the latter asked.

The answer, "Because you are speaking about a friend of mine."

Chapter Twenty-three

1997: For a time I sat in the car looking at the fence. Only affluent country club members were allowed beyond. It was too high to climb, at least not without drawing attention. I walked across 20th East and there it was: the creek flowed free and unfettered, above ground. But I could not reach it, could not place my hand in its cold waters. Through the chain link I could see into the water and it was clear. Over there...a golf ball. Instinctively, I looked around for the cop in his cart. Among the yellow rocks, glowing like gold where the current eddied, I saw no trout, no living thing. Parleys Creek was there. But it was lifeless.

Quickly, I ran down the fence line to the waterfall hole. It was not there. The stream had been channeled to bisect the golf course fairway and neither the waterfall nor the diversion behind it, or even the ditch which once coursed to the prison, remained. The prison itself had been moved. A lot of time had elapsed. But... How could something so vivid in my memory no longer be there?

What was that...movement behind the willows? A pair of mallards! The hen in front, male close behind. The two were inseparable, the hen darting from flow to slack water, the male close behind, both nurturing the other, not only in a Darwinian replenishing of species it would seem, but in companionship, even among so-called emotionless animals.

It had been years since I first walked here, drawn like iron filings to a giant magnet. I was now a middle-aged man. Maybe more. I must have no regrets with the passing of time. I must spend more of it with present friends, while looking up past ones. And with my mother, nearing 90...she who told me at one time she would have withheld me from the creek, but rejoiced at what I learned from its banks. More time with my children and theirs.

A long time later, I stirred, climbing numbly into the car, driving to the canyon mouth, or as close as the maze of new streets and private fences would allow. Three freeways filled the gully of my youth, one to downtown, one leading to southside suburbs and one into the canyon. It held a large sign which read, "Cheyenne, 425 miles." I stopped, looked, turned and finally found a trail from rim to gully bottom. Shading my eyes, I could see a ribbon of water below and clamored toward the glimmer, hastening my pace when detecting the first sound of gurgling flow. The trail was steep but finally, I was at the bottom, gazing into the creek where the Gravel Pit Hole should have been, studying the new landscape for the home where Crazy Mary lived, where...but it was all gone.

Turning to walk upstream toward the old Suicide Rock pool, I saw that the fill which was now I-80 halted my path. A new pool had been carved by water falling from a pipe below the freeway fill. But it was not the same. The scene was human-cut, barren, devoid of vegetation. Several boys and their dogs came to swim in the clear water and for a moment it seemed as if the stream were alive again. True, the man-cut falls were higher, the water deeper than Suicide Rock or Gravel Pit holes. But it would be like saying *Homo sapiens* could build a higher, better geyser than Old Faithful. And maybe an engineer from MIT could even make it blow twice as often.

Peering into the deep riffles , probing with a stick, nothing moved. The dark rocks, overturned, to be sure, were replete with caddis and may fly larvae. The food was there. Cutthroat trout could live here once more, but where were they? By what catastrophic event had they disappeared? Had construction of the freeway for a time dried up the waterway? No, the creek would have been placed in a pipe for a time and then...man had disrupted nature, leaving without even noticing.

I walked downstream as if in a spell and noticed several plaques, one commemorating the D &RGW Railroad which the words on the metal plate said once ran through here...and another memorializing the pioneers which used this canyon 150 years before. I followed several trails, some dead- ending in a tangle of oak brush, becoming entangled in it, forcing a smile. I came upon hikers and bikers and heard them say no vehicles were allowed in the gully as they once were. Beautiful. It showed wise planning by the city or county, rare and wise planning for someone in government. And at top of the rim in a place I'd somehow missed, a park named after a person named "Tanner," where all the trails and paths converged by the road, with picnic tables and grass for quarter of a mile and kids flew kites.

As a boy, I'd almost never seen anyone else in the gully, beyond end of the golf course, seldom another human soul. Now, ladies walked dogs and kids gamboled and tried to walk the stream over fallen trees without getting their feet wet. A few more contemplative types, including one couple, sat on the bank dangling their feet in the water, withdrawing toes quickly because the water was so cold. Some things had not changed.

So, now the gully belonged to everyone and everyone was invited. That was good. Very good. I lay back, drew a long breath, sat up and looked again. I should have brought Jessica with me. I would do that next time.

I sat there for awhile. Then, I walked up the creek. There…there! The tail of a cutthroat trout. Two of them! Some had survived the engineering asault.

I looked on in amazement. And for a long time I was a boy again. A 12-year-old boy.

Appendix

How I rig:

Bait and spin fishing: I prefer a precision-made, durable, open- faced reel, with a rod tip sensitive enough to handle a light strike, yet strong enough to cast for distance. (You want a flexible but not a weak rod tip.) I use monofilament line in 6-lb. test (light for longer casting) to smaller fish, as in alpine lakes. (If water-filled casting bubble is used, mono less than 6-lb. can't handle weight. I might, however, tie 4-lb. test below bubble so that if snagged, I don't lose the bubble.) This rig is used for casting lures or bait to mossy water where buoyancy is needed to avoid deep fouling. As for lures, I like a No. 3 Mepps spinner for trout of 12 inches or more, no. 2 for pansize fish like white bass.

If fishing water with boat where long casting is not necessary, or if the fish are larger, use 8-lb. test. Seldom is heavier test line needed, except for trolling to lake trout, and even then, light line gives more vibration and action to any lure. Use stouter mono if fishing for bass or walleyes in murky water where fish must be "controlled" away from snags.

Fly fishing: I use three rods of different size, all about 8-9 feet long. I recommend no 3 or 4, 5 or 6, 7 or 8, made of graphite or boron. (Both are now superior to split bamboo.) One does not want to sacrifice quality in a fly rod that one will be wielding day after day. The no. 3-4 is used for small stream and low water dry fly fishing, the no. 5-6 primarily for nymphing in rivers of medium size or more, the 7-8 (a very heavy rod) for pike-size fishing in large water. Likewise, I use a matching (4 weight) line for the lightest rod, heavier line (say , 6) for the second heaviest rod, 8 for the heaviest. In all cases, I prefer weight-forward (rocket taper) line for long-distance casting. Double taper (less expensive) will work for the lightest rod in tossing a dry fly. I would not recommend a level or single taper line, however cheap the price, even for beginners. Both are difficult to cast and could discourage even the most experienced veteran.

On the lighter rod, leader is best tapered from about .020-.030 on butt end to .007 diameter on the business end. (Leader thicker than .007 won't fit into the eye of size 18-20 flies, which are often called for in most trout fishing.) I go to .008-9 final taper for the medium weight rod, and whatever leader strength is needed (metal tippet is a possibility) for the heavier rod in pursuing larger fish such as pike, Coho salmon etc.

For a time I used extremely light leaders, such as 2-lb. test for alpine lakes, but one must realize that even with the best of knots, up to one fourth of leader strength is lost; a dozen back casts in wind might snap off the 2-lb. leader. I go with 4-lb. test if casts of length are required. But with thinner diameter leaders being developed nowadays, 6-lb. test in .007 is seldom detected even by wary fish. While I believe in ultra-light for maximum fish fight, I also like to release the fish without exhausting it. (Studies show fish not battled to a complete standstill have a better chance of surviving.) Nets are also helpful in landing fish with some energy remaining, enhancing their survival.

For dry fly fishing on clear water I use at least 10-12 feet of leader, shorter for nymphing or wet fly angling. Often I use a dry fly on 10 feet of leader, using that pattern as a "strike "indicator, with a nymph tied on about three feet below. However, a fish may hit the topside fly as well.

I don't like using sinkers but if necessary, I keep some tiny splitshot on hand for deep nymphing.

A fly fishing vest is very helpful in keeping artificials and supplies, scissors, etc. handy while hip-deep in the water. I use a XXlarge, not because I'm that big but because I may want to wear it on the outside of warm clothing.

When buying hip boots or chest waders, check very carefully for workmanship around seams and connections, especially along the sole. Some boots habitually pull loose about the third time you tug them off or on. Be sure to buy a little big to allow for two pair of socks.

In buying a fly-tying vice, be certain to get a strong clamp-type that holds the lightweight fly hook snugly. A wobbly vice just won't keep you at it very long. Nymphs and streamers can be tied with a little practice but I recommend taking a fly-tying class for winged, dry flies.